IN DEFENSE OF GOOD TEACHING

What Teachers Need to Know About the "Reading Wars"

Edited by

Kenneth S. Goodman

Stenhouse Publisl
York, Maine

D0143850

This book is dedicated to all the courageous and highly professional teachers, administrators, and teacher educators who have borne the brunt of these attacks. A lesson that those mandating curriculum and methodology have not understood is that only teachers can change what happens in classrooms. And teachers will find ways of continuing to act on what they know on behalf of their pupils. The saddest part of these attacks is that the most dedicated, hardest-working, and best-informed teachers are being blamed for the failures of a system being continuously eroded by politicians.

Things will get worse before they get better, but eventually good teaching will drive out bad and teachers will achieve the respect they deserve.

Stenhouse Publishers, 431 York Street, York, Maine 03909
www.stenhouse.com

Copyright © 1998 by Whole Language Umbrella

Library of Congress Cataloging-in-Publication Data
In defense of good teaching : what teachers need to know about the "reading wars" / edited by Kenneth S. Goodman.
    p.   cm.
    Includes bibliographical references.
    ISBN 1-57110-086-5 (alk. Paper)
    1. Reading—United States—Language experience approach. 2. Politics and education—United States. 3. Reading—United States—Language experience approach—Religious aspects. 4. Education and state—United States. I. Goodman, Kenneth S.
LB1050.35.I5   1998
372.4—dc21   98-11218
                                                  CIP
Manufactured in the United States of America on acid-free paper
03 02 01 00 99 98 9 8 7 6 5 4 3 2 1

Contents

Acknowledgments

In this strange age, with literacy under attack and technology being heavily supported, I need to begin by acknowledging the advent of computer networks. Just a few years ago, few of us were computer literate. Now we could not function without the listservs and the Internet. They made it possible to share knowledge and documents rapidly with groups of people who have connections to other networks that produced an informed group who could spread the knowledge of what is happening in states and nationally. We informed each other through e-mail, cried on each other's collective virtual shoulders, and shared our attempts to reach legislators and other decision-makers. When a crisis occurred, we could mobilize many people to respond immediately, as happened when the Reading Excellence bill was to be voted on. Rep. William F. Goodling, head of the House Education Committee, complained of being awakened at night by California phone calls.

As this book was developing, events followed each other so rapidly that only the Internet made it possible to keep up with the latest phrasing of a bill and the horror stories of California and Texas. So I acknowledge Lois Bridges and Margaret Moustafa, who organized a marvelous listserv to keep up with California happenings and mobilize opposition; Jim Burke, who put our messages on CATENET, the California English teachers' network; and Barbara Guzzeti, who kept the National Reading Conference network going.

Gerry Cole, P. David Pearson, Steve Krashen, Richard Allington, Brian Cambourne, and Denny Taylor have been active in informing the discussion and leading resistance to the imposition of curriculum and methodology.

Debra Jacobson, Marie Ruiz, Yetta Goodman, Steve Bialostok, and others at the Program in Language and Literacy at the University of Arizona were very helpful in producing this book. Many others lurking on the Internet provided valuable information and feedback.

Finally I'd like to thank the contributors to this book, who were willing to go through multiple revisions to make their chapters current and up to date.

This opening chapter represents Ken Goodman's political education over a three-year period that began with an attack on whole language and Goodman in the December 1994 Atlantic Monthly. Goodman documents what happened next in the aftermath of a strong conservative sweep nationally and in many states in the 1994 elections. A crisis in reading was manufactured based on misunderstandings and misrepresentations of the 1994 National Assessment of Educational Progress.

The attacks took a political turn as California, Texas, and many other states began to enact laws and/or establish state educational mandates to force a shift away from whole language and other curricular innovations in language arts and literacy and toward simplistic phonics programs. That brought the force of law in on one side of a long-term paradigm battle in education over whether to teach reading as meaning construction or word recognition.

But this political battle is clearly over more than how reading should be taught. The scope of the movement has expanded to include math and bilingual education as its targets. And it has moved from the states to the federal scene, with laws in the process of enactment aimed at controlling methodology, curriculum, and research in every state and district. Several very different groups have played major roles in the attacks. Each group seems to think it can control the others. There is something gripping in how the events this chapter recounts have led to these ends. But the "reading wars" are just a preliminary skirmish in the conspiracy to control and diminish public education.

Who's Afraid of Whole Language? Politics, Paradigms, Pedagogy, and the Press

Kenneth S. Goodman

Australians say, "It's the tall poppies that get cut down." And whole language has become a tall poppy indeed. It is the most powerful grassroots pedagogical movement ever to have developed in education. In North America it spreads from teacher to teacher until it has affected in some way the vast majority of classrooms. Its influence has spread throughout the English-speaking world; whole language has caught the imagination of educators in Latin America, Asia, Oceania, and Europe. I'm not suggesting that the majority of teachers in North America are whole language teachers. What I am suggesting is that whole language has had a profound influence on how curriculum, materials, methodology, and assessment are viewed. Publishers have had to rethink their textbooks and tests. Whole language has helped to redefine teaching and its relationship to learning. It has revealed that children, all of them, are powerful learners of written as well as oral language, that they are capable of using language to think, to learn, to solve problems. Given the opportunities of whole language classrooms, all of us have had to reevaluate our expectations of what children are capable of learning and doing.

It is the visible success of whole language, not its weaknesses, that has made it the major target of a powerful coalition of forces, which for varying reasons fear its success. Part of the power of whole language stems from the base of knowledge it builds on—bringing together constructivist psychology; functional linguistics, psycholinguistics, and sociolinguistics; ethnography; literary theory; semiotics; and child development research and theory. Whole language integrates scientific knowledge and an understanding of how humans use language to make sense—to express and to comprehend meaning in both oral and written language. It is built on a respect for what young learners have already accomplished in their use of oral language and their awareness of written language when they come to school.

3

The broad base of knowledge that whole language has brought to education has become the basis of official national, regional, and local school policies in many parts of the world and, more specifically, of curriculum and practice in much of the English-speaking world, including Great Britain, New Zealand, Australia, and Canada. National and local literacy education policies in many other parts of the world reflect holistic and constructivist views, though turning that into classroom realities has been difficult because of the minimal levels of professional education of teachers and the lack of financial resources for staff development.

In the United States, the broad base of knowledge from which whole language stems would not have affected schooling in the ways that it has if it were not for the development of a large number of self-empowered, professional teachers who have internalized this knowledge and used it to build, individually and collectively, a pedagogy to which they gave the name "whole language." The term first became popular among teachers in Canada to differentiate the integrated and holistic pedagogy they were developing from what they saw—and were rejecting—as a part-language pedagogy built around a technology of textbooks and tests growing out of the behavioral psychology that had come to dominate schools, particularly in the United States. American teachers eagerly responded to the term as they took control of their classrooms from the bloated and demeaning teachers' manuals of the text publishers. In fact, when California authorities in 1987 adopted a state framework that integrated reading with the other language arts and put real literature in reading programs, they were only following what many teachers were already doing. This large, growing base of informed, professional teachers is the driving force behind the spread of whole language as a true grassroots movement. But it is also what the forces combining to attack whole language most fear. A major goal these various opponents share is to deprofessionalize and control teachers and teacher education.

A key aspect of the whole language movement has been the emergence of powerful, knowledgeable teachers, tall poppies, who are now suffering the full force of the attacks on whole language.

The NAEP Reports

Some of the best indicators of how many American teachers have been influenced by whole language comes from the National Assessment of Educational Progress (NAEP) tests for 1992 and 1994 (Mullis et al. 1993a, 1993b; Campbell et al. 1996; Miller et al. 1995; Williams 1995; as of this writing, the 1994 NAEP reading results are the most recent ones reported). In the 1992 NAEP assessment, 97 percent of fourth-grade students had teachers who said they gave at least moderate emphasis to the integration of reading and writing. A majority of students were being taught by teachers who said they have embraced aspects of whole language and literature-based reading as part of their reading instruction (Mullis et al. 1993a, pp. 33–34).

The 1994 NAEP questionnaire asked teachers about topics they had "training in." Three of the topics relate to whole language: teaching critical thinking, combining reading and writing, and "the whole language approach to reading." Nationally, in 1992 83 percent said yes, they had training in critical thinking; in 1994, 79 percent said they did. On combining reading and writing, 89 percent in both years said yes, they had training in this area. On whole language, 80 percent in 1992 said they had such training, and 85 percent in 1994 said they did (Miller et al. 1995, pp. 126–28). There is no information in the 1994 reports on actual use of whole language.

These reports by teachers on their awareness and/or use of whole language in their classrooms do not in themselves indicate the extent of actual changes in their classrooms. But there is strong data from the NAEP reports that show the influence of whole language on students.

Most striking in the NAEP data is evidence of the trend away from primary reliance on basals (see table). This trend, which has continued, is related to higher scores on the NAEP. Estimates before 1992 indicated that 95 percent of classrooms used basal readers either exclusively or as the major material in reading instruction (Goodman et al. 1988). In 1992, 12 percent of teachers said they used primarily trade books, and 49 percent reported using both trade books and basals. In 1994 these figures had moved to 19 percent and 57 percent. Only 1 out of 5 teachers in 1994 said they used only basals. Furthermore, pupils whose teachers were using primarily trade books showed higher mean scores on the NAEP assessments than pupils whose teachers were using primarily basals. The advantage of using trade books is clear in 1994, with those in trade-book-dominant classes showing a mean score of 219, compared to 212 for those in basal-dominated classes.

Use of Basals and Trade Books

	Basal Primary		Trade Primary		Basal and Trade		Other	
	1992	1994	1992	1994	1992	1994	1992	1994
% reporting use	36%	21%	12%	19%	49%	57%	3%	3%
Mean score	216	212	223	219	218	215	208	202

Source: Campbell et al. 1996, p. 68

In addition to the shift away from basals, other strong evidence of the influence of whole language is shown in the NAEP data.

Reading at Home for Fun

In both 1992 and 1994 almost half of fourth graders nationally (44 percent and 45 percent) said they read almost every day for fun. Not surprisingly, the more kids read for fun at home, the higher the mean scores on the NAEP tests. Nationally, in both 1992 and 1994, those reading almost every day averaged about 25 points higher than those who never or hardly ever read for fun at home.

Reading Silently and Choosing What They Read

A major feature of whole language is that students read books of their own choice, silently, in school. Nationally, and in every state, approximately two-thirds of fourth-grade pupils in both 1992 and 1994 reported that they are asked to read silently almost every day in school. Kids who read silently almost every day scored better than kids who rarely read silently in school. The latter unlucky students scored about 30 points lower on average in both years than daily silent readers.

Both 1992 and 1994 assessments show that more than half of all fourth-grade pupils nationally report having time to read books of their own choosing almost every day in school. And, like silent reading, there is strong evidence in the relative mean scores that choice is beneficial. In 1992 there was a 20 point mean difference between those who chose their own reading daily and those who rarely got to do that and a 16 point difference in 1994.

Three Books a Month

One major impact of the whole language movement has been the increased sales of trade books and increased use of children's rooms in libraries. Book sales have increased tenfold in ten years. This is reflected in the NAEP reports. Students were asked in both 1992 and 1994 how many books they had read in the previous month. Nationally, 68 percent of fourth graders in 1992, and 69 percent in 1994, said they read three or more books a month. Over 40 percent reported reading five or more books a month in both years. Those who read no books had the lowest mean scores. And there was a wide difference in scores between those who read no books and those who read five or more books per month. Happily, only 7 percent of pupils in 1992 reported no books read. In 1994 9 percent read no books.

I've cited this NAEP data mainly to show the influence of whole language on American students. But in addition, the NAEP evidence provides robust support for the effectiveness of whole language. It's clear from the data that the attacks on whole language are not based on any demonstrable failure. So what *is* motivating the attacks? Careful consideration of the agendas of several different whole language opponents will shed some light on why each fears whole language and how these varied groups have come together in a common focus on using state and federal laws to control teachers, curriculum, and methodology.

The Far Right

For well over half a century the far right has used a campaign for phonics to elect ultraconservative school board members and attack both public education and teacher education. The Reading Reform Foundation is a group with a long history of dedication to what they call "systematic intensive phonics." The Foundation's *Basic Information and Catalog* includes an article entitled "The Epidemic of Reading Disabilities" by Canadians Carl Kline and Carolyn Lacey Kline. It exemplifies the rhetoric of the "phonics first" campaign:

> When 35% of the population is affected by a disability, it is an epidemic. When that disability is the leading cause of emotional problems in children and adolescents in North America, we are talking about a serious public health problem. Consider also that this epidemic is a major etiological factor in school-dropouts and in juvenile delinquency. Furthermore, . . . it seems likely that teenagers who can't read or spell and who consequently hate school are easy targets for drug dealers.
>
> We already have the vaccine to attack reading disability, but we can't get the educators to use it. Samuel Orton, Rudolf Flesch, Jeanne Chall, Patrick Groff and numerous other researchers have urged the educators to prevent this massive problem by inoculating primary students with a steady injection of synthetic, explicit phonics. (p. 6)

Here is simplistic logic dressed in medical metaphor. (1) Huge numbers of people aren't learning to read. (2) That produces many other problems: emotional difficulties, school dropouts, delinquency, and drug use. (3) All that could be easily avoided with a shot of "synthetic, explicit phonics." (4) Teachers and others who don't agree are part of a conspiracy to deprive children of literacy and destroy North American society.

Some of those who believe in this simplistic logic are no doubt sincere. But others see the issue of reading as a means of frightening and politicizing rural and working-class parents. They use "phonics first" campaigns to elect local school board members, to lobby for state "choice" and voucher programs, and to influence federal policies and laws. Lest you think that those who march under this far-right phonics banner are easily dismissed as irrational extremists, you should know that they are the same groups that have been able to take over much of the local organizations of the Republican Party in such states as Iowa, Arizona, and Texas (see, for example, the national and state 1996 Republican platforms); they are the ones tirelessly campaigning for phonics bills nationally and in most states. They pack state and local board meetings and hound legislators as they enter and leave their offices. In educational circles, they operate under names like "Parents for Better Education" or "Concerned Citizens for Educational Reform." As we'll see later in this chapter, they are the ones who widely publicize the attacks on whole language from those within the research communities, bringing "experts" who support phonics into their state and local campaigns. They publish newsletters, run clearinghouses, and have access to far-right talk shows, right-wing columnists, and television evangelists. And they bring enormous pressure on particular school boards, principals, and teachers. They are the engine that drives the attack on whole language. (See Chapters 5 and 6 for details on how this agenda operates at the state and local level.)

It wasn't always whole language that they proclaimed the enemy. Rudolf Flesch (1981) coined the term "Look, say" as a catchall phrase for any approach to reading instruction that didn't begin with a strong focus on phonics. In England, where the principles of whole language are widely used but the term is not, the attack was on "the real books approach."

Those of the far right campaign against control while at the same time wanting themselves to control. In Arizona, for example, they pushed for strong phonics requirements in the proposed state reading standards while they opposed the adoption of any state standards. The key focus of the far right is phonics in reading, but they have also invented a derisive term for modern math curricula, rejecting "the new 'new math.'"

They oppose developmentally appropriate experiences and what they term "politically correct" history. In reading, they want skills taught while controlling and censoring what kids are permitted to read. They oppose the idea of reading involving meaning construction as a dangerous idea and threat to religious belief. Currently in California and elsewhere they have unleashed an all-out attack on Reading Recovery, the remedial reading program developed by Marie Clay (1971).

On July 17, 1996, Robert Dole announced his education agenda, which included his "Education Consumers' Warranty," an answer to what he called the "failure, frustration, and futility" in public education. He blamed education bureaucrats and teachers' unions for running public schools into the ground and proposed to divert $2.5 billion of current federal support for education to funding a voucher system that would require states to provide matching funds (which of course would also be diverted from funds supporting public schools). Here's how the *Washington Post* reported his "warranty":

> Carefully following a prepared text, which he read from a Teleprompter, Dole unveiled the warranty, which says children

have the right to a safe school, freedom from incompetent bureaucrats, and to "learn the three R's through proven methods." And
he ridiculed modern trends in education . . .

Dole denounced "modern education experts" who had what
he called "an amazing gift for making simple things complicated."
He said the tried-and-true phonics reading method has been widely replaced with the "whole-language" method, in which children
are taught to read with open-ended exercises that emphasize creative writing, inventive [sic] spelling and literature.

"It's very interesting, very sophisticated, very new and exciting," Dole said. "The only problem is—it doesn't work." (Hardin
1996)

Whole language is the tall poppy Dole could single out in a broad
attack on "modern education experts" and their "amazing gift for making
simple things complicated." And by attacking whole language and coming
out for the "tried-and-true" phonics reading method, Dole aligned himself
with a major far-right group that has made its campaign for "direct, systematic instruction in phonics" the linchpin of its political agenda. (Note
also the misnomer for invented spelling. The far right has somehow turned
this into "inventive" spelling; the incorrect usage has become a marker for
the source of the information.) Politically, Dole's conservative, back-to-
basics call was meant to calm social and religious conservatives turned off
by his overtures to abortion-rights supporters. "Any time that Dole is going
to get out on an issue that is a high priority for social conservatives, it's
going to help him," said Mike Russell, spokesman for the 1.7 million-mem-
ber Christian Coalition (*USA Today*, July 18, 1996).

Business and Privatization

The agenda Dole espoused for education is also part of the general goal of
a major segment of American business to privatize all government func-
tions except the military—even prisons. In adopting a far-right education
agenda Dole came out against public education, using the far-right label of
public education as a "vise-like monopoly." That's the term groups like the
Heritage Foundation have used in proposing the privatization of education.
They want to open up certain segments of education to profit-making busi-
nesses. Writing in *The Nation* (September 8–15, 1997), Phyllis Vine exposed
widespread attempts of profit-making corporations to make money out of
charter schools and privatization. She quotes two investment analysts:

Mary Tanner, managing director of Lehman Brothers . . . compares
it [education] to health care—"a local industry that over time will

become a global business." Montgomery Securities' Michael Moe claims that "the timing and entry into the education and training market has never been better."

But more important than making profits from school takeovers, big business wants to reduce school taxes in order to increase profits. The idea of a free common public school system is so widely supported, however, that in order to achieve the goal of privatizing education it becomes necessary to convince Americans that public education has failed and that this is the fault of teachers failing to teach and students refusing to learn.

This attack on public education is driven by a business ethic that has eliminated millions of jobs in order to maximize profits. It's a mean-spirited policy that rejects the view that the education of young people is the responsibility of society in favor of the much older view that education should be the responsibility of parents and, as is true in many countries, that children should get the education their parents can afford to give them. Legislating on the basis of this position would lead to the abolition not only of the federal role in education but of the state role as well.

Politicians' Failure to Support Schools

There is another aspect to the role of politicians in both parties in the attack on whole language. Politicians have for years failed to provide sufficient support for effective education. The California legislature almost unanimously agreed that there was a relationship between whole language and the state's low NAEP test scores. As a result, they gave immediate support to two so-called ABC bills, which require, in part, "systematic, explicit phonics, spelling and basic computational skills" (Eastin 1996, p. 1). But the NAEP data, supplemented by *Education Week* (Wolk 1997), actually suggests that what's really to blame is the legacy of California's Proposition 13, which resulted in drastically constricted support for public education and a deemphasis on professional teacher education in teacher certification. Lack of support, not whole language, has much to do with the decline of education in California and other states with low means.

One way to consider how states support schools is to look at how much per-capita income each state spends on education. Nationally the 1996 figure was $41 per $1,000. (The NAEP 1994 data was updated by 1996 data in *Education Week*'s report.) High-scoring Maine, Wisconsin, and North Dakota spent $45 to $49 per $1,000. California's $34 per capita was higher than miserly Hawaii ($28) but less than many states poorer than California.

Another statistic to consider is spending per pupil. Nationally, this figure in 1996 was $5,541. California spent $4,753. That's higher than

---

California: The Legacy of Proposition 13 and Deprofessionalizing Teaching

Spending Per Pupil (adjusted for costs)
National average: $5,541. Arizona: $4,222; Hawaii: $4,394; California: $4,753; Maine: $5,854; Wisconsin: $6,345; Connecticut, New York, and New Jersey: over $8,000

Spending Per $1,000 Per Capita Income
Hawaii: $28; California: $34; Arizona: $36; North Dakota: $45; Maine and Wisconsin: $49

Teacher Salaries (NEA 1995–96, adjusted for cost of living)
National average: $36,744. Hawaii: $28,259; Arizona: $31,908; California: $36,110; Michigan: $50,224

Class Size (percent of classes over 25 pupils)
National: 41%. California: 93%; Utah: 76%; Florida: 73%; Arizona: 51%; Texas: 0%; Maine: 5%

Teacher Preparation
Undergraduate Major in Education
National: 69%. California: 39%

Degrees Above the Bachelor's
National: 41%. California: 29%; Indiana: 84%

Temporary and Uncertified Teachers
National: 5%. Hawaii: 12%; California: 11%*; Arizona: 9%

*This figure is deceptively low because of the minimal amount of professional education required prior to initial certification.

Sources: Miller et al. 1995; Wolk 1997

Arizona and Hawaii, each of which spent under $4,500. Maine and Wisconsin spent $5,854 and $6,354 respectively per pupil. Connecticut, New York, and New Jersey each spent over $8,000 per pupil.

In 1996, California teachers were paid at about the national average (adjusted for cost of living). But these salaries were achieved at the price of very large classes (Williams 1995; Wolk 1997). Only 7 percent of California teachers in 1994 reported having fewer than 25 pupils in their classes. This contrasts with a national figure of 59 percent. Only Utah, with 24 percent of teachers, and Florida, with 27 percent reporting classes of fewer than 25 pupils, come close to California (Wolk 1997). Class size is a measure of financial support as well as state policy. All of the Texas teachers and 95 percent of the Maine teachers reported classes under 25 pupils (Williams 1995, p. 55).

In the fall of 1996 California Governor Pete Wilson announced a massive campaign to reduce class size in the primary grades. That campaign led to immediate aggravation of another problem. California's percentage of uncertified teachers was reported as 11 percent before the class size reduction. The mandate brought a movement of experienced teachers from inner-city to suburban positions as jobs opened in the suburbs raising the ratio of uncertified teachers with the lowest achieving inner-city pupils.

In California in 1994, only 39 percent of teachers had education majors (as compared to 69 percent nationally). Only 29 percent of California teachers have advanced degrees; the national figure is 41 percent, and Indiana's is 84 percent (Williams 1995; Wolk 1997).

In joining the attack on whole language, politicians have shifted the blame for shortcomings in public education from themselves to teachers, some of whom are underprepared and most of whom are working in crowded, poorly maintained, and underfunded classrooms.

Paradigm Politics

Let's shift our focus now to another group: researchers who conduct experiments on reading. These researchers work within a paradigm that requires that experiments be tightly controlled, with only one or a small number of variables being permitted to vary while everything else is held constant. Most of their research is done in laboratories, with their subjects in controlled experiments. When the research is done in classrooms, highly constrained instruction over short time spans is given to experimental groups of students while other statistically comparable groups are treated as control groups. But control in the real world of the classroom is much harder to achieve than in the laboratory. These researchers' experiments are designed to show how specific instructional interventions affect specific, controlled aspects of reading. Often the intervention is use of a commercial reading program.

The methodologies, designs, and findings of this research paradigm stand in direct succession to decades of such research, and while the terms they use may have evolved ("phonemic awareness," for example) these researchers' current findings and beliefs are consistent with those of experimental researchers of the 1960s, '70s, and '80s. This point is worth making because this experimental research stance has always stood in contrast to the research that has served as the foundation of whole language. As P. David Pearson has said, "there is really nothing new in this debate. In one form or another, it has been going on for decades, perhaps centuries" (1997, p. 24).

The experimental researchers' view of reading has been summarized by Marilyn Adams:

> It has been proven beyond any shade of doubt that skillful readers process virtually each and every word and letter of text as they

read. This is extremely counter-intuitive. For sure, skillful readers neither look nor feel as if that's what they do. But that's because they do it so quickly and effortlessly. Almost automatically, with almost no conscious attention whatsoever, skillful readers recognize words by drawing on deep and ready knowledge and their connections to speech and meaning. In fact, the automaticity with which skillful readers recognize words is the key to the whole system . . . The reader's attention can be focused on the meaning and message of the text only to the extent that it's free from fussing with the words and letters. (quoted in McPike 1995, p. 4)

Keith Stanovich carries this view of the reading process into a view of reading instruction.

That direct instruction in alphabetic coding facilitates early reading instruction is one of the most well-established conclusions in all of behavioral science . . . Conversely the idea that learning to read is just like learning to speak is accepted by no responsible linguist, psychologist, or cognitive scientist in the research community. (quoted in McPike 1995, p. 4)

Two things stand out from these two statements. First, this view of reading, reading development, and reading instruction depends on word recognition (not phonics), in sharp contrast to the principle that underlies whole language, that the construction of meaning is the basis of reading. Second, these statements suggest these researchers' absolute belief that they are right and that their views in fact are the only "responsible," scientific ones.

Marilyn Adams and Maggie Bruck (1995) summarize the researchers' view of reading as word recognition:

Over the last few decades, reading researchers have developed a far better understanding of the print processing and how it feeds and fits into the rest of the reading system. They have learned why poor word recognition is a stumbling block for so many young readers and why, too, it is so frequently associated with poor comprehension. They have also learned much about how children learn to read words and help them do so. Educators can and should keep the positive initiatives of the whole language revolution. But it is also time to put this knowledge about word recognition into college classrooms and into practice. (p. 18)

Balancing as a Political Strategy

This bow toward "balance" between whole language and reading as word recognition culminates in an article in which Adams and Bruck analyze the appeal of whole language to teachers. They quickly reject the idea that its appeal could have to do with its view of reading as meaning construction and learning to read as learning to make sense of print. They reduce the differences between whole language and the "scientific" word recognition view to the "[whole language] movement's stance on phonics and code instruction" (p. 19).

But why have teachers been led to such a "wrong" view and why are they so resistant to the truth according to Stanovich, Adams, and their colleagues in scientific word recognition? Why, Adams and Bruck ask, have "the attitudes about teaching and learning phonics and about the naturalness of reading acquisition that characterize the whole language" approach continued to be so appealing to teachers if they are so wrong? The answer, they say, is that "they were tightly connected to the other issues of teacher empowerment, child-centered education, and the reading-writing connection. We believe, moreover, that it is these latter issues that inspire the deepest commitment and passion of the movement" (p. 17). Later, after exploring the practices of whole language, they reach this conclusion:

> If, in fact, these are goals that drive the whole language movement, then they must be supported whole-heartedly by all concerned. These goals are of paramount importance to our nation's health and progress. At the same time, however, they are strictly independent of the issues of the nature of the knowledge and processes involved in reading and learning to read. On these issues the research is resoundingly clear. Only by disentangling these two key sets of issues can we give either the attention that each so urgently deserves. (p. 18)

But if Adams and Bruck can so clearly separate the good parts of whole language from its wrong, unscientific views of the reading process and learning to read, why can't teachers also separate them? It is not because teachers themselves are convinced that the whole language view of reading as meaning construction and of learning to read as natural is right—how could they be, since it is wrong? Here Adams and Bruck are caught in their own paradigm. They have not examined the research base of whole language. In particular, they have not read the huge amount of literature written by teacher researchers that has supported the whole language view of written language and its development. They have not understood that whole language literacy curriculum and instruction is built on this research, with teachers the major contributors to the evolving knowledge base. Instead, they tell themselves it is the whole language extremists' refusal to accept scientific truth that explains the unwillingness of teachers to see that truth. And since there can be only one scientific truth, rejection of their position is a rejection of science itself. Thus, though Adams and Bruck call for a balance between whole language and word-recognition positions, a "disentangling" of the broad goals of whole language and the nature of reading,

> this disentanglement cannot take place as long as there exists an anti-research spirit within the whole language community. Many of the leaders of the movement actively discredit traditional scientific research approaches to the study of reading development and more specifically to the evaluation of their programs. The movement's anti-scientific attitude forces research findings into the backroom, making them socially and, thereby, intellectually unavailable to educators who are involved in whole language programs. (p. 18)

It must have been terribly frustrating for these "scientists" to see the widespread enthusiasm among teachers for whole language and the overt rejection of what they regarded as proven truth. By themselves they could not seem to get their message to teachers, even when they claimed to be in favor of a balanced approach, in which they would permit the inclusion of many aspects of whole language if only teachers would agree to change their view of reading as meaning construction to the scientific view of reading as rapid and accurate word recognition, and if only teachers would devote considerable time to direct instruction of the alphabetic code.

In Bed with the Far Right

At this point we should examine the tenuous, but long-standing, relationship between experimental researchers and the far right. When Richard Anderson, a University of Illinois psychologist, was given a grant from the National Institute of Education to begin the Center for the Study of Reading he brought together a team that had a common interest in schema theory as a means of explaining comprehension and little interest in reading instruction, particularly in beginning readers. (Bolt, Beranek, and Newman, a private, profit-making research group in Cambridge, Massachusetts, was co-grantee in the Center.) In subsequent refundings, Anderson managed to avoid the grant agency (NIE) shifting the focus away from comprehension to beginning reading through political strategies. In 1985 his center issued a report, *Becoming a Nation of Readers*, "with its clear support of 'phonics first and fast,'" according to Pearson (quoted in Adams 1990b, p. 9). In producing this report Anderson hoped to get the phonics lobby off his back and on his side by laying "to rest once and for all some of the old debates about phonics and comprehension," as Robert Glazer put it in his foreword to the Anderson report. Though the report professes a view of reading as meaning construction, it unequivocally states that "every reader must break the code that relates spelling to sound and meaning." It also states that readers must be able to "decode words quickly and accurately" (Anderson et al. 1985, pp. 10–11). Phonics is defined as "instruction in the relationship between letters and speech sounds" (p. 38). The report recommends that phonics should be taught early, be made explicit, and be kept simple (pp. 43, 57).

The "phonics first" lobby greeted the Anderson report as total vindication of their position. Newspaper editorials proclaimed that the center had proven phonics the method of choice. *Readers Digest* and the Reading Reform Foundation ran a full-page ad in the *New York Times* announcing the victory. Copies of the Anderson report were sold by professional organizations and distributed free by basal publishers.

But the phonics lobby in Washington wanted more. They wanted federal law to mandate phonics in reading instruction and teacher education. And they wanted a new report to go even further, including listing the most "cost-effective" phonics programs. According to Pearson, "it was *Becoming a Nation of Readers* . . . that spawned the legislation (authored by the late Senator Zerensky of Nebraska) commissioning this [Adams] report on phonics" (quoted in Adams 1990b).

So Anderson's attempt to avoid getting caught in the politics of phonics by issuing an endorsement of phonics only got him further in. The 1986 refunding of the Center explicitly required a new phonics report as a condition of the refunding by the federal government in response to the Zerensky legislation. Marilyn Adams, then a psychological researcher at Bolt, Beranek, and Newman, was commissioned by the Center to prepare the report.

In 1989, the Senate Republican Policy Committee issued a white paper, *Illiteracy: An Incurable Disease or Education Malpractice?* Senator William Armstrong is listed as the author, but the actual writer was Robert Sweet, head of the Right to Read Foundation and currently on the staff of the U.S. House Committee on Education and the Workforce. Here's what Senator Armstrong said about the white paper:

> For too long, we have been unwilling to deal with the root cause of the problem of illiteracy in America: the flawed methods we have used to teach our children to read. Research shows phonics is the most effective way to teach people to read. It's the way most of us learned to read. But it fell out of use in the last 20 years, with disastrous consequence. (Armstrong 1990, p. 1)

This chain of events brought the "phonics first" lobby into a new relationship with a major group of reading researchers. Never before had any research center or researcher accepted a direct federal commission to marshal the research literature in support of phonics and its political advocates. The "findings" of the Adams report were determined in advance by a federal government agency acting on instructions from Congress.

Not surprisingly, the sponsor found the report acceptable. Within a few days of the release of Adams's book, Senator Armstrong has this to say on the floor of the Senate:

> In a major new study on reading instruction released in January 1990 entitled *Beginning to Read: Thinking and Learning About Print,* Marilyn J. Adams, a researcher at Bolt, Beranek, and Newman, Inc., in Cambridge, Massachusetts, recognizes phonics as an essential ingredient of early reading instruction. She concludes that: "Research indicates that to become proficient readers, children need to learn and be able to use the relationships between letters and sounds and that explicit instruction of these relationships leads to improved reading achievement." (*Congressional Record,* February 5, 1990)

But neither *Becoming a Nation of Readers* (Anderson et al. 1985) nor Adams's *Beginning to Read* (1990a, 1990b), both published with enormous fanfare and very broad distribution, has made any visible impression on teachers, their classroom practice, and their beliefs about reading. Adams, Anderson, Stanovich et al. must have been disturbed to see whole language spreading and having enormous impact while the "scientific truth" they possessed was being ignored if not overtly rejected.

The National Institute of Child Health and Human Development (NICHD)

Another body of research that had little impact on teachers and was also little known in the reading research community was that funded by the National Institute of Child Health and Human Development (NICHD), an agency within the National Institute of Health (NIH), the major federal funder of medical research. NIH is part of the federal Department of Health and Human Services. The rationale for funding research related to reading within the broad mission of NIH is that it would deal with children whose reading was limited by disabilities. Research funded by NICHD has been conducted by experimental psychologists who work in medical or clinical settings. Most of these researchers were not much interested in the teaching of reading or reading curriculum. Reid Lyon, Acting Chief of the Child Development and Behavior Branch of the NICHD, has taken an aggressive stance on applying findings from the NICHD research to decision-making on reading instruction. He has used his connections with the American Academy for the Advancement of Science (AAAS) and other such eminent groups to create the view, picked up by the press, that the NICHD research is the only scientific research on reading and that it all leads to a single conclusion: phonics is the essence of successful reading programs.

Lyon permitted himself to be introduced to a legislative committee in Sacramento, California, as the chief authority in the federal government on reading research (videotape of testimony).

In testimony before the House Committee on Education and the Workforce on July 10, 1997, Lyon characterized the NICHD funded research as "extensive research on the process of learning to read in our nation's schools" (p. 24). P. David Pearson (1997) has expressed concern about how Lyon and NICHD have

> tried to capture the scientific mantle. Reid Lyon says quite openly and without equivocation that we have once and for all proven, beyond a shadow of a doubt, that reading is NOT . . . a psycholinguistic guessing game as Goodman and Smith would have us believe. Even more disconcerting is the assertion by many followers of the NICHD work that we now have incontrovertible proof that early systematic attention to the code is the most effective way to teach reading. (p. 24)

Pearson objects to these claims:

> [P]erhaps . . . this is the most fundamental concern for me, those who report the NICHD research seem either hopelessly ignorant or intentionally dismissive of the last 20 years of research on early literacy within the educational community, not to mention the earlier generation of educational research comparing different approaches to early reading." (p. 24)

Lyon organized a panel at the AAAS in 1996 in which all panelists agreed that whole language had no scientific base whereas phonics did. In reporting the North American press put a heavy focus on one study funded by NICHD and conducted by a team led by Barbara Foorman and others at the University of Houston. Though the study was not complete and no report had been published in a refereed journal, newspapers reported that it proved conclusively that phonics was superior to whole language in teaching first- and second-grade at-risk children to read.

The Foorman Study

The only published version of the Foorman study as of this writing is a short article in a learning disability journal that included it as part of a research program of several loosely related studies done in the Alief School District in suburban Houston. The study involved 375 first- and second-grade Chapter I pupils in over sixty different classrooms (no data is provided on the approximately 1,300 other pupils in these classes who apparently got the same instruction). Almost 60 percent of the target pupils are

African American, a far higher percentage than in the district school population generally. As with most of the NICHD-funded studies, the subjects were the lowest ranked of the Chapter I children. The subjects were divided into four groups according to the in-class instruction they received. Three of the four groups of target pupils also were given a pullout program.

One group received what Foorman and her colleagues called "whole language instruction." We have only their word that what they received was truly whole language instruction. A second group received an adaptation by Foorman and her colleagues of a program developed by Elfrieda Heibert that Foorman labeled "embedded phonics." The third group were given Open Court, a commercial reading program. The fourth group, which was not really part of the study, were referred to as the "unseen" whole language group; they received the district's regular program. The original proposal called for one group to get Distar instruction; Foorman told a Texas group how she came to use Open Court instead (coincidentally, both Distar and Open Court are now published by the SRA division of McGraw Hill):

> We were going to use the reading mastery program many know here as Distar because the literature supported that program with children of low socioeconomic status . . . I called my friend Marilyn Adams, and I said, "Help I'm not allowed to use Distar" . . . Well, to equip 18 classrooms and teacher training would have cost me close to $100,000 . . . And she said, "Well, I happen to know of a program you might try. It seems to have good components of instruction based on sound research," and that's the story of how we got this program. (Governor's Business Council, p. 51)

She didn't tell the Texas group that her "friend Marilyn Adams" is the major author of Open Court. Open Court appears to have provided both the materials and "teacher training" for those teachers using their materials (by Foorman's estimate $100,000 worth). Although the published report (Foorman et al. 1997) refers to the Open Court group as receiving "Direct Instruction [caps theirs] in a balanced approach," the *Houston Chronicle* (May 5, 1996), citing an *LA Times* report, called it "intensive phonics," "concentrated phonics," and a "phonetic-based reading program." The *Toronto Globe and Mail* reported that Foorman said at the AAAS session that "children taught phonics were six times as likely to be reading more than one word at the end of the year as whole language children." Later the article refers to "the pure phonics group students taught to sound out each letter in an 'A equals ahhh, B equals buh' way."

Foorman and her colleagues have been highly selective in reporting their findings. The strange claim reported in the *Toronto Globe and Mail* about how many children could read more than one word comes from their use of two subtests in the Woodcock-Johnson test that test only word recognition and the ability to read nonsense words. In her testimony in Sacramento for the state legislative committee and in Texas for the Governor's Business Council, Foorman made an equally strange claim. Here's what she said in Texas as she showed histograms:

> This is a histogram of the growth, the frequency of who were growing in a certain—their growth in word reading across the year. This is the Open Court Curriculum. This is the control whole language, our seen whole language group, and this is the embedded phonics group. The most important thing is the embedded phonics and the two whole language groups' growth rates are bunching around zero—zero growth rates. A large percentage of the children don't show any growth in reading in those programs. (Governor's Business Council, p. 54)

Foorman is giving her listeners the impression that large numbers of children had not learned to read a single word at the end of the second grade! (She is also saying that reading words on a list is reading.) I know of no program, however bad, that has readers at the end of second grade unable to read a single word.

The Foorman study does not provide evidence that phonics is successful or that whole language isn't. The researchers found only what they planned to find: that they could make a heavily supported direct instruction basal program look better on word list tests than other, weakly supported programs. Even so, they could only provide evidence of differences in word recognition and not in comprehension.

The study ended after the first year in a dispute between the district and the researchers. That should have made the results of even more dubious value, since it was planned as a five-year study. Reid Lyon says NICHD only funds long-range studies. So the question is, how does a study that is poorly designed, not yet reported to the funder, and unpublished except in the most minimal way get so much attention? The answer is that Reid Lyon showcased it to call particular attention to the NICHD. The publishers of Open Court also widely publicized it well before any results had been reported elsewhere. Another author of the study has told me, through e-mail, that they asked those responsible for Open Court to stop making claims for their program based on the study. But those claims were a factor in their problems with the district.

The "success" of the program in "Houston" (now embellished to include the whole city) has been widely exploited in California and elsewhere. Marion Joseph, now a member of the state Board of Education in California, was instrumental in getting the Packard Foundation (Hewlett Packard) to provide a grant of $4 million to the Sacramento school district conditional on their suspending text adoption procedures and adopting

Open Court. (See Spring 1997 for details on the intricate connections between private foundations, neoconservative thinktanks, and the right-wing agenda in education.)

The Distar Disinformation Group

Over thirty years ago, in the period when minority learners were being called "culturally deprived," Siegfried Englemann developed a program in reading and math he called Distar. It was rooted in behavioral learning theory and deficit views of low-achieving, poor, and minority children. One characteristic of Distar's promotion was the persistent claims of fantastic success based primarily on data provided by the program's developers. Over the years the popularity of the program waxed and waned. It was sold with special state and/or federal funding including a tutorial aspect (one tutor per five pupils) and was usually abandoned when outside funding disappeared. Over the years it became a kind of pariah program among educators, seen as an exemplar of deficit-view programs.

Englemann and his associates at the University of Oregon have developed a disinformation program built around a theme: only direct instruction programs such as Distar are research based. All other programs, particularly whole language, they contend, have absolutely no research base. In addition, research-based programs (namely, Distar) teach kids to read; all others, particularly whole language, do not—in fact they produce dyslexia, illiteracy, delinquency, and so on.

When the political tides changed in California, the Distar disinformation group shifted into high gear. Douglas Carnine became an influential advisor to the state legislature and the Board of Education. He found a similar role in Texas. Jean Osborne, a Distar author, was given a major official role in staff development in Texas. Bonnie Grossen, their Oregon colleague who edits a direct instruction journal put out by the group, edited a "research summary" of NICHD purporting to show that direct instruction in phonics (Distar) is directly supported by NICHD research. This disinformation scenario has become law in every particular in California. It has been given urgency in that all the laws based on the disinformation are given immediate effect, a quite unusual procedure for any law. In all this there is a clear conflict of interest with legal decisions based on information supplied by those most likely to profit from them.

Capturing Teachers by Force:
Disinformation Becomes Law

In the aftermath of a strong conservative sweep in the elections of November 1994, the far right in California succeeded in ending the innovative statewide performance-based assessment program and forced the formation of a Reading Task Force. The Distar disinformation group, the experimental research scientists, and NICHD's Reid Lyon stood ready to join in blaming the 1987 California English–Language Arts Framework and its supposed espousal of whole language for a crisis in literacy. As the report put it, "The task force concluded that the 1987 English–Language Arts Framework did not present a comprehensive and balanced reading program and gave insufficient attention to a systematic skills instruction program" (California Reading Task Force 1995, p. 2). The attack on whole language by those on the far right created a new opportunity to bring their positions to the attention of teachers and in fact to mandate that teachers adopt them. It came in the aftermath of the release of the 1994 NAEP *First Look* (Williams 1995) and the press's subsequent reporting that whole language had failed to teach kids to read because California's mean on the NAEP test among fourth graders had dropped from the 1992 test results, putting the state near the bottom of the rankings among participating states with Guam and Louisiana.

> National and state reports indicate that a majority of California's children cannot read at basic levels. This reading failure begins in early grades and has a harmful effect for a lifetime. Only a call to action at the highest levels, one that can marshal both human and fiscal resources and bring this story to the public, can be expected to address this crisis. (California Reading Task Force 1995, p. 1)

New allies were found. Albert Shanker, president of the American Federation of Teachers, offered a forum for the "scientific" word recognition message in a special issue of *American Educator* (Summer 1995). And William Honig, former California State Superintendent of Instruction, found redemption from his disgrace in being convicted of misusing his office by recanting his prior support of whole language and endorsing the scientific truth of Adams and Stanovich. Subsequently, his felony conviction was reduced to a misdemeanor, allowing him to do business with the state (he couldn't as a convicted felon).

The Distar agenda was touted as the solution to the crisis:

> Skills development is critical in beginning reading. These skills should be directly taught and each child's ability should be assessed. Kindergarten students need to develop phonemic awareness. (California Reading Task Force, p. 4)

> In kindergarten, at least one third of the day should be devoted to language arts. In early primary grades, students should spend at least one half of the day in reading and or other language activities. (California Reading Task Force, p. 11)

In an "Advisory" (1996) from Delaine Eastin, the California State Superintendent, the task force recommendation moved from *should* to *must*:

> [A]ny early reading program must include the following instructional components: phonemic awareness; letter names and shapes, systematic, explicit phonics, spelling, vocabulary development; comprehension and higher-order thinking; and appropriate instructional materials. (p. 4)

The total certainty of the experimental researchers was translated into strong promises in the Advisory:

> There is sufficient guidance now available from research about how children best learn to read and about how successful reading programs work to ensure that virtually every child will learn to read well, at least by the end of third grade. (p. 2)

The Reading Task Force and the State Department Advisory in California both explicitly called what they proposed a balanced program. But the press reported it as a rejection of whole language and a mandate for phonics.

The disinformation group now has the ear of the state legislature. "Research-based programs" such as Distar and Open Court are ready and waiting, and the bills recently passed by the California legislature have no elements of balance, despite some of their titles. That's true also for bills the far right is pushing in many other states. They mandate back-to-basics curriculum and the methodology and content of teacher education programs. The so-called scientific truth of Adams and Stanovich has come out of the back room and into the legislative committee room. Adams has shifted from her role as "scientist" to one of program author of Open Court, a legislative advisor, and a program implementer as she roams California, Texas, and other states promoting "research-based reading programs." In imposing on teachers explicit constraints on how and what they teach, however, promoters like Adams run a strong risk of alienating teachers from the views they are trying to get them to accept. They're playing another dangerous game as well. No doubt they believe that because their views are "scientific" they will be persuasive in the power plays of the far right in the current political scene. But the far right is upping the ante, broadening its attack and the demands it is making on mainstream politicians and educators.

The Media: Creating News

In considering the role of the media in the attacks on whole language, we must differentiate the far-right newsletters, magazines, and ultraconservative columnists and radio and TV talk shows, whose bias is explicit, from mainstream media. The former have been consistently against whole language or any kind of progressive reform or innovation in education. They speak for the far right, particularly the religious right. This press needs specific targets, such as witchcraft in basal readers or Ken Goodman. Whole language did not become an important target to them until its popularity among teachers increased sufficiently that it began to be mentioned outside of professional journals and conferences. The far-right media have certain favorite "scientists" they quote. Patrick Groff is a favorite, with Jeanne Chall a close second. They report every morsel from their favorite scientists, interweaving it with Distar disinformation.

Here's a documented example to illustrate how the process works: A group of linguists and closely associated psychologists in Massachusetts become aware of a proposed state language arts framework. It offends them because it defines reading as meaning construction. These linguists, who have shown no interest in written language or school curricula for decades, believe that written language is not language but an encoding of oral language. They write a letter to the state Commissioner of Education and circulate it among many prominent linguists at MIT, Harvard, Brandeis, the University of Massachusetts, and several other universities in the state. Forty of them sign it. With the letter goes a much longer cover letter that explicitly attacks whole language and cites its failure in California, which they read about in the *Boston Globe*. (Never mind that Massachusetts and the other New England states did very well on the same NAEP state-by-state comparisons.) The commissioner schedules a meeting with David Pesetsky and a colleague who wrote the letters and organized the signings. He thanks them for their interest and assures them that their views will be considered.

But then the letters take on a life of their own. The signed letter (usually without the cover letter) is distributed on several e-mail networks by those who support the sentiments and those who are alarmed by them. Samuel Blumenfeld (1995) reprints the letters and several pieces of related correspondence in his *Blumenfeld Education Letter*. The material is picked up by the phonics lobby. (Now they have not only research psychologists but also distinguished linguists on their side.) Newspaper columnists also use the linguists' letters. Right-wing commentators use them to silence teachers who complain about their misrepresentations of whole language.

Shifting to the Mainstream Press

An important change in the media's coverage of literacy education took place when the *Atlantic Monthly* published an article on whole language in December 1994 (Levine 1994). The scientific word recognition group found a new forum in the national press in the context of the phonics lobby's attack on whole language. The author of the *Atlantic Monthly* article reported that whole language "theories" have been discredited, that "in the two decades since the whole language philosophy first became influential in academic circles, a considerable amount of research has been showing Goodman's and Smith's psycholinguistic theories to be wrong" (p. 43). A pattern was thus set for subsequent treatment of whole language in the popular press.

High-Tech Journalism

The information superhighway has brought a new form of investigative reporting to journalism—a high-tech version of the old children's game of Telephone, or Gossip, where someone whispers a message to the person next to him or her, which is whispered to the next person and the next, until it gets all the way around a circle, at which point the last person says the message out loud. Everyone then laughs at how the original message has changed in the transmission.

Let's say that an editor of the *New York Times* says to a stringer in Los Angeles, "Do a story on this phonics–whole language thing going on in California." This freelance reporter doesn't start the story from scratch. He sits down at his computer, gets onto the Web, and in a few minutes is browsing through what many other reporters have recently written on the subject. He outlines "the facts" as represented in the several previous stories, notes who is quoted as saying what, then picks the angle he will take in his own story. He then writes his story, in the process phoning a few of the individuals previously quoted in order to get fresh statements. If the people he calls don't give him the lines he needs for his story, that's all right—he can pick some older lines out of quotes he's found in other reporters' stories. His assignment is facilitated by the thick stack of material he has received from his editor and the CEO of the paper's parent corporation—all attacking whole language and lauding phonics.

When the reporter finishes writing, he reads the piece over and realizes that it sounds a little one-sided, so he finds a name of a whole language advocate in the materials he's accumulated and calls that person for a "balancing" quote. Then he files his story. In return, he gets a nice note from the editor complimenting him on the story's balance and the quality of the research. The CEO compliments the reporter too.

Because the article appears in the *New York Times* on Wednesday in the Education section, for the next week or two the article is reprinted by many other cities' newspapers, which have recently downsized and fill their news columns with features from other papers. Perhaps the editor of the *Christian Science Monitor* sees the piece in the *Times* and assigns its own stringer to do a story. She in turn gets on the Internet to research her story . . .

The net effect (so to speak) is twofold. First, the agreement among all these stories creates a synthetic reality. Even the reporters begin to believe that there is a core of truth in all the stories simply because they're all saying the same thing:

> Data from the 1994 NAEP study shows that 60 percent of kids can't read at a basic level; the stress educators have placed on whole language while neglecting real reading instruction in the form of phonics is to blame.

That must be true because so many papers have reported it.

But there is another effect of this practice. As each reporter changes in minor ways the original story, the details shift a bit. When an Orlando reporter calls me and says he saw my name in the Chicago paper, I'm not surprised later to see in his article that his quote from me is not anything I said to him but a paraphrase of what I said to the *Tribune* reporter.

Here's an example of how whole language was reported on in an "alternative" newspaper, the *LA Weekly:*

> But whole language, which sounds so promising when described by its proponents, has proved to be a near *disaster* when applied to—and by—real people. In the eight years since whole language first appeared in the state's grade schools, California fourth-grade reading *scores have plummeted* to near the bottom nationally according to the National Assessment of Educational Progress (NAEP). Indeed, California's *fourth-graders are now such poor readers* that only the children of Louisiana and Guam—both hampered by *pitifully backward education systems*—get worse reading scores. (Stewart 1996, p. 20) (Italics mine: these ideas were her twist on the story.)

There are a number of misstatements both in this paragraph and in the rest of the article. What did this reporter actually research about whole language or education in Guam, Louisiana, or California? How does she know about "pitifully backward education systems"? Still, the article was reprinted a few weeks later in more mainstream newspapers: the *Sacramento Bee,* the *San Jose Mercury-News,* and others.

Bill Honig is extensively quoted in this article as are representatives of the scientific word recognition group. Here's a quote from Honig:

> Things got out of hand. School administrators and principals thought they were following the framework when they latched onto whole language and our greatest mistake was in failing to say, "Look out for the crazy stuff, look out for the overreactions and

the religiously anti-skills fanatics." We totally misjudged whose voices would take charge of the schools. We never dreamed it would be driven to the bizarre edge. (p. 21)

There are villains in the article, fanatics, gurus, and theorists, though they were not interviewed for the piece.

> [A] revolution was brewing in the classroom. Whole language gurus like Ken and Yetta Goodman of the University of Arizona were selling the romantic notion that childhood reading was a "natural" act that was being repressed by teachers hooked on low-level issues like word recognition and letters . . .
>
> Unfortunately, the theorists were operating without the benefit of methodologically accepted research. According to articles published by the American Federation of Teachers no meaningful research has verified their claims. (p. 23)

It's the movement of the controversy into the mainstream media that has had the greatest impact on the image of whole language. That, in turn, has encouraged the far right to step up its attack at state and local levels, waving newspapers in front of boards, superintendents, and legislators that purportedly tell the story of the failure of whole language in California and, by implication, everywhere.

Richard Colvin, an education writer for the *Los Angles Times,* crossed the line from reporter to advocate when he joined an expert panel at the American Educational Research Association and invented a reading crisis in New Zealand. He wrote, "New Zealand showed America—and the world—how to abandon phonics. Now its own students are struggling and some critics question the methods that made the nation's literacy legend" (Colvin 1997, p. A28). Colvin finds calamity if New Zealand nine-year-olds slip from first place to sixth in an international reading study, ignoring that the difference between the national scores of those in second to sixth place are statistically equivalent.

Fundamentalism in Reading

We live in an age in which there is a resurgence of fundamentalist views in many parts of the world. It crosses religions. Christian fundamentalism was mentioned earlier in this chapter. In the Moslem world fundamentalists are forcing their views on every aspect of life in Iran, Afghanistan, and Algeria. And Jewish fundamentalists physically interfere with other Jews coming to the Wall in Jerusalem to pray. What these movements all have in common is a clinging to old ways, old beliefs, and an overwhelming fear of change, of modernity itself. In education, fundamentalism takes the form of "back-to-basics" movements, a longing for the good old days when all children behaved in school and learned fundamental, safe skills and truths. For fundamentalists, change in public education involves an imposition of dangerous new ideas and experiences on their children. Those who advocate such change are seen as agents of evil. There is even fundamentalism among researchers, in the belief that research that does not involve controlled experiments is not just nonscience but antiscience.

Whole language is a threat to all these fundamentalists. To those who, for any reason, believe that everything is explicitly good or evil, right or wrong, true or untrue, seeing the teaching of literacy as a simple choice between fundamental phonics and innovative whole language makes sense. Though fundamentalists have a strong distrust of science, putting a scientific blessing on this dichotomy greatly strengthens their position and gives them much more political clout. And, as mentioned earlier, among the scientists supporting fundamentalism in reading is a strange research fundamentalism that rejects all nonexperimental research as nonresearch.

Their "true science" can produce "research-based programs." The far right can concentrate on keeping pressure on politicians and administrators at all levels, on being ready to pack a hearing room or school board meeting, while the disinformers and "scientists" push the "truth" on teachers and administrators.

Hijacking America Reads

As part of his 1996 reelection strategy President Clinton, echoing the California task force report, promised in his "America Reads" program to have every child a reader by age eight. His plan included administering a national reading test in fourth grade and instituting a massive program of volunteer tutors. During 1997, the House Education and Workforce Committee held hearings around the United States ostensibly on the subject of "what works." The Republican majority, under Rep. William F. Goodling of Pennsylvania, carefully orchestrated who got to speak. Hearings in Washington in September 1997 featured Reid Lyon.

Lyon set up the "crisis" in reading:

> In the state of California, 59% of fourth grade children had little or no mastery of the knowledge and skills necessary to perform reading activities . . . compared to a national average of 44%. (Lyon 1997, p. 3)

To learn to read, Lyon asserts, the scientific word recognition view must be used:

> What our NICHD research has taught us is . . . the would-be reader *must* understand that our speech can be . . . broken into small

sounds (phoneme awareness) and that the segmented units of speech can be represented by printed forms (phonics). This understanding . . . (termed the alphabetic principle) is *absolutely necessary* for the development of accurate and rapid word reading skills. (p. 4)

And why do children have trouble learning to read?

Invariably, it is difficulty linking letters with sounds that is the source of reading problems . . .

Unfortunately, there is no way to bypass this decoding and word recognition stage of reading . . . In essence, while one learns to read for the fundamental purpose of deriving meaning from print, the key to comprehension starts with the immediate and accurate reading of words. (p. 8)

And what about the teacher?

A major impediment to serving the needs of children demonstrating difficulties learning to read is current teacher preparation practices. Many teachers lack basic knowledge and understanding of reading development and the nature of reading difficulties. (p. 13)

Lyon's recommendations include the following:

■ Major efforts to ensure that colleges of education possess the expertise and commitment to foster expertise in teachers (pre-service and in-service).
■ Competency-based "training programs" with formal board certification for teachers.
■ A formal procedure to assess the current status of scientific research-based knowledge relevant to reading development and effectiveness of various approaches to teaching children to read.
■ Strategies for rapid dissemination of this information to facilitate teacher preparation and effective reading instruction in our nation's schools.

This translates into a national reading curriculum and methodology mandated for all teacher-educators and teachers. "Rapid dissemination" translates into use of state and federal power to enforce the curriculum, and justifies bypassing all of the usual safeguards, such as review processes for funding, state and local text selection procedures, and teacher participation in state, district, and school decision-making. California law sets up a paradigm police authority to determine who may teach and what may be taught in programs funded with state and federal support.

Lyon's proposals provide similar controls and fit neatly into a plan that is the base for legislation coming out of the House Committee on Education and the Workforce. Robert Sweet, founder of the Right to Read Foundation, is now a staff coordinator for the committee. His predecessor in that position, Hans Meeder, joined with Douglas Carnine to propose a plan they published in *Education Week,* September 3, 1997.

Essentially, Carnine and Meeder put the educational community and the nation on notice that having captured literacy education in California they intended to use the same blueprint to capture the nation by taking over the America Reads program. In California, Carnine and others have succeeded in convincing key decision-makers that there is only one kind of reading research—the kind that tests published programs on learners—and that commercial programs based on direct instruction of explicit synthetic phonics are the necessary and only way to teach reading. Most of the proposals in their *Education Week* commentary are already law in California.

They would hijack America Reads and all its funding in the service of "a research-based approach." Then they would, by early 1998, have a national "expert panel" announce a synthesis of research knowledge about reading (direct synthetic phonics). This panel was funded by an amendment to the 1997 appropriations bill and applications for membership were invited in December 1997. Reid Lyon, the head of NICHD, would become reading czar with authority to order two cabinet members, the Secretaries of Education and Health and Human Services, to disseminate the accepted knowledge about reading research by imposing it on Head Start, Even Start, and Title I. The Secretary of Education would impose "scientifically based research on reading" on the Office of Educational Research and Improvement (OERI), particularly the regional labs, which would not only disseminate the scientific truth but issue "a 'product recall' of previously disseminated information not 'scientifically validated'" (p. 41).

A single authority, presumably under Reid Lyon, would coordinate all federal agencies to make sure that parents, grandparents, and caregivers would know "what a research-based reading program looks like" (p. 41). As in California, that program would look like Distar.

The plan includes a role for Carnine like the one he enjoys in California and Texas: chief paradigm policeman. Federal funds would be given to almost anybody (no qualifications needed) to develop programs for disseminating research knowledge to teachers; "an independent third party evaluator would establish whether the model embodied scientific research principles about reading" (p. 43).

The Carnine-Meeder plan provides a scapegoat: whole language. "It is confounding why, even in an area as well researched as early reading, there has been such enormous difficulty in turning that into widely replicated practice. On the contrary, poorly researched programs, such as an extreme whole language approach, have been quickly and widely adopted across many states, most notably California" (p. 43). Early reading is indeed well researched, but most of it would be in line for "product recall" in the Carnine-Meeder plan.

As in California, there is no middle ground in this plan: you're either for research-based scientific programs or you're a whole language lover.

Not surprisingly, at the time the Carnine-Meeder plan was published the House Committee on Education and the Workforce staff began floating a draft for potential federal legislation that was based on, and in some parts copied from, the Carnine-Meeder plan. Things moved very fast. HR2614, which embodies most of the Carnine-Meeder plan, was passed by the U.S. House of Representatives by voice vote on a Saturday afternoon as Congress was hurrying to adjourn for the 1997 year. The chamber was virtually empty, and no negative votes were recorded. A few days earlier the president had met with Rep. Goodling, and the administration and the Department of Education told the committee they could accept the bill. At this writing the bill is in committee in the Senate waiting for committee action.

As HR2614 went to the floor of Congress, *Time* (Collins, October 27, 1997), *Newsweek* (Wingert and Kantrowitz, October 27, 1997), *U.S. News and World Report* (Toch, October 27, 1997), *Atlantic Monthly* (Lemann, November 1997), and *Policy Review* (Palmaffy, November–December 1997) all published articles on the "reading wars"; all came out squarely for phonics. The *Baltimore Sun* and the *Washington Post* also published major coverage. None of these articles mentioned HR2614, but all slammed whole language and promoted phonics.

> After reviewing the arguments by the phonics and whole-language proponents, can we make a judgement who is right? Yes. The value of explicit systematic phonics instruction has been established. (Collins, October 27, 1997, p. 81)

> The evidence is overwhelming that kids with reading problems need phonics-based instruction. Why aren't educators getting the message? (Palmaffy, November–December 1997, p. 32)

Achieving Change Through Force of Law

P. David Pearson (1997) expresses concern with the drive to use state and federal power to win the "great debate":

> In the ascendancy of whole language, literature-based reading and process writing as cornerstones of the elementary school language arts curriculum, the forum for promoting these new views and their accompanying teaching tools was the marketplace of ideas.

Part of the momentum of the movement was to find any and every way possible to "get the information out" so that teachers would have access to it. The other part of the logic was to create forums, such as TAWL (Teachers Applying Whole Language) groups and teacher research networks, to sustain teachers who had begun to make these changes and to assume the curricular authority to which they were entitled. (p. 8)

Dissemination, the marketplace of ideas, and professional support groups are conspicuously absent from the back-to-basics counter movement. The strategy of the movement is simpler and more direct: work through legislative and policymaking bodies to mandate the changes deemed necessary. Prey upon the crisis mentality that policymakers find so appealing . . ." (p. 24)

Two Major Concerns

I want to bring this review of the forces involved in the virulent attacks on whole language to focus on two major concerns.

Will Teachers Turn Away from Whole Language?

First, let's consider the impact on whole language and whole language teachers. Here I believe the most important issues are how whole language achieved the success it has among teachers, and the potential of the attacks for dislodging whole language and its effects from classrooms and replacing it either with the scientific word recognition of Adams and Stanovich or the mandated agenda of the far-right phonics lobby.

The success of whole language lies partly in the solid knowledge base it has built, but mostly in the translation of that knowledge base into successful classroom reality by highly professional, committed classroom teachers. What Adams, Stanovich, Honig, Lyon, and others who oppose whole language have never understood is that whole language teachers are not the dupes and pawns of whole language "gurus." They are professionals who base what they do in their classrooms on what they know and who themselves continue to contribute to the knowledge base of whole language. They actively reject the scientific word recognition paradigm as well as simplistic phonics programs because they have tested their knowledge base with their pupils in their classrooms and confirmed the validity of whole language, not because they have been deprived of access to scientific knowledge. These are teachers who have "been there and done that" and who are not in need of enlightenment from on high. They are confident in their knowledge and dedicated to using it to support their students. They are offended and insulted by attempts to force them into narrow phonemic awareness and skill-and-drill phonics programs. They think of themselves as professionals.

So in the end the effect of the attacks may be limited. Without the coercion of laws and board mandates there is little chance of converting the core of teachers who have identified with whole language. And with the coercion there is a strong chance that an even larger number of teachers will be offended and respond negatively. This rejection by teachers is not likely to take the form of mass demonstrations or highly organized campaigns. More likely, American teachers will do what they have always done—close their doors and keep doing what they believe in. Even changing the textbooks will not dislodge the changes whole language has brought. Too many teachers are now aware that they can teach without basals and texts. They know, without seeing the NAEP data, that having kids silently read real literature of their own choosing is much more effective than following the sequenced skills and tortured texts of the basals. These teachers will not stop their students from writing until they have mastered the spelling book lists. They will not willingly subject kindergarten and first-grade children to phonemic awareness drills. Those who fear whole language have seriously underestimated the professionalism of whole language teachers. And they have seriously overestimated the ability of laws to force change on any North American teachers.

In California and Texas, and now nationally, as coercive attempts to force changes on teacher educators are taking place, these attempts have only insulted and outraged these professionals. Teacher educators in the United States have never been a unified group, but these strong-arm tactics may be uniting them.

Researchers who have supported "balance" find no ground left to stand on. Those with the state power to push for phonics have given researchers an ultimatum: "You're either for us or against us." Clearly, the issue is not whole language, and it is not whole language that is the target.

Moreover the far right is so heady with its recent successes that it has broadened its attacks and made many groups within professional education aware that whole language was only the first visible target. The developments in Washington have made it clear to reporters that the attacks on whole language are political.

That doesn't mean that I am totally optimistic. Support for whole language among state and local administrators was never very strong. Already administrators have become nervous about even using the term "whole language," substituting euphemisms or dubbing their programs "balanced." An advisory from the state department of education becomes a mandate on principals and teachers. There is no doubt that waves of pressure are reaching many whole language teachers. Particularly where they are already teaching in difficult situations with large classes, meager resources, and challenging pupils, some of these teachers may choose to leave the classroom rather than continue to be beaten up. That would be a great loss, because it will mean that the more successful professionals would leave. There is some evidence that this loss of experienced teachers has begun to happen in California: between the 1992 and 1994 NAEP assessments the percentage of teachers with less than ten years' experience increased sharply, while the percentage with ten to twenty-five years dropped sharply (Miller et al. 1995, pp. 122, 123).

Despite these real problems, however, the boldness of the attempt to take over reading education in the United States has resulted in the coming together of a wide range of researchers and teacher educators on a common agenda:

1. *Neither Congress or any state legislature nor any federal or state agency should establish a national or state reading methodology.* What is being pushed is a hard-line version of Distar and Open Court, code-named "research-based programs." Their merit or lack of merit is not the issue. Congress should not pass laws requiring schools or local education agencies to use *any* specific program or methodology.

2. *Neither Congress or any state legislature nor any federal or state agency should establish a single definition of reading or single reading paradigm in funding programs for pre-service or in-service teacher education programs.* There are both historic and contemporary differences among literacy educators. There are adequate procedures and forums for the profession to debate the merits of a range of alternate views. Using federal laws and federal bureaucracies to push any one view to the exclusion of all others is unwarranted and will do more harm than good, regardless of the merit or lack of merit of the favored definition or paradigm.

3. *Neither Congress or any state legislature nor any federal or state agency should impose on research funding programs any single definition of reading or any single reading paradigm.* There is no consensus among researchers in literacy on what has been learned from past research that would warrant limiting federal funding, or who could be funded by federal programs, to studies that support a single view of reading and reading instruction. Such an imposition would impose a dangerous antiscientific constraint on research and limit what can be learned.

4. *Neither Congress or any state legislature nor any federal or state agency should bypass traditional standards and procedures for peer review or centralize authority for decision-making or review of decision-making in the hands of a single individual or extraordinary authorities.* In California, and in the discussion documents the House Education Committee has circulated, preexisting procedures and agencies are bypassed and decision-making is concentrated in the hands of special-

ly created agencies and single individuals with the clear intention of controlling who and what will be funded without going through well-established agency peer review procedures.

5. *There should be no blacklisting or stigmatizing of paradigms, people, pedagogies, universities, research agencies, or instructional programs, either directly or indirectly, through establishing a single paradigm or narrowly drawn set of criteria for eligible programs or grantees.* In California, Texas, and a number of other states, legislation has been introduced or passed that specifically proscribes certain pedagogies, instructional practices, or materials; among these are using a whole language approach, teaching use of context in reading, and accepting invented spelling in writing. In other cases criteria for acceptable practice are so specific and narrowly drawn that they have the effect of excluding certain approaches.

6. *No federal or state law or program should be framed in such a way that its effect would be to provide substantial advantage to any commercial reading program. No person should hold an advisory position with any federal or state agency or with Congress or any state legislature who would personally profit from any legislation or regulation.* Several people who are authors of Distar and Open Court (both published by SRA/McGraw Hill) have played key advisory roles or have actually been on the payroll of states whose legislation and/or regulations they have advised or controlled.

The Real Target: Public Education

The underlying objective of those who attack whole language is to bring down public education itself. This is not a battle that can be won by teachers closing their doors. It requires rebuilding at least part of the historic coalition that fought for and won universal education in the first place. Defeating the most serious attack on public education since it first was won will take a united profession supported by parents and responsible community groups.

References

Adams, M. J. 1990a. *Beginning to Read: Thinking and Learning About Print.* Cambridge, MA: MIT Press.

———. 1990b. *Beginning to Read: Thinking and Learning About Print: A Summary.* Champaign, IL: Center for the Study of Reading.

Adams, M. J., and M. Bruck. 1995. Resolving the Great Debate. *American Educator* (Summer).

Anderson, R. C., et al. 1985. *Becoming a Nation of Readers: The Report of the Commission on Reading.* Champaign, IL: Center for the Study of Reading.

Armstrong, W. 1989. *Illiteracy: An Incurable Disease or Education Malpractice?* Washington, DC: U.S. Senate Republican Policy Committee.

———. 1990. Senate Approves Armstrong Amendments to Improve Literacy. News from Bill Armstrong. Press release, February 6, 1990.

Back, E., et al. 1995. Forty Massachusetts Linguists and Psycholinguists Blast Whole Language. *Blumenfeld Education Letter* (November).

Barrs, M., and A. Thomas. 1993. *The Reading Book.* Portsmouth, NH: Heinemann.

Binkley, M., and T. Williams. 1996. *Reading Literacy in the United States.* Washington, DC: U.S. Department of Education, National Center for Educational Statistics.

Blumenfeld, S. L., ed. 1995. Forty Massachusetts Professors of Linquistics and Psycholinguistics Blast Whole Language. *Blumenfeld Education Letter* (November).

California Reading Task Force. 1995. *Every Child a Reader.* Sacramento: California Department of Education.

Campbell, J. R., et al. 1996. *NAEP 1994 Reading Report Card for the Nation and States.* Washington, DC: Educational Testing Service for National Center for Educational Statistics, Office of Educational Research and Improvement, U.S. Department of Education (January).

Carnine, D., and H. Meeder. 1997. Commentary: Reading Research into Practice. *Education Week* 17, 1: 41, 43.

Clay, M. 1971. *The Early Detection of Reading Difficulties.* Portsmouth, NH: Heinemann.

Collins, J. 1997. How Johnny Should Read. *Time* (October 27).

Colvin, R. L. 1997. Trouble in the Mecca of Reading. *Los Angeles Times* (May 5).

Eastin, D. 1996. *Teaching Reading: A Balanced Comprehensive Approach to Teaching Reading in Prekindergarten Through Grade 3.* Sacramento: California Department of Education (May 10).

Elley, W. 1992. *How in the World Do Students Read?* The Hague: International Association for the Evaluation of Educational Achievement (July).

Flesch, R. 1981. *Why Johnny Still Can't Read: A New Look at the Scandal of Our Schools.* New York: Harper & Row.

Foorman, B. R., D. J. Francis, T. Beeler, D. Winikates, and J. M. Fletcher. 1997. Early Interventions for Children with Reading Problems: Study Designs and Preliminary Findings. *Learning Disabilities: A Multidisciplinary Journal* 8, 1: 63–71 (Winter).

Glaser, R. 1985. Foreword. In R. Anderson et al., *Becoming a Nation of Readers: The Report of the Commission on Reading.* Champaign, IL: Center for the Study of Reading.

Goodman, K., et al. 1988. *Report Card on Basal Readers.* Katonah, NY: Richard C. Owen.

Governor's Business Council. 1996. *Picking a Research Based Reading Program* (April).

Hardin, E. 1996. Dole Hits School "Monopoly" and Its "Pliant Pet." *Washington Post* (July 18).

Houston Chronicle. 1996. UH Study: Phonics Approach Makes Pupils Better Readers (May 5). Staff and wire reports.

Iserbyte, C. 1990. Focus: Reading Is the Civil Rights Issue of the '90s. *AFA Journal* (March).

Kline, C., and C. L. Kline. n.d. The Epidemic of Reading Disabilities. In *The Reading Reform Foundation Basic Information and Catalog.* Tacoma, WA: Reading Reform Foundation.

Lemann, N. 1997. The Reading Wars. *Atlantic Monthly* (November).

Levine, A. 1994. The Great Debate Revisited. *Atlantic Monthly* (December).

Lyon, G. R. 1997. Statement of G. Reid Lyon, Ph.D. Washington, DC: Committee on Education and the Workforce, U.S. House of Representatives (July 10).

McPike, E. 1995. Learning to Read, Schooling's First Mission. *American Educator* (Summer).

Miller, K. E., et al. 1995. *Cross-State Data Compendium for the NAEP 1994: Grade 4 Reading Assessment.* Washington, DC: Educational Testing Service for National Center for Educational Statistics, Office of Educational Research and Improvement, U.S. Department of Education (December).

Mullis, I., et al. 1993a. *Executive Summary of the NAEP 1992 Report Card for the Nation and the States: Data from the National and Trial State Assessments.* Washington, DC: Educational Testing Service for National Center for Educational Statistics, Office of Educational Research and Improvement, U.S. Department of Education.

———. 1993b. *NAEP 1992 Report Card for the Nation and the States: Data from the National and Trial State Assessments.* Washington, DC: U.S. Department of Education.

Palmaffy, T. 1997. See Dick Flunk. *Policy Review* 86 (November–December).

Pearson, P. D. 1997. The Politics of Reading Research and Practice. *Council Chronicle* (September): 24, 8.

Republican Party of Iowa. 1996. *The Republican Party of Iowa State Platform, as Adopted June 15, 1996.* Accessed from Internet.

Smith, J. W. A., and W. B. Elley. 1995. *Learning to Read in New Zealand.* Katonah, NY: Richard C. Owen.

Spring, J. 1997. *Political Agendas for Education.* Mahwah, NJ: Lawrence Erlbaum.

Stewart, J. 1996. The Blackboard Bungle: California's Failed Reading Experiment. *Los Angeles Weekly* (March 7).

Toch, T. 1997. The Reading Wars Continue. *U.S. News and World Report* (October 27).

Vine, P. 1997. "To Market, to Market . . . The School Business Sells Kids Short." *The Nation* 265, no. 7 (September 8–15).

Williams, P. L. 1995. *NAEP 1994 Reading: A First Look,* rev. ed. Washington, DC: Educational Testing Service for National Center for Educational Statistics, Office of Educational Research and Improvement, U.S. Department of Education (October).

Wingert, P., and B. Kantrowitz. 1997. Why Andy Couldn't Read. *Newsweek* (October 27).

Wolk, R. J., ed. 1997. Quality Counts: A Report Card on the Condition of Public Education in Fifty United States. Supplement to *Education Week* (January 22).

Carole Edelsky set out to find the stories of how individual school systems, administrators, and teachers have been attacked and how they've fought back. Each story is as individual as the communities and participants are; yet each shows the overlapping elements of a much larger campaign to take control of public education, to reshape it and narrow its focus and impact. Each story is itself part of a larger, longer story of attacks that recur or resurface in a school or district near or far.

Even when battles are won, there are major casualties: fired teachers and administrators, smeared reputations, marginalized curricula, self-censorship of those not even attacked.

2

It's a Long Story—
And It's Not Done Yet

Carole Edelsky

Once upon a time (to begin in story mode, since it is stories that I want to tell), I set out to find stories of successful efforts by whole language educators to counter the increasingly powerful rightist attacks on education (and ultimately on democracy). I hoped that hearing details of particular stories would inspire and instruct more of us on fighting back. I chose cases I had heard about, those involving school board elections, state-level educational policies, and attacks on particular individuals. Then I read published analyses of the activity of the far right. I didn't seek out stories about whole language people winning right-led attacks on curriculum or resisting attempts to remove certain books from reading lists or to block purchase of particular textbooks. And I didn't know of stories set in extremely poor or minority communities. My own story, then, and whatever I make of it, must be understood as unfinished.[1]

Background Information

I interviewed people from Glendale, Arizona; Lake County, Florida; Littleton, Colorado; Bowling Green, Ohio; Kalamazoo, Michigan; and Peekskill, New York.[2] I also read published accounts regarding Vista, California; La Mesa–Spring Valley, California; and Round Tree, Texas. Before telling the stories of these communities, however, I must begin with some background information.

Goals and Tactics

It is important not to confuse the tactics of the far right with its goals. One of its tactics is to smear whole language. But its goal is to eliminate public schools entirely. The far right's love affair with phonics is a tactic, not a goal. They tout the benefits of phonics, but what they are really pushing is control of teachers, texts, and readers in a universe of moral absolutes.

The far right has a theocratic strand and a business strand. Sometimes the two strands are in opposition. But not when it comes to schools. The goal of the far right is to take control of education for the sake of God (the theocratic strand) and gold (the business strand). The business right is interested in taking over education so as to increase profits, both directly (through selling stock in privatized ventures) and indirectly (through cutting local property tax bills, which largely fund public schools). The theocratic right is interested in winning the supernatural battle it believes is occurring between the forces of God and the forces of Satan, and this involves putting schools on the side of (the Christian) God. It is this religious zeal wrapped in a balance sheet that makes the tone of far-right activity reminiscent of both the Crusades and the conquest of the New World (Berlet and Quigley 1995).

The far right is influenced greatly by Christian Reconstructionists, a small group whose ideas have broad appeal among others on the right. Christian Reconstructionists insist that church comes before country or family and that the U.S. public schools must be run according to the biblical law of the Old Testament rather than the "natural" law of the U.S. Constitution. Christian Reconstructionists call for the death penalty for heresy, blasphemy, astrology, adultery, homosexuality, and a wide range of other "crimes" (Clarkson 1995). But the core belief of the far right, regardless of sect, is moral absolutism, which stems from the absolute hierarchical authority of God and leads to the "proper" hierarchical arrangements in families, schools, and government. Democracy and pluralism are anathema to the far right (Berlet and Quigley 1995). Its goal of taking control of education includes promoting such beliefs along with "ordinary" Christian theism.

Tactically, the far right has focused its efforts on winning elections—primarily thousands of lower-level public offices (on school boards, library boards, water commissions, and so on)—in order to impose its views and also to use these positions as springboards for higher offices (People for the American Way 1994). By using the "15 percent solution" (15 percent of the electorate is all that is needed to win an election—for elections with particularly small turnouts, only 6 or 7 percent is needed), the far right has been able to concentrate its electoral efforts. If the public in a given election is not sufficiently mobilized to turn out in large numbers, the right gets its 6 to 7 percent to the polls and wins (Freeman 1993).

Believing it is working for God, the religious right feels justified in using whatever tactics will advance its agenda. That includes deceit and contradictory rhetoric or outright lies. Just one example of its underhanded techniques is hiding the positions and associations of electoral candidates depending on the targeted voters, either by keeping candidates "under wraps" or tailoring mailings so that, for instance, voters identified as favorable to abortion are sent campaign literature that omits a candidate's anti-abortion stance while those who oppose abortion get literature that includes it (Galst 1995).

The Basis of the Far Right's Appeal

The Right taps into widespread legitimate anger, fear, and alienation. Decreases in real income, fewer full-time jobs with benefits, a greater need to piece together several jobs leaving less time for friends, family, and solitude, a deteriorating physical and social environment, increasing gratuitous violence—the crises in this country are exceedingly complex. Their solutions are equally complex. But not according to the far right. They can explain the crises simply and easily. Unemployment is due to affirmative action programs and a lack of phonics in schools. A worsening economic situation is the fault of dark-skinned immigrants. Violence is due to the media's being controlled by Jews and homosexuals. This scapegoating deflects blame from the economic system and places it on already stigmatized groups: women, ethnic minorities, gays and lesbians, the poor (Sklar 1995).

Particularly devastating for whole language educators, the religious right has joined the business right and added a new scapegoat to the list: public schools. First, the Right established the lie that the schools were failing (Barlow and Robertson 1994; Berliner and Biddle 1995). Then it blamed the supposedly failing schools for problems in the economy and society at large. The far right's coup de grâce in "reinventing" public schools as villains was to play with the word "public." It minimized the notion of public access and public interest and highlighted the idea of public governance, now widely associated with bureaucratic waste and ineptitude. As a result, the Right was able to snidely label public schools "government schools."

The Right scapegoats minorities, but its appeal is growing among minorities. This is due to clever, if cynical, outreach to minority communities (People for the American Way 1994). Despite the Right's actual record of lobbying and voting against civil rights legislation and opposing court challenges on behalf of minorities, far-right radio and television shows direct much broadcast time to minority audiences. These shows whip up anti-gay sentiment in minority communities (according to right-wing propaganda, discrimination against gays is not a civil rights issue; rather, homosexuality is a moral issue). Those on the Right pretend to have an altruistic desire to improve conditions for minorities (according to the Right, it is in minorities' interests to support a voucher system for school choice, since the public school system has failed them). Most cynical of all, the Right cashes in on symbols of a movement whose successes it is bent on undoing: the civil rights movement. It features Martin Luther King, Jr. and Harriet Tubman in anti-abortion ads. It compares Operation Rescue tactics to civil rights activity. And it paints Christians as oppressed victims, kin to those forced to go to the back of the bus (People for the American Way 1994).

Rhetorically, the far right wins acceptance of its agenda by appealing to people's fear and anger with time-tested tactics of scapegoating and with calculated outreach, regardless of the obvious inconsistencies (that is, that the outreach is often directed at the scapegoats). But rhetoric explains only part of the far right's success.

The Infrastructure of the Far Right

Religious-right rhetoric can reach so many and be so effective because of the movement's infrastructure. For the last thirty years, "secular, corporate and religious branches of the Right have spent hundreds of millions of dollars" on building this infrastructure (Berlet and Quigley 1995, p. 23). The infrastructure is what permits organizing day in and day out, year after year, the kind of organizing that does not stop after either an electoral victory or a defeat. Day-in and day-out organizing is directed at individuals through the mail, by phone, and on the Internet. Mass audiences are reached through a $2.5 billion religious broadcasting industry, many independent publishing companies, and dozens of religious monthly newspapers (Diamond 1995). These corporate entities are aided by think tanks, law firms, and public relations firms that conduct research, publish studies, shape issues, and groom syndicated columnists and "experts" for radio and TV shows (Berlet and Quigley 1995). It is this infrastructure that permits the Right to conduct research with focus groups in order to test out winning slogans and rhetoric (such as "government schools," "local control," "choice"). And it is this infrastructure that has succeeded in lobbying legislators and the public at large on everything from taxes (equating raising taxes on the wealthy with raising taxes in general—Sklar 1995) to teaching (equating drill and direct instruction with educational excellence; equating phonics with reliable, replicable, research-based programs).

Some Stories

This, then, is some of the context for the stories that follow.

Challenging the Far Right in Elections

There are many ways the far right has been challenged, and one way is at the polls.

GLENDALE, ARIZONA Almost ten years ago, the far right won a majority on the Glendale, Arizona, school board with "stealth" candidates, previously unknown people who refused to talk to reporters, did not appear at candidates' forums, and did not publicize their agenda. After the election the first act of the new right-wing majority was to announce a statement of philosophy: Glendale would be a back-to-basics district, with its schools emphasizing phonics and direct instruction. Soon after this announcement, they hired an outside consultant (whose qualifications were prior experience as a travel agent) to conduct a "curriculum audit." In the course of their tenure, the new board fired the superintendent and two progressive principals; they harassed teachers with excessive scrutiny and administrators with demands for lengthy reports on short deadlines. Attendance at school board meetings increased dramatically, as did the length of meetings (meetings that had drawn ten people and lasted for two hours began to draw hundreds and last past midnight).

A small number of articulate parents organized a recall campaign; it failed. These same parents continued to organize for the next election. They orchestrated which parents and which teachers would speak on what topics in the two-minute time slots allotted for visitors at the end of board meetings. They ran a slate (nothing less than a majority would turn things around) with a positive campaign, focusing on what they stood for. They got teachers, administrators, and other parents to campaign door-to-door through the neighborhoods in 110-degree heat. A few administrators and teachers videotaped board meetings as a strategy of counterscrutiny. A tiny liberal weekly ran an exposé on the takeover of the school board by the far right. The small daily newspaper in Glendale expanded to publish the increased volume of letters to the editor concerning education. The parent-led group held fundraisers for campaign expenses (while the right-wing candidates put flyers on cars in church parking lots). A couple of teachers and administrators kept interactive journals with each other throughout the period for mutual support.

The parent-led group did win the election, ousting the far-right majority. But almost ten years later, district schools still feel repercussions from those events. According to one of the major participants, many Glendale educators now display a "turtle syndrome," afraid to come out of their shells and try anything new. And the community in general seems to have lost a measure of trust of school board members as a result of having been lied to repeatedly. Recently, another right-wing board was elected. A key curriculum person in the district was demoted and then fired. This time the state attorney general intervened. Four members of the board resigned rather than be prosecuted for violating the state open meeting law.

LAKE COUNTY, FLORIDA Like Glendale, Arizona, Lake County, Florida, experienced a successful stealth campaign. Low voter turnout in the 1992 election coupled with effective organizing by the religious right resulted in a loss for the supposed shoo-in candidates. The community was startled to find itself with a school board that overnight refused to permit Head Start programs on school campuses (because young children should be home with their mothers) and demanded that Lake County schools teach the "superiority of U.S. culture." (With this policy the AFT union local brought suit against the school board for violating state law concerning multicultural education. The policy also attracted national media attention.) School board meetings began to last five to ten hours; attendance at some meetings grew to over one thousand. Board members obstructed the work of teachers and other professionals by derailing faculty meetings and demanding reports that required vast amounts of documentation.

By 1993, the community began to fight back in preparation for the next election. A nonpartisan PAC, People for Mainstream Values, was organized. This coalition of business leaders, parents, teachers, and other education professionals brought in a speaker from Vista, California, to give an account at a community forum of Vista's victory over the religious right. The coalition monitored board meetings, sent out questionnaires, publicly endorsed candidates, identified "stealth" candidates by publicizing all the candidates' positions, operated a phone bank to contact voters, and did "all the good ol' stuff you do" to campaign person to person (G. Burry, personal communication). They received favorable press coverage through news articles informing people of how the board was spending its time and taxpayers' money, editorials supporting the Mainstream Values candidates, and pointed, sophisticated political cartoons.[3] Besides working in the coalition, teachers also worked with students and parents to get parents to vote.

Voter turnout was high in Lake County's 1994 election. The candidates supported by the coalition won. After the election, coalition members agreed on the importance of not becoming complacent (the two far-right candidates who won in 1992 were up for reelection in 1996). The PAC therefore continues to exist. Members want to evaluate and improve their own efforts to raise public awareness of the issues and to increase public participation. But with the spotlight off (the "American superiority" policy was repealed, so the AFT local dropped its lawsuit and the press dropped its frequent coverage), attendance at board meetings is again low. The coalition's concern is that people will congratulate themselves ("we whipped 'em"), sit back—and invite a return victory by the religious right.

LITTLETON, COLORADO Until the 1993 election, the Littleton, Colorado, School District was noted statewide for its openness to new ideas. The abrupt turn taken by the newly elected school board in 1993, however, was no surprise. The winning slate had run an explicitly back-to-basics campaign, aided by the Christian Coalition. It intended to appeal both to those who were nostalgic but uninvolved with current schools and to religious conservatives who were extremely concerned with educational practice (mothers' prayer groups met weekly to pray that teachers would teach more phonics).

The back-to-basics slate's victory brought more than a return to basics. It prompted the canceling of conflict resolution programs and ungraded primaries. It also sparked an exodus of professionals: many of the good teachers and nearly half the principals left for bordering districts. It also marked the start of six-hour-long board meetings with hundreds in attendance. As in Glendale, Arizona, a lawsuit was brought against the Littleton School District for violating Colorado's open meeting "sunshine law." The presiding judge agreed with the plaintiffs, saying that some school meetings did indeed have to be "open," with an agenda published twenty-four hours in advance. However, the judge stopped short of declaring that the public could take part in all school activity, including participating in faculty committee meetings and having access to teachers' mailboxes. Still, the ruling was enough to provide moderates in the district with a wake-up call to organize and act.

Within months of the election, parents at individual schools got together and organized a group called Partners for Littleton Schools (PLS). They established committees: a legal committee (twenty-six lawyers donated their time) to watchdog the Right to make sure the sunshine law and Roberts' Rules of Order were being followed; a speaking committee to prepare statements and speak at school board meetings; a writing committee to compose press releases and letters to newspapers; and a research committee to track board meetings and document, among other things, how the board was damaging the district through micromanagement (deciding on the use of ruled or unruled paper in the kindergartens, for example, while virtually ignoring the personnel crisis). PLS divided the district into sections and designated parents who would be responsible for organizing each section.

The day the new school board was to vote on the terms of the superintendent's departure, PLS held a rally in her honor. The rally, attended by 1,500 people, was the first major PLS publicity move for the upcoming 1995 election. To reach the 73 percent of the voters in the district who had no children in the system, the parents organized a grandparent group to approach older voters. They also solicited teachers to help behind the scenes (in the 1993 campaign, local talk shows had discredited the teachers' endorsement of other candidates, saying teachers were simply manipulated by the union).

With leaflets and street-corner banners, PLS was a visible presence. At district-sponsored forums on local cable television, PLS parents made sure to get to the front of the line at the microphone and asked pointed questions. This time they were determined to force far-right candidates to show their true colors on such issues as "local control" at school sites versus school-board-imposed policies for all schools.

In the 1995 school board election PLS-backed candidates won a majority. Board meetings are once again smaller and of shorter duration. Well-qualified professionals are once more applying for positions in Littleton schools. But PLS has not completely disbanded. A steering committee still meets, and a phone tree stands ready. A parent representative from each school building attends each board meeting. The writing committee continues to send letters to newspapers, board members, and legislators. PLS members volunteer for every district committee; once on the committee, they volunteer to do the work. And at every opportunity, they work to rebuild the community's image of its teachers.

SAN DIEGO COUNTY SCHOOLS A similar story has been told in great detail about several of the school districts in San Diego county in California (Freeman 1993): a right-wing takeover of the board followed by sudden interest in public school affairs, huge attendance at lengthy board meetings, parents taking the lead in mobilizing the community well before the next election, individuals and professional organizations or national citizens' organizations volunteering legal and public relations expertise, one or more persons devoting nearly full time to the effort, coalitions working to use multiple means to reach every potential voter.

Challenging the Far Right Through Supporting Public Education in State Politics

Another category of success story is less dramatic. This category can be called general, ongoing support of public education. In Michigan and Ohio, ultraconservatives' control of state legislatures and state boards of education has produced legislation favoring vouchers and charter schools and resolutions or policies that effectively deprive teachers of the right to exercise their professional judgment (for example, policies rejecting all but abstinence curricula for sex education and those demanding intensive systematic phonics for reading instruction). In each state, the issues that are deemed important and politicians' rhetoric and positions on those issues point to associations with the religious right.

MICHIGAN The organization Michigan for Public Education (MPE) is about three years old. It started as a small group of strongly committed educators who solicited the advice of people in the Michigan Department of Education and public relations experts. After some initial floundering, the group began to focus on state-level activity. Their meetings become working sessions, as they decided who would address which issues at state board meetings and how those statements should be shaped, who would network with which other groups on which topics, who would go to public hearings to provide testimony, and how such testimony should be framed. Members wrote a brochure to attract a wide dues-paying membership, and they started publishing a newsletter. They began issuing score cards on candidates' agendas for the League of Women Voters. Through networking with other groups (such as People for the American Way, the American Civil Liberties Union, the Parent Teachers Association, the Michigan Education Task Force, the League of Women Voters, and the Michigan Education Association), they have been invited to speak about education at various groups' meetings and on radio talk shows.

MPE has become a legitimate contributor to the public conversation on education in Michigan. Newspaper articles on state actions involving education now routinely report MPE's position on those actions. Their work has also led to a general increase in activity on the part of Michigan's professional education organizations.

OHIO Phonics is a "cause" for conservative Republicans in Ohio. The state legislature has passed laws requiring phonics in teaching reading and resolutions about providing teachers with in-service on intensive systematic phonics; it has even inserted language about phonics into the agriculture budget. Not surprisingly, general ongoing efforts to promote public education in Ohio revolve largely around the issue of phonics.

Combined efforts on the part of OCTELA (Ohio Council of Teachers of English Language Arts), the Ohio Department of Education, and individual educators have slowed but not halted the Right's achievement of its objectives. These professional educators helped write the model course of study for reading (although the legislature then passed a bill releasing schools from an obligation to comply with the model). They are working to minimize such legislative actions as appropriating $300,000 for ten demonstration projects on intensive systematic phonics while reducing funding for Reading Recovery and other programs. OCTELA sends its members regular legislative updates with suggestions for action. Public education supporters who are teacher educators are having students study state activity relating to reading instruction so that new teachers will begin their careers with an understanding of how politicians control teachers' professional activity. Some of these public education supporters make lunch dates with legislators to discuss phonics. A few years ago, they formed an organization called LEAF (Literacy Educators and Advocates Forum) to keep members up to date on current literacy research. They are now trying to interest business leaders and parents in attending bimonthly LEAF meetings. Ohio supporters of public education have not blocked the Right's efforts, but they have succeeded in preventing an easy and complete return to "flat earth" reading instruction.

Challenging the Far Right by "Hangin' in There"

The third category of story I have to relate may be dramatic, but is not easily seen as a success. It concerns efforts to thwart far-right attacks on individuals. When right-wing rhetoric and/or organizations are used to "get" an educator, the educator is almost always "got." Religious-right majorities on school boards have ousted superintendents and principals. Religious-right parents have forced tenured teachers to change their practice or to transfer.

The case of a whole language principal in a New York City suburb is both an example of this type of story and an exception. The community prided itself on having an excellent and forward-looking elementary school. In this community are many competitive parents who believe that if their children do not "test out" as "gifted" they must be "learning disabled," because "average" is not acceptable (a somewhat odd modification to the Lake Woebegone effect).

Some years ago, the new elementary school principal, after receiving tenure at the end of her third probationary year, attended a summer whole language conference with some teachers from her school. They returned energized, eager to begin teaching from this new perspective.

The next years were exciting. Parents began to report that their children loved going to school and dreaded vacations because there was no school. But not everyone was happy. A few traditional upper-grade teachers with great stature among parents worked to sabotage the new program. They played on parents' insecurities, warning them that their children would not succeed later if they weren't given skills worksheets, spelling tests, and a demand for "best handwriting" on all papers. When a newly hired superintendent, in an effort to demonstrate openness, held a meeting with parents and asked them for their "concerns," parents rightfully took that as an invitation to complain. Those who had heard the upper-grade teachers' warnings complained about the lack of traditional spelling and handwriting practice. Even though they knew their children now loved the exciting work they were doing at school, these parents—themselves schooled in traditional ways and lacking conventional measurements of what their children were learning (for example, spelling tests)—were susceptible to the upper-grade teachers' "skills" rhetoric.

Into that setting came an anonymous letter signed "Concerned Parents." It later became known that fewer than thirty parents of the 220 families in that school constituted the "Concerned Parents." It also appeared that they received help from outside strategists. The letter expressed concern about students not having enough drill in math, about their not being taught grammar and spelling, and about their having careless handwriting. Newspaper articles that fanned the flames ("What's going on at that elementary school?") and vague petitions that garnered hundreds of signatures ("Sign this if you want to see improvements at the elementary school") followed.

In less than a year, "Concerned Parents" had managed to overturn the curriculum and pressure the superintendent and the school board to find grounds to bring dismissal charges against the principal. In New York state, a teacher's working with particular views on curriculum does not constitute grounds for dismissal, but withholding special education services from learning-disabled children does. The principal was identified as the party responsible for sponsoring an open-ended, meaningful, hospitable-to-all curriculum rather than sending "average" children to LD worksheet practice if they didn't qualify as "gifted." The principal was duly charged on 125 counts (mostly instances of denial of special services), suspended as principal, and assigned to a desk in the district office. For over two years, she has been given busy work, and is not permitted to take phone calls or to see visitors during the work day.

Where, you ask, is the success here? The principal was offered a settlement (bribe?) if she would resign. She refused. The district sued her and two supporting parents to keep them from talking, claiming it was doing so in order to protect the students named as being denied special services. These two parents have filed a countersuit in federal court, claiming infringement of their First Amendment rights. The hearings have dragged on since 1994 with so many delays that the formal defense—which will be the first opportunity for the principal and her supporters to speak—has, as of this writing, not yet begun. Meanwhile, the local press has switched sides, printing articles about the district's and the school board's already wasting over a million dollars of taxpayers' money on this case.

Again, the question: where's the success in this story? The school with excited teachers and learners is gone. Faculty have left. Families are moving or sending their children to private schools. But—here's the success— the principal has not crumbled. She has received moral support from NCTE. She has found social, aesthetic, and spiritual ways to retain strength and dignity and to achieve some serenity. And she is determined to hold out for the start of her formal defense so she can tell the whole awful story.

The Moral(s) of the Story(ies): Some Suggestions

Now that I have told my stories, what can be learned from them? What are the morals of these stories? Several points come to mind.

First, since it is largely through local elections that the Right has gained control, we whole language educators must concern ourselves with elections. That means organizing local communities, neighborhood by neighborhood.

We must also attempt to find and expose candidates' often hidden ties to the far right. Unfortunately, in the eyes of many voters, a candidate's far-right connections are not an obvious liability. It is important, therefore, to spell out what those connections mean: opposition to diversity, pluralism, and democracy; acceptance of bigotry.

Exposing the Right also means emphasizing its hypocrisy. Several of the success stories I have heard involved taking such action as the following: contrasting far-right board members' calls for lowering costs, cutting "frills," and saving taxpayers' money with their unnecessary purchases of extras for their own offices; publicizing the Right's willingness to waste taxpayers' money on million-dollar legal battles to destroy an individual or to silence critics. Also deserving an intense spotlight is the Right's chutzpah in claiming the moral high ground while engaging in a variety of lies and dirty tricks. Certainly democratically inclined educators must show that appealing-sounding slogans about "local control" and "choice" in fact mean imposing a single worldview on everyone.

An important strategy of the far right in gaining control is to use laws to harass or obstruct. It is essential, therefore, for legal counsel to be a part of some of the success stories—sometimes for protection, sometimes for beating the Right at its own game. Educators should seek out like-minded lawyers for pro bono help.

We should also seek help from our own professional organizations. NCTE and some of its state affiliates have had a hand in some of the success stories. National mainstream citizens' organizations with experience in fighting the Right (for example, People for the American Way, Citizens United for the Separation of Church and State, and a relatively new organization called Parents for Public Schools) have also been willing and able to help. Clearly, we should not only ask our professional organizations for help, we should also press them to develop more effective ways to support local struggles against the Right and to make such efforts one of their primary activities.

At the same time, we should rethink demonizing the Right as extremists. Aspects of the far right's message have such broad appeal that we undermine our own chances when we dismiss the message and, by implication, all who accept it as extremist. Extremists are the fringe. But it is many more people than a fringe group who can be enticed to look away from the real source of their legitimate fears (runaway global capitalism) and instead blame welfare mothers and first-grade teachers. Moreover, the "extremist" label will soon be less obviously applicable. As part of the Right's base-broadening effort, the Christian Coalition is now urging supporters to stay away from so-called extremist issues (G. Burry, personal communication).

One of the Right's most popular and seemingly nonextremist issues is phonics. To millions of people, phonics evokes (distorted) memories of their own schooling. It also fits folk notions of what reading is. To the far right, however, phonics means decoding what is "there." It means appropriate hierarchies—the authority of text over interpretation and ultimately of (the Christian) God over man. To the theocratic right, promoting phonics is a tactic for asserting Christian control of schools.

But phonics is invested with even more than that. Associated with a romanticized, idyllic earlier America, a push for phonics is a push for undoing the social justice gains of the 1960s and replaying Vietnam, this time with the U.S. victorious.

Logical argument, theory, and research, therefore, are not what persuades school boards and legislatures to mandate phonics instruction (though research may be used after the fact as justification). And logical argument, theory, and research will probably not convince them (or the public) otherwise. Therefore, I suggest that we stop trying to change minds by finding just the right research on phonics and the tightest of arguments about reading. (I'll come back to the issue of changing minds in the section on overall considerations.) Still, it is important to have material available to refute the Right's push for phonics—and that material is available. Ken Goodman's Phonics Phacts (1993), and Connie Weaver's Understanding Whole Language (1990) provide useful information.[4]

Tactically, we can make use of material such as Goodman's and Weaver's books again and again, repeating it as the Right repeats its sources. We can also begin to "advertise" in weekly classroom newsletters to parents the ways we teach phonics each week (B. Chambers, personal communication). And we can try to shift the argument from the "truth" about phonics to the rights of teachers and the dangers of politicians who micromanage instruction.

Suggestions for the Long Term

The leading protagonists in several of the success stories I have heard have been parents. Teachers have tended to join the effort in fewer numbers and at a later date. Like much of the general population, teachers do not see politics as something that concerns or interests them, nor do they see themselves as activists. That situation must change. Professional preparation should include a study of current struggles over public schooling. Educators should learn how to act politically on behalf of teachers and students.

Of course the problem isn't only that educators tend to stay silent, it is also that they are ignored or dismissed when they attempt to be heard. One of the most noteworthy accomplishments of educators involved in Michigan for Public Education is that they have won a respected place in the conversation. A definite long-term need for teachers is to reproduce that accomplishment many times over, to organize so that we are not only heard but sought out as having legitimate positions on educational issues.

Suggestions for Overall Considerations

It isn't only fear and anger that attract people to far-right positions. On issues concerning education, the far right's position can resonate among citizens who have a sincerely held (if naive) perspective on literacy. That perspective is widely shared; people who would otherwise find little to agree on often agree on a need for phonics. This popular perspective is also notably stable. We have learned how long it takes for people to shift their perspective on literacy.

It seems, then, that we must do two things as we attempt to undercut the appeal of right-wing proposals for phonics. On the one hand, we cannot let ourselves be discouraged by a failure to make quick inroads in consciousness. On the other hand, we must become better at public relations. That entails coming to understand that our potential audience is hardly monolithic. It isn't only the Christian Coalition that pushes a phonics orientation to reading (Harste and Burke 1977). So do many otherwise progressive academics in nonliteracy fields. Despite intensely investigating and exposing right-wing activity, progressive media (such as *The Nation*) and authors (for example, the contributors to Berlet 1995) consistently fail to even mention, let alone appreciate, the role phonics plays in the right-wing agenda.

Once we recognize the heterogeneity of the audience, we must tailor our message about what's wrong with mandated phonics accordingly, highlighting infringement on professional rights with some audiences and loss of society's (as opposed to an individual parent's) interests with others. Our discussions about literacy should be moved to the background in the context of these political arguments. We cannot expect to completely overturn folk notions about reading, even among progressives. We may have more success making professionalism the main argument (especially as people begin to appreciate, with the advent of managed medical care, what it's like to have nonprofessionals making decisions in a specialized field).

We should begin to look seriously at our own rhetoric. When we pit "proactive" against "reactive" we establish an underanalyzed dichotomy. As with other buzzwords, these two work to short-circuit our actions rather than to guide. This categorizing can invalidate potentially productive efforts while idealizing those that might not be particularly effective. Currently, as the most powerful political movement in the United States, the far right is able to establish the terms of the game. If we don't react to their activities (for example, by challenging their candidates for elected office) or their issues (for example, by lobbying against vouchers), we are simply out of the game.

In the current climate, it isn't reactive to organize against a far-right legislator or to solicit support in protecting one's job when under attack. Right now, democratic educators need to engage in all kinds of activity. We need to assess local situations (which is where we can have the most impact), diversify our actions, and not worry about whether we are being reactive or proactive.

Another bit of rhetoric we should examine is our use of the term "political." In an effort to persuade and educate, many of us (myself included—Edelsky 1994) have discussed the political nature of all educational activity. I still believe that idea is correct but also think that we need to make that point with greater care. We have to start distinguishing the ideological and power meanings of "political" from the wheeling-and-dealing meanings. Just as the far right has made use of the negative meanings associated with the word "government," we can make use of negative meanings (greed, corruption) associated with "political" (D. Bloome, personal communication). But we can do this only if we are careful to separate the various meanings of "political." If we can do this, we can tap into ready reservoirs of support when we argue that reading instruction should not be political—that is, that politicians motivated largely by self-serving opportunism should not mandate by law how to teach reading (Bloome 1995).

Democratically minded educators must also develop a deep appreciation for the fact that it is not only that the personal (family relationships, home budgets, and so forth) is political (in the sense of power and ideology), but that the political (in all senses) is also personal. Individual people, with individual names and faces, are the carriers of trends, the mouthpieces for positions, the objects of attacks, the defendants in court. It is very difficult not to "take it personally" when we are blacklisted, shunned, criticized, baited, fired, or sued. After all, it is me, you, her, or him by name who suffers. We must connect with and support each other so that we can weather the attacks. And we must come to deeply understand that we each live in history, caught in cross-currents not of our making but also capable of joining with others to redirect the flow.

To return to story discourse, we must give up the idea of "happily ever after." Even where the Right loses battles, it "leaves behind durable right-wing coalitions poised to launch another round of attacks" (Berlet and Quigley 1995, p. 42). To paraphrase a slogan about freedom, education—for democracy and for critical citizenship—is a constant struggle.

Endnotes

1 "Unfinished" is an understatement. Since 1996, when this chapter was written, the plots of the stories I report have certainly thickened. Because the local situations in several of them are extremely sensitive (for example, at least two new lawsuits have been filed), I will not identify which of the following plot twists go with which stories, but will instead note some details. One community's school board and its superintendent ousted key holistic administrators, charging the administrators with causing philosophical "disruption and division." The politically conservative board members themselves have been accused of meeting secretly to conduct board business. They agreed to resign when the state attorney general intervened. In another district, an award-winning, popular whole language principal was fired by the right-wing school board. She has since been blacklisted (or so it seems) by neighboring districts and has not yet found another administrative position. In 1997, two

districts continued to experience rifts between neighbors and ruptured professional relationships over the "sides" that were taken.

The setting of the stories has changed too. More overt right-wing domination (in the national sphere and in media blitzes on literacy and education) has affected the daily lives of those featured in each of these stories. The Right is now so well-positioned within local, state, and national governments and also in quasi-governmental agencies and institutes, and the media is so fine-tuned to do its bidding (which turns out to be its own bidding—the bidding of corporate media owners and the bidding of ideologies that support media owners' class interests) that it has been able to accelerate its anti–public education activity. That activity may seem contradictory—on the one hand, privatization (a hundredfold increase in charter schools, national and state voucher legislation near passage); on the other hand, centralization (attempts to install a national curriculum in reading, national criteria for research on reading). But it is not contradictory: both privatization and centralization are strategies in ultraconservative attempts to control education. Through legislating right-wing views on reading for the poor who will remain in public schools and through permitting right-wing views of religion and profit to prevail in the private schools now to be supported by tax dollars, the Right will be able to put an end to one of the few remaining democratizing features of U.S. society: a system of free public education for all. Educators in each of my stories know this. They have grabbed onto electronic media "life preservers" to try to halt the Right's recent onslaughts. Finding themselves working full-time at school and then full-time again on e-mail to oppose multiple simultaneous four-alarm blazes ("brush fires" does not suggest the seriousness of the problem), educators in each story are strained as never before.

2 Thanks to Ellen Brinkley, Gail Burry, Bonnie Chambers, JoAnn Falinski, Kitty Kazmarek, Lynn Peach, and Vicki Winterscheidt for taking time to tell me their stories. The characters, plots, and settings each deserve a novel rather than the brief summary reported here.

3 Many of these cartoons appear in a booklet, *Saving Our Schools from the Religious Right: The Lake County, Florida, Story*. Written by two members of People for Mainstream Values, Mary Smith Fletcher and Frances Ann Meador, the booklet is available for $4.95 from Saving Our Lake County Schools, P.O. Box 492124, Leesburg, FL 34749-2124.

4 In addition, Stephen Krashen has informally assembled a summary of experimental studies on the fallacies of phonemic awareness training. He sent these via e-mail to a closed listserv on November 15 and 16, 1997. And Denny Taylor (in press) has critiqued the research on phonics touted as "replicable and reliable."

References

Barlow, M., and H. Robertson. 1994. *Class Warfare*. Toronto: Key Porter.
Berlet, C. 1995. *Eyes Right*. Boston: South End Press.
Berlet, C., and M. Quigley. 1995. Theocracy and White Supremacy. In C. Berlet, ed., *Eyes Right*, pp. 15–43. Boston: South End Press.

Berliner, D. C., and B. J. Biddle. 1995. *The Manufactured Crisis: Myths, Fraud, and the Attack on America's Public Schools.* Reading, MA: Addison-Wesley.

Bloome, D. 1995. Unpublished letter in response to letters signed by 40 linguists.

Clarkson, F. 1995. Christian Reconstructionism. In C. Berlet, ed., *Eyes Right,* pp. 59–80. Boston: South End Press.

Diamond, S. 1995. The Christian Right Seeks Dominion. In C. Berlet, ed., *Eyes Right,* pp. 44–49. Boston: South End Press.

Edelsky, C. 1994. Response to Letter to the Editor. *Language Arts* 7, no. 1: 550–51.

Freeman, M. 1993. *The San Diego Model: A Community Battles the Religious Right.* Washington, DC: People for the American Way.

Galst, L. 1995. Pious Moralism. In C. Berlet, ed., *Eyes Right,* pp. 50–58. Boston: South End Press.

Goodman, K. 1993. *Phonics Phacts.* Portsmouth, NH: Heinemann.

Harste, J., and C. Burke. 1977. A New Hypothesis for Reading Teacher Research: Both Teaching and Learning of Reading Are Theoretically Based. In P. D. Pearson, ed., *Reading: Theory, Research, and Practice: Twenty-Sixth Yearbook of the National Reading Conference.* St. Paul, MN: Mason.

People for the American Way. 1994. Religious Right Efforts at Outreach to Ethnic and Minority Communities. Brochure. Washington, DC: People for the American Way.

Sklar, H. 1995. The Dying American Dream. In C. Berlet, ed., *Eyes Right,* pp. 113–34. Boston: South End Press.

Taylor, D. In press. *Beginning to Read and the Spin Doctors of Science.* Urbana, IL: National Council of Teachers of English.

Weaver, C. 1990. *Understanding Whole Language.* Portsmouth, NH: Heinemann.

In this chapter Ellen Brinkley lays out how religious Christian fundamentalists place a high value on literacy because it provides access to the Bible and, through the Bible, the truth as revealed by God.

Fundamentalist parents worry about possible satanic influences their children can encounter. The political right plays on these fears and uses them in attacks on public education in general and whole language teachers in particular. Brinkley suggests that whole language teachers can ease the fears of such parents by understanding their beliefs and showing respect for their religion and moral values. She also shows that there is much in common between whole language and core religious values, and that this has led to many Christian fundamentalists becoming enthusiastic whole language teachers.

Brinkley differentiates between the political agendas of the religious right and the religious beliefs of Christian fundamentalists. Teachers and educators need to be aware that nothing they do can please those whose agenda is ultimately the destruction of public education.

3

What's Religion Got to Do with Attacks on Whole Language?

ELLEN H. BRINKLEY

Schools across the nation are being blamed for violence in our society, for unemployment, and for a decline in morals. The public hears almost daily from politicians, and from national organizations that influence politicians' agendas, about how rotten the public schools are. Meanwhile municipalities exempt local corporations from tax responsibilities, which reduces local funds for schools. Legislators mandate educational policy with little understanding of the likely consequences. So-called pro-family groups advocate school curricula that alienate and disenfranchise students whose heritage and perspectives differ from the majority. The rhetoric of fear and divisiveness, often unfounded and used to promote purely partisan agendas, is a threat to whole language and to public education for all students (*Michigan for Public Education* 1995). It is within this accusatory atmosphere that I consider attacks on whole language and ask "What's religion got to do with it?"

Parents of all faiths and of no faith are persuaded by media coverage of education issues that their children's learning is being shortchanged at school (Berliner and Biddle 1995). The "education in crisis" message is often enhanced for parents who are members of politically conservative Christian congregations, where the pastor may promote phonics from the pulpit (Thogmartin 1994, p. 121) and where the Christian Coalition may have liaisons working in churches to help members carry out their activist agenda (Christian Coalition 1995). Parents of the religious right, comparing what they hear with their own school memories, are also likely to be influenced by a deluge of anti–whole language mail they receive regularly from at least half a dozen nationally organized religious-right groups, such as Citizens for Excellence in Education, Concerned Women of America, and the Eagle Forum. In the midst of so much disinformation, it's no wonder that parents, influenced by the religious right, become desperate worriers and outspoken protesters fighting against what they've been led to believe is "educational malpractice" (Blumenfeld 1984, p. xii). They may even come to think of their children's teachers as ungodly, or part of a satanic conspiracy to take over the world (Cumbey 1985). Given such possibilities, we might wonder that there hasn't been more controversy than there is.

Whole Language Flash Points

Attacks on whole language seem to focus primarily on three flash-point issues: phonics versus whole language; invented spelling; and basal readers versus literature. Clearly, the misnamed phonics–whole language controversy is the hottest issue; for decades phonics-first and meaning-first advocates have been pitted against each other. Many of the parents I encounter can't remember how they were taught to read, except to recall workbook fill-ins and round-robin read-alouds. The focus on phonics among attackers of whole language doesn't therefore appear to spring from parents' memories of their own school experience so much as it is stirred up by "experts" and sales pitches on the radio that convince parents that systematic, intensive phonics is the only way their children will learn to read. The overattention to phonics depends in part on views about texts held by fundamentalist Christians, who can be seen as members of an influential, religiously strict group, many of whom are aligned with the religious right.

The use of invented spelling is another flash point. This growing controversy emerges whenever whole language teachers ask students to write. In spite of the cliché about the three Rs—reading, writing, and 'rithmetic—being essential parts of the traditional curriculum, many parents can recall little if any writing instruction or experience from their own early school days, except perhaps for engaging in penmanship drills and copying sentences. What they do recall is a heavy dose of spelling lessons, spelling bees, and tests with lots of spelling and vocabulary words to memorize. The focus on invented spelling among attackers of whole language seems to originate in parents' perception that conventional spelling is an important goal in and of itself, not primarily a tool for writing. Understandably then, if parents don't find weekly graded spelling tests in their children's backpacks, they're likely to complain. In addition, some parents' overattention to conventional spelling too early in the learning process, like overattention to phonics, stems in part from fundamentalist Christian views about written texts (see below, and Chapter 7 in this volume).

Another whole language flash point is the use of literature in the classroom—authentic works of literature that replace the "fractured language" of basal readers as the chief source of classroom reading materials

(Goodman et al. 1988, p. 88). Sadly, many parents don't recall being given the opportunity to read "real books" in their early elementary classrooms unless (as in my case) it was after all their "work" was done. Thus, attacks on whole language that focus on literature grow partly from parents' discomfort that their children's school experience isn't like their own. More significantly, attacks on literature are often grounded in parents' knowledge that young readers are more likely to remember and be influenced by what they read in "real" books. When children in whole language classrooms read a variety of trade books rather than a simple basal, parents can't easily monitor which books their children will read and what impact their reading might have.

Reading, Meaning-Making, and Religion

On the surface, these flash-point issues seem to have little to do with religion. But whole language attackers who embrace Christian fundamentalism hold views about written texts that are grounded in theology—that is, views that grow out of their beliefs about and experiences with the Bible. One reason that fundamentalist Christian parents value reading so highly and favor an emphasis on phonics and spelling is that they believe these skills will lead to a more careful reading of the Bible. Studying biblical texts closely, attending to precision of language, and carefully weighing the meaning of each word are especially valued, since fundamentalists depend on their accurately reading and interpreting Bible messages as a way to keep them focused on God's will for their lives. From the start, then, biblical literacy is a primary goal for these parents. In fact, when a baby is born, one of the first gifts given is often a book of Bible stories, which may become one of the first books shared by parent and child.

When I was growing up I attended a nondenominational, fundamentalist Christian church called the Bible Center Church. In Sunday school we sang "The B-I-B-L-E—yes, that's the book for me. I stand alone on the Word of God, the B-I-B-L-E." As children we were challenged to "learn" the books of the Bible—that is, to be able to name, in order, all sixty-six books of the Bible from memory. There were prizes, often a Bible, for those who could do it. We were encouraged to memorize selected verses, to "hide" the Word of God in our hearts (Psalms 119:11, King James Version) as a comfort and as a source of strength when our faith was tested. Today, as a whole language educator, I might refer to my education as a back-to-basics church experience that placed great emphasis on the words of the sacred text.

Although fundamentalist Christians believe that "God gave every word of Scripture, not just the thoughts" (Chapman 1986, p. 14), they see the

Bible as God's vehicle for speaking directly to religious truth-seekers. In this view, it is God who constructs the meaning through inspiration. Actually, it's not only fundamentalist Christians who view Bible reading as more than a transaction between reader and text (Rosenblatt 1978). D. J. Furnish (1975), a United Methodist seminary professor, explains: "The Bible is not only a record of Divine–human encounters in the past, but by its very nature it has the power to bring God and persons together in encounters today. When we willingly open ourselves to it, we risk opening to ourselves, to one another, and to God in such a way that we cannot escape a Divine–human encounter" (p. 38). Meaning from sacred texts, therefore, emerges from the interaction of reader, text, and God.

Many fundamentalist Christian parents, and mainline Christians as well, share the belief that redemption and eternal life depend on specific experiences—turning away from sin, asking for and accepting God's forgiveness, and trying to live a life faithful to the example of Jesus Christ. The stakes are high, but parents know that no matter how much they'd like to do so, they can't control what their children decide to do about God. Many religious-right parents consequently become fearful of any possible temptation that might lead their children away from the faith (Dobson and Bauer 1990). They fear that just as children are subject to God's influence, they also can be influenced by demons with potentially grave consequences as children approach an age when it's believed God holds them "accountable" for their actions (Beeson and Mills 1993, pp. xxvii, 77). Therefore, parents with especially strong faith, or especially strong fears, sometimes place their children in private, parochial schools if they can afford to do so. Many, however, choose instead to try to control and change the public school curriculum.

Ultimately, however, I believe that what lies at the deepest level of parents' complaints and fears about phonics, invented spelling, and classroom literature, and what turns fundamentalist Christian parents into whole language attackers, is their perception that literacy learning in their children's classroom fails to recognize the parents' religious worldview, a view that places religious beliefs and practices at the center of their lives. No doubt partly influenced by the crisis messages of the mass media and the highly charged rhetoric of those who claim to be on God's side, parents fear that classroom experiences that ignore their theological worldview will influence their children to think that religion and God don't matter and that therefore the schools will lead children away from their parents' faith.

Making a Place for Religious Views

As whole language educators we have learned to be inclusive, to celebrate cultural diversity, and to honor multiple ways of knowing. Because most whole language classrooms *are* inclusive classroom communities, it seems likely that children in such classrooms may already feel free to discuss religious ideas and experiences at school. Nevertheless, there is widespread belief that, in most classrooms across the country, information about the role religions have played, and continue to play, in society and throughout history is generally omitted from the curriculum. Many believe that classroom discussion of religious ideas seldom, if ever, takes place.

National religious-right groups have for years complained about the omission of religion from the classroom. Christian Coalition publications, for example, regularly cite cases that demonstrate "intolerance toward public expression of faith," such as a recent example in which a third-grade student's artwork and writing were not displayed in the school hallway with those of her classmates because she had included what school officials labeled an "inappropriate" message: "Jesus loves us" (Thomas 1996, p. 12). Similarly, a recent issue of the *AFA [American Family Association] Journal* reports on several public school incidents that appear to restrict religious freedom unjustly, including the case of a Virginia parent who removed her daughter from the public school after the principal had barred her from reading the Bible on the school bus (Religious Freedom Amendment 1996, p. 20).

Whole language educators are more likely to take note of scholarly research and opinions on the subject. One often-cited study was conducted for the U.S. Department of Education in the mid-1980s by Paul Vitz, a professor of psychology at New York University. Vitz studied forty social studies texts for grades one through four and found "not a single 'primary' textual reference to a religious activity in contemporary American life" (Vitz 1986, cited in Nord 1995, pp. 153–54). Of the forty texts, twenty-one made "no textual mention" of religion (Nord 1995, p. 154). Vitz's research is sometimes questioned, however, on the grounds that "its conclusions seemed to have been reached before research began" (Menendez and Doerr 1991, p. 46).

A smaller but somewhat similar study at the Baylor University Center for Christian Education involved twenty-four social studies and reading textbooks that had been approved for third- and fifth-grade students in Texas. The authors of the study looked for examples of religious values, individual values, and social-secular values and found in the social studies texts numerous examples of "commentary on religious freedom" and "the fact that the church has been the center of community life in many nations" (Sharp and Wood 1992, cited in Berliner and Biddle 1995, pp. 109–10). The reading texts had fewer expressions of values, though they were not value-free (p. 110). David Berliner and Bruce Biddle discuss this research study within a section describing as "myth" the notion that public schools and textbooks do not promote moral values, but they seem to hedge a bit, explaining that it is "difficult to tell" whether there is less classroom attention to values now than in the past (p. 111). There is also a 1987 study of U.S. government and civics textbooks conducted by People for the American Way, a national public interest organization, that led to the conclusion that "the texts too often are static descriptions of dynamic processes, ignoring questions of belief and value at the heart of people's 'lives and fortunes and sacred honor'" (Carroll et al. 1987, cited by Gaddy, Hall, and Marzano 1996, p. 62).

Others who have recently spoken out on the issue of religion in the classroom include Barbara B. Gaddy, T. William Hall, and Robert J. Marzano (1996), who are, respectively, an education consultant, a Methodist minister, and an educational trainer who was once a monk. Regarding religion in the classroom, they say, "In spite of Supreme Court approval—even encouragement—of teaching about religion, and in spite of a plethora of available resources, study materials have been far too silent on the subject of religion" (p. 199). Nel Noddings (1993), a professor of education at Stanford University, insists that in the second half of this century educators have ignored religion entirely (p. xiii). Nord (1995), a philosophy professor at the University of North Carolina, contends that "in American public schools and universities students can—and most do—earn high school diplomas, college degrees, M.B.A.'s, J.D.'s, M.D.'s and Ph.D.'s without ever confronting a live religious idea" (p. 1). Similarly, in *The Culture of Disbelief* (1993), Stephen Carter, a Yale law professor, describes a pervasive "trivialization" of religious beliefs and practices and explains the problem teachers face, saying, "the concern to avoid even a hint of forbidden endorsement of religion has led to a climate in which teachers are loath to mention religion" (p. 206).

Clearly, the prevailing opinion is that religion in the classroom is absent or invisible. When classroom teachers don't know what to do or say, they operate in default mode: When in doubt, leave it out. My own school experience supports this conclusion. As I grew up, I didn't expect my public school teachers to understand or respect my religious beliefs and practices. It's possible that some of my teachers shared my religious perspective, but day by day in the classroom religion just didn't come up as a topic for discussion or instruction. Only those who were a part of my faith community shared my beliefs and proposed answers to life's biggest questions. Thus, I feel some kinship with students today who find no authority figure at school who understands their religious ways of knowing (at least no one willing to talk about it), and I understand what drives religious-right parents to lash out in frustration (Brinkley 1994, 1995).

So, what's all this got to do with whole language? I propose that one way to reduce the attacks on whole language, and perhaps to begin resolving the broader conflicts about public education as well, is to find a place within whole language classrooms for religion (and for moral values, a related topic beyond the scope of this chapter). Such a proposal leads immediately to questions about how it might be done. Again, there is substantial consensus: first, religion should be acknowledged as an important part of many people's day-to-day experience; and, second, religions and the role they have played and continue to play in such fields as social studies and the arts, including language arts, should be taught (Nord 1995; Carter 1993; Noddings 1993; and Carroll et al. 1987).

I suggest making a place for religion because I believe that if we do so, we might begin to address the deepest, sometimes unspoken fears of fundamentalist Christian parents. However, let there be no mistake. When I say that religion should be acknowledged and discussed in the classroom, I am not advocating that public prayer be returned to the classroom. Nor am I advocating that creationism be taught in science classes. And perhaps even more important, I do not support proposed legislation for a constitutional "religious freedom" amendment or passage of a Parental Rights and Responsibilities Act. I don't believe politically conservative Christians are being persecuted or that there is an "incredible war being waged against religious freedom in America" (Thomas 1996, p. 12). Instead, I simply agree with Nord, Noddings, Carter, and others who argue persuasively that, generally speaking, religion is invisible or treated as irrelevant in public schools today, that this is a problem that needs to be addressed even in whole language classrooms, and that it can be done while preserving the separation of church and state.

Discussing religion and religions in the classroom may not, of course, dramatically change fundamentalist parents' attitudes about whole language and public education. By speaking to their deepest fears, however, such action might reduce some of the explosive tension between parents and schools today. Still, there's a chance that introducing religion as a topic of study might intensify the controversies about whole language, since religious-right parents might not be pleased with the necessarily pluralistic classroom discussions of religion that would ensue. There's a chance they might not be happy with the prospect of "ungodly" teachers explaining religion. Despite the fact that discussing religion and honoring religious pluralism may frighten or anger extremists from both the political right and the political left, however, I believe that the vast majority of parents and citizens will approve and support whole language educators' intention to include religion in the classroom in these ways.

Untangling and Rethinking Religion and Pedagogy

Although acknowledging religious beliefs and discussing religion may address some of fundamentalist Christian parents' deepest fears, that action alone will not dismantle the "manufactured" crisis (Berliner and

Biddle 1995). Responding to parents' theologically based concerns is a place to start, but whole language educators need also to consider a broad range of issues in order to deal with the attacks on whole language. At some point it becomes necessary to try to disentangle the religious issues from those of whole language pedagogy and philosophy.

Religious-right parents have a constitutional right to hold whatever religious views they like. As citizens we might be tempted to criticize extremists' theological views, but as whole language professionals, we should not—no matter how beleaguered we feel—respond by counterattacking fundamentalists' religious views. Religious beliefs and practices are constitutionally protected in almost every case, even when worshipers handle poisonous snakes as an expression of their faith. Thus, we must respect the right of parents to hold whatever religious beliefs they like, but we can take a strong stand for what we know and believe about teaching and learning. Pedagogy is the area where whole language educators can have the greatest impact, because we understand these issues better than anyone else. We can and should address anti–whole language views about pedagogy, even when those views are held and acted on by religious persons or groups.

Perhaps another way we can defend whole language pedagogy against religious-right attacks is to call attention to the fact that whole language is consistent with, and in some cases even embodies, Christian theology. In fact, many whole language teachers of religious faith see whole language as one of the best ways to put their faith to work. Although I've set aside the fundamentalist Christian orthodoxy I grew up with (and thereby take the chance that I'll no longer be considered a "real" Christian by some), I embrace whole language partly because it is consistent with the tenets of my faith. Both place great value on respecting students as individuals with needs, interests, and talents. That is, both value the promise of each child. We can also take hope from statements made about whole language by conservative Christian educators, such as Arden Ruth Post (1991), a professor of education at Calvin College (a Christian Reformed college in Michigan), who explains to parents that whole language provides Christian parents and teachers "a wonderful opportunity to foster children's language development in an exciting, dynamic, instructionally sound—and most important—consistently Christian way" (p. 26). Post supports her pro–whole language position by grounding her pedagogical perspective in theology: "The whole language philosophy gives teachers the opportunity to acknowledge the nature of God-given communication and the holistic nature of the child" (1996, p. 14). (Whole language teachers from a more liberal or progressive Christian faith perspective similarly can see parallels between critical literacy, or critical pedagogy, and liberation theology, both of which promote an alliance with the poor, emphasis on cultural diversity, and a philosophy or theology of hope and possibility.)

In light of these connections, whole language educators should, I believe, welcome fundamentalist Christian parents into whole language, not ridicule their faith and drive them away. We might, for example, demonstrate that even fundamentalist Christians, who believe in the inerrancy of the Bible, construct meaning when they read the Bible, because they believe that God speaks to them through their inspired reading of biblical texts. Like young language learners, they may build on their individual reading by considering the meaning that's constructed by other readers. They may participate in a Bible study circle, where a small group of laypersons get together periodically to study and discuss a portion of the Bible. In that setting, one person may serve as discussion leader, though this role may be rotated among group members. During their discussions participants may read particular passages aloud, with each person sharing the meaning that she or he believes God inspires from the reading. They may focus on particular words, discussing a range of possible meanings, and they may discuss implications of the texts for their lives. The purpose of these study circles is different from that of a language-arts classroom, of course, but whole language teachers will recognize a striking parallel between such experiences of faith and literature study circles that play such an important role in many whole language classrooms.

Religion, Pedagogy, and Politics

I encourage whole language teachers to find ways to explore faith-based connections with parents whenever appropriate. But even if it were possible to address all of religious-right parents' pedagogical concerns, it still wouldn't be enough to lay to rest the attacks on whole language. Ultimately, it is crucial that whole language teachers untangle and rethink the connections among religion and pedagogy *and politics*. Many people have in the past acted politically because of their religious faith; this can be entirely justifiable. What we should contest, however, are anti–whole language and anti–public education political agendas, even when those agendas are held and acted on by religious persons or groups.

Much that I've discussed in this chapter grows out of my personal experience with the most sincerely religious among those who embrace Christian fundamentalism. That is, I've focused on those who care deeply about their faith, about doing God's will, and about their responsibility to be God's representative within their family, their community, and the world. But some who claim the deepest faith demonstrate that they are driven primarily not by faith but by a desire for political control. For example, Ralph Reed, former executive director of the Christian Coalition, developed a plan that involved placing workers in each voting precinct and in 100,000 churches, with the promised result that "we will be larger and more effective and will reach more people than the Democratic and Republican parties combined" ("The Right Hand of God" 1995, cited in Gerzon 1996, p. 13). Such initiatives surely are motivated more by a political quest for power than by religious faith. Even more chilling are discussions of "dominion theology," a theory that "believers" are "entitled to 'dominion' over all the world's institutions" (Cox 1995, p. 66). Harvey Cox reports that comments made by Pat Robertson, founder of the Christian Coalition, carry "a strong impression of being a dominion-theology voice" when Robertson summarizes his political theology by saying, "There will never be world peace until God's house and God's people are given their rightful place of leadership at the top of the world" (quoted by Cox 1995, p. 66). Although people like Robertson and the Christian Reconstructionists (Cox 1995, p. 68) may claim to ground their actions in religious faith, their political goal seems clear: to make America into a theocracy, a country ruled by their particular brand of Christianity.

Fortunately, many people who align themselves with the religious right are not extremists who mingle politics and religion to accomplish oppressive ends. But such frightening ideas and rhetoric call for swift rebuttal, which is probably most effective when offered by persons of faith. Jim Wallis, progressive Christian author of *The Soul of Politics* (1994), condemns the religious right and their destructive uses of religion: "It has been a white religion, has fueled the backlash against women's rights, and has used blatant caricatures and attacks on homosexuals as highly successful fund-raising techniques" (p. 36). The result, Wallis contends, has been confusion and rejection of the Christian faith by many people who are repulsed by this pervasive "unholy alliance of religious appeals and right-wing politics" (p. 36). Carter (1993) likewise rejects the divisive distortions of the religious right, explaining that "Christ's message . . . is one of love and inclusion, not of hatred and division. It is painful for me as a Christian to watch the perversion of this message by the far right wing of my own faith into a call for holy war" (p. 90).

What's religion got to do with attacks on whole language? Given the agendas, the strategies, and the power of the religious right, there seems to be almost nothing these days that doesn't have something to do with religion. Whole language is no exception, but many of the attacks on whole language launched by the religious right are motivated more by politics than by faith. The attacks ultimately promote an agenda focused on controlling public school curricula and using public money to pay for private schools. In Michigan, for example, major contributors to nationally organized religious-right groups have been identified as providing the primary financial support for a multimillion-dollar media campaign to promote a state constitutional amendment that would authorize public funding for private schools, both nonsectarian and parochial (Guyette 1996).

As whole language educators, we simply must not take the chance that the voices of religious-right extremists might be the only ones heard on these issues. The issues of religion are not only part of the problem but can also be part of the long-term solution. Thus, we can take several courses of action to make a positive difference:

1. We can acknowledge religion and teach about religion and religions in whole language classrooms—action that may speak to the central fears of sincere religious-right parents.
2. We can work patiently with individual parents to demonstrate the effectiveness of whole language learning—action that may generate new support and new whole language defenders.
3. We can boldly challenge the pedagogical inaccuracies disseminated by the religious right—action that may better inform the general public and thereby diminish the attacks.
4. We can challenge and resist the religious right's use of their religious beliefs as a smokescreen to cover and promote grossly intolerant and inequitable political ideologies.

Whole language educators aren't by nature combative. What we care most about is what happens to kids and to learning. The last thing most of us want is conflict. But these days whole language teachers are feeling besieged. This is one of the reasons that we in Michigan have started a grassroots organization, Michigan for Public Education (see Chapter 11, this volume). It's why people in Pennsylvania have formed the Freedom to Learn Network and why parents in Mississippi formed what is now a national organization, Parents for Public Schools. Defending against attacks on whole language will take a commitment to do whatever all of us, individually and together, can do to support and strengthen whole language and public education.

Suggestions for Rethinking Religion and Whole Language Classrooms

In closing, I offer some ideas for supporting religion in the whole language classroom.

1. Include realistic fiction, historical fiction, biography, and nonfiction that contain religious and spiritual themes and information. The Spring 1996 issue of *The ALAN Review* (published by NCTE's Assembly on

Literature for Adolescents) features an article entitled "Spiritual Themes in Young Adult Books" (Mendt 1996, pp. 34–36) that explains the benefits of inviting students to explore spirituality and to learn about the many religious systems in today's world. The author cites more than a dozen titles on the subject.

2. Accept, neither discouraging nor encouraging, student writing about religion or religious experiences. The wide range of expressive writing experiences (personal reflections and narratives, journal and log entries, to name a few) and inquiry projects that whole language teachers include should not be limited to nonreligious topics. Learners should feel free to research religious topics and issues if such a project fits within curricular guidelines. An article by F. Todd Goodson (1994) provides a candid discussion of a student research project involving witchcraft, the author's subsequent examination of his decision as teacher to reject that topic, and his recommendation that students be asked instead to research opposing positions when controversial topics are selected.

3. Children in elementary whole language classrooms should learn through reading and social studies about religious pluralism, studying (not experiencing) religious customs, basic beliefs, holidays, and histories of major religions (Nord 1995, p. 386). At the middle and high school levels, school districts might consider offering a course in comparative religions. David Ruenzel (1996) discusses the design and development of such classes being offered by a couple of public schools in North Carolina.

4. Given fundamentalist views about biblical texts that place great value on precision of language, plan literacy events for families that will engage them and their children in writing. Parents may not understand the learning benefits of invented spelling until a generation of parents can recall their own whole language school experiences. In the meantime, if at all possible, engage them in writing and teach them about writing as process as well as product so that they will know that writers in whole language classrooms do attend to spelling and conventional usage. Some religious-right parents express a preference for "true" information and stories; therefore, make a point to show parents the range of reading and writing experiences planned for their children, including informational texts (biography, inquiry reports, personal narrative, observation logs, letters, and so on). They're probably right to complain if unlimited classroom choices result in reading and/or writing in a single genre.

5. Realistically, whole language teachers don't have the time or probably the desire to become First Amendment scholars. Still, such educators need to consider how the Bible and other sacred texts might be appropriately used in the classroom. These texts cannot be read devotionally in the classroom (that is, religion cannot be practiced in the classroom), but they can be studied as literary or historical works (Nord 1995, p. 117). Before

proceeding, whole language educators should refer to a resource that spells out religious rights and responsibilities. One source I find useful and user-friendly is Barry Lynn, Marc D. Stern, and Oliver S. Thomas's *The Right to Religious Liberty*, Second Edition (1995), a pocket-sized ACLU handbook written in question-and-answer format.

6. Finally, proposed legislation deserves special attention. Parents' rights bills may sound reasonable until we begin to realize some of the potential implications, such as the possible requirement that all curriculum materials, even last night's newspaper, be cleared with the school board before being used in the classroom. An even greater threat exists from pressure to use such bills as the Parental Rights and Responsibilities Act to force school vouchers to pay for private schools, thus giving parents unlimited freedom to decide where their children will go to school. Whole language educators urgently need up-to-date information (see, for example, Isaacs 1996)) to stay informed and to help others understand the threats that are sometimes posed by proposed state and national legislation.

References

Beeson, R., and K. Mills. 1993. *Spiritual Warfare and Your Children: When Your Child Is Under Attack and What to Do About It.* Nashville, TN: Thomas Nelson.

Berliner, D. C., and B. J. Biddle. 1995. *The Manufactured Crisis: Myths, Fraud, and the Attack on America's Public Schools.* Reading, MA: Addison-Wesley.

Blumenfeld, S. L. 1984. *N.E.A.: Trojan Horse in American Education.* Boise, ID: Paradigm.

Brinkley, E. H. 1994. Intellectual Freedom and the Theological Dimensions of Whole Language. In J. Brown, ed., *Preserving Intellectual Freedom: Fighting Censorship in Our Schools,* pp. 111–22. Urbana, IL: National Council of Teachers of English.

———. 1995. Faith in the Word: Examining Religious Right Attitudes About Texts. *English Journal* 84: 91–98.

Carroll, J. D., W. D. Broadnax, G. Caontreras, T. E. Mann, N. J. Ornstein, and J. Steiehm. 1987. *We the People: A Review of U.S. Government and Civics Textbooks.* Washington, DC: People for the American Way.

Carter, S. L. 1993. *The Culture of Disbelief: How American Law and Politics Trivialize Religious Devotion.* New York: Basic Books.

Chapman, J. 1986. *Why Not Teach Intensive Phonics?* Pensacola, FL: A Beka Book.

Christian Coalition. 1995. *Citizen Action Seminar Manual.* Chesapeake, VA: Christian Coalition.

Cox, H. 1995. The Warring Visions of the Religious Right. *Atlantic Monthly* 276, 5: 59–69.

Cumbey, C. E. 1985. *A Planned Deception: The Staging of a New Age "Messiah."* East Detroit: Pointe Publishers.

Dobson, J., and G. L. Bauer. 1990. *Children at Risk: The Battle for the Hearts and Minds of Our Kids.* Dallas: Word.

Furnish, D. J. 1975. *Exploring the Bible with Children.* Nashville, TN: Abingdon Press.

Gaddy, B. B., T. W. Hall, and R. J. Marzano. 1996. *School Wars: Resolving Our Conflicts over Religion and Values.* San Francisco: Jossey-Bass.

Gerzon, M. 1996. *A House Divided: Six Belief Systems Struggling for America's Soul.* New York: Putnam.

Goodman, K. S., P. Shannon, Y. S. Freeman, and S. Murphy. 1988. *Report Card on Basal Readers.* Katonah, NY: Richard C. Owen.

Goodson, F. T. 1994. Culture Wars and the Rules of the English Classroom. *English Journal* 83, 5: 21–24.

Guyette, C. 1996. Onward Christian Scholars. *Detroit Metro Times* (June 26–July 2): 10, 12, 14–15.

Isaacs, R. 1996. Parental Rights and Wrongs: Dangerous Legislation. *People for the American Way News* 2: 3, 7.

Lynn, B., M. Stern, and O. Thomas. 1995. *The Right to Religious Liberty: The Basic ACLU Guide to Religious Rights.* 2d ed. Carbondale, IL: Southern Illinois University Press.

Mendt, K. L. 1996. Spiritual Themes in Young Adult Books. *The ALAN [Assembly on Literature for Adolescents,* NCTE] *Review* 23, 3: 34–36.

Menendez, A. J., and E. Doerr. 1991. *Religion and Public Education: Common Sense and the Law.* Silver Spring, MD: Americans for Religious Liberty.

Michigan for Public Education—Why and Why Now? 1995. Portage, MI: Michigan for Public Education.

Noddings, N. 1993. *Educating for Intelligent Belief or Unbelief.* New York: Teachers College Press.

Nord, W. A. 1995. *Religion and American Education: Rethinking a National Dilemma.* Chapel Hill, NC: University of North Carolina Press.

Post, A. R. 1991. Whole Language: A New Approach to Teaching. *Christian Home and School* 69, 1: 22–26.

———. 1996. The Whole Language Debate. *Christian Home and School* 74, 2: 11–14.

Religious Freedom Amendment. 1996, January. *AFA [American Family Association] Journal* 20 (January): 21.

The Right Hand of God. 1995. *Time* (May 15): 35.

Rosenblatt, L. 1978. *The Reader, the Text, the Poem: The Transactional Theory of the Literary Work.* Carbondale, IL: Southern Illinois University Press.

Ruenzel, D. 1996. Old-Time Religion. *Education Week* 15 (March 27): 30–35.

Sharp, P. T., and R. M. Wood. 1992. Moral Values: A Study of Selected Third- and Fifth-Grade Reading and Social Studies Textbooks. *Religion and Public Education* 19: 143–53.

Thogmartin, M. B. 1994. The Prevalence of Phonics Instruction in Fundamentalist Christian Schools. *Journal of Research on Christian Education* 3, 1: 103–32.

Thomas, G. 1996. Does Religious Freedom Have a Prayer? *Christian American* 7, 2: 12–13.

Vitz, P. C. 1986. *Censorship: Evidence of Bias in Our Children's Textbooks.* Ann Arbor, MI: Servant Books.

Wallis, J. 1994. *The Soul of Politics.* New York: New Press.

David and Yvonne Freeman spin out the history of a remarkable decade in California education. The story begins in 1987 with a new state language arts framework through which the Department of Education moved away from text-based curriculum in reading and writing and moved toward holistic, literature-based programs. It ends with the repudiation of that framework and a swing, through law, to mandated phonics programs and affirmations of loyalty to those mandates. At both ends is William Honig, State Superintendent in 1987 and reborn phonics expert and advocate in 1997. In California laws were passed essentially without opposition; and the state Board of Education, appointed by a conservative governor, has taken decision making and implementation out of the hands of the Department of Education, which has been effectively neutralized in the swift changes taking place.

4

California Reading:
The Pendulum Swings

DAVID FREEMAN AND YVONNE S. FREEMAN

Consider the following two quotes:

> An analysis of the way reading has come to be taught reveals that we have been relying on an almost assemblyline approach . . . Instead of teaching a skill-based program using brief, unfocused narratives which lack meaningful content, we suggest a teacher utilize a program that encourages reading significant literary works which reflect the real dilemmas faced by all human beings (Honig 1988, pp. 237, 239).

> Some of the newest reading texts reflect a balanced approach and utilize the powerful research on effective reading strategies and practitioner best practices accumulated during the past decade. In one, for example, the first grade begins with two weeks of letter, sound, print awareness and language review, primarily through game activities with students. Next, all students start working through approximately 100 lessons which provide enough basic letter/sound correspondences, sight words, word attack skills, and language structure knowledge to enable students to read trade books and a reading anthology which is part of the program. (Honig 1996, p. 67)

In 1987, California introduced a revolutionary English–Language Arts Framework that called for a shift in emphasis from skills-based reading programs to programs in which good literature was the keystone. As a result of this shift, the state's official position for the teaching of reading supported a whole language approach.

The first quotation above comes from a 1988 article by Bill Honig, then State Superintendent of Public Instruction, which outlined the new initiative California had undertaken. According to the 1987 Framework,

73

which was to guide reading instruction in California, skills were out; literature and values were in.

Ten years later, Honig is taking a very different view. The second quotation comes from a book he recently authored. Although he still calls for the use of literature and stresses the importance of reading to learn, he insists that students must first learn to read. This involves a heavy dose of skills and the use of books that "must also include words which correspond to the phonics and word attack lessons taught" (Honig 1996, p. 62). For young readers, at least, literature and values are out; skills and controlled texts are back in. The pendulum has swung, and teachers who embrace a whole language philosophy are now under attack.

Honig is no longer State Superintendent of Public Instruction. He left that office in disgrace, having been convicted of a felony. Honig's felony was subsequently reduced to a misdemeanor, which coincidentally made it legal for him to do business with the state. His influence in shaping California's educational policies is stronger now than when he was superintendent (for more on this, see D. Freeman 1996). His book and his testimony as an expert witness had a clear and direct impact on the California Reading Task Force report *Every Child a Reader* (1995). This report, in turn, resulted in a Reading Program Advisory, *Teaching Reading: A Balanced Comprehensive Approach to Teaching Reading in Prekindergarten Through Grade Three* (Eastin 1996). The Advisory was sent out by California's Department of Education to all the state's prekindergarten and primary-grade teachers, and it helped to guide the committee working to rewrite the Framework itself.

These dramatic swings in the official position on English–language arts instruction from the state Department of Education during the last ten years have left school districts and individual teachers perplexed and anxious. The current state of reading instruction in California is extremely confusing. Adding to the disarray are twelve new laws from the state legislature that are designed to legislate the teaching of explicit, systematic phonics, to eliminate funding for any program associated with "whole language," and to ban references to use of context cues or "inventive spelling" during staff development. In addition, the Commission on Teacher Credentialing has set out guidelines to ensure that universities prepare prospective teachers to teach reading through a phonics approach. New teachers will have to pass a test on teaching reading using phonics, and the universities themselves will be evaluated on how well their students perform on the test.

Ten years ago, when California introduced its new Framework, educators across the country took notice. The shift that California made in 1987 toward a greater emphasis on literature was followed in many other states. Literature became a key component in most reading programs. But now California is swinging back toward what has been traditionally called the basics. Literature programs are being called inadequate for teaching children to read. The California scene is indeed confusing, but California is setting national patterns, as it did ten years ago. So it is important to try to sort out what has happened and what is happening now.

In this chapter, we first briefly review the history of California reading policy over the past ten years. We then examine pressures that prevented full implementation of the 1987 Framework. We compare the 1987 Framework with the new documents by contrasting the two views of reading and the two views of research that they represent. We conclude by assessing the likelihood of the implementation of the mandated approach and by reflecting on its impact on California's teachers and children.

California's Reading Initiative: The Beginnings

Educational reform efforts in California began in the early 1980s with the development of model curriculum standards, which provided "one of the first steps in the process of revitalizing the English–language arts curriculum" (in the words of the 1987 English–Language Arts Framework). In May 1986, Bill Honig launched the California Reading Initiative in response to "alarming new research on illiteracy in America" which indicated "that without a profound change in direction, most American school children will not become lifelong readers" (Honig 1988, p. 236). The Initiative was a comprehensive plan to "revitalize the teaching of reading and the language arts through curriculum and resource development" (p. 236). The basic themes of the Initiative were the following (p. 237):

- Reading should be enjoyable as well as educational.
- Learning to read is a means toward the goal of becoming a lifelong reader.
- Teachers should inspire students as well as teach them.
- Parents are teachers, too: when they read aloud, listen to children read, and encourage reading, they enhance the learning process.
- Literature should be the core of the language arts curriculum.

The Initiative included "Recommended Readings in Literature, Kindergarten Through Grade Eight," a listing of 1,010 books that California educators suggested to help create reading programs that would "involve students in the excitement of learning" (p. 236).

The English–Language Arts Curriculum Framework and Criteria Committee met over a two-year period to draft and edit the English–Language Arts Framework. As the opening lines indicate, this document represented a change in curriculum based on research:

> We are in the midst of a revolution—a quiet, intellectual revolution
> spinning out dramatic insights into how the brain works, how we

acquire language, and how we construct meaning in our lives. (1987, p. 1)

California's reading initiative in the 1980s was launched with fanfare and high expectations. It was developed in response to a reported crisis in reading test scores. The 1987 Framework called for a strong emphasis on teaching literature and values. School districts bought books on the recommended reading list. Teachers were asked to change their practice to reflect current research. Into this reading revolution, some educators injected doubts. Were teachers prepared to implement this new kind of reading program? Could they be prepared adequately in a short time? How would results be judged? Just what form would the new tests take? How would all this be funded? And what about the growing population of English-language learners? As the eighties ended and as other states looked on, California began its educational experiment.

Impediments to Implementation

Four key factors combined to impede successful implementation of the 1987 Framework: pressures from testing; pressures from administrators, parents, and some teachers; pressures from changes in the student population; and pressures from limited school budgets. In the following sections, we consider each of these forces.

Testing

Perhaps the strongest of the pressures came from the push for high scores on standardized tests. The recommended changes in instructional approach had come in response to low test scores. The new documents called for both a change in teaching methods and a change in testing. Soon, some teachers began experimenting with portfolios, observation checklists, or miscue analysis, but schools were still required to give standardized reading tests, and administrators and parents judged success by the scores on those tests.

The mean scores for California students were among the lowest of the states that took part on both the 1992 and 1994 National Assessment of Educational Progress (NAEP) tests. (A number of states elected not to participate or failed to meet the sample requirements.) Using literature to teach reading, an approach associated with whole language, was blamed for the low scores. However, as Regie Routman (1996) points out, on the 1994 NAEP "the difference between California, the lowest scoring state, and the highest scoring state was only about 15 percent" (p. 6). Jeff McQuillan (1995) suggests that many factors contributed to the poor test results, among them limited access to public or school libraries, reduced per capita income, and low per-pupil expenditures. Routman adds two other factors: that California has the largest class size in the nation and has no uniform or mandatory staff development for teachers.

Actually the 1994 NAEP results could be used to show the success of whole language because they revealed that in California 66 percent of the students reported they read at least three books a month, and 42 percent said they read five or more books each month. And those who read more had higher test scores (Goodman 1995). Nevertheless, the low test scores were used by those who called for reforms in teaching reading.

Parents, Administrators, and Teachers

The apparent failure of the Framework to effect dramatic improvements in mean scores on standardized tests was one source of the pressure to abandon literature that came from parents, administrators, and some teachers. Many teachers resisted the top-down state recommendations for a process approach to teaching reading and writing and for the establishment of studentcentered classrooms with built-in opportunities for choice. In addition, some administrators were not prepared to trust teachers to create literate classroom communities and made it clear that they were more comfortable when teachers followed a predictable, structured commercial program. Even when they wanted to trust the teachers, few administrators knew how to support them as they attempted to shift their teaching orientation.

The vast majority of California schools adopted literature-based basal programs in the late 1980s. Because they contained more authentic literature than previous programs, they were often referred to as whole language programs. Teachers were expected to implement these new programs with only minimal in-service suggestions on how to teach reading using real literature. Many teachers tried to use one story at a time from the anthology for all their students or have all their students read the same piece of designated core literature. A common confusion that arose was that whole language meant whole-class instruction, with every student reading the same story at the same time. When not all students could read the literature independently, teachers became frustrated and blamed whole language.

Even in cases where teachers understood how to use literature and how important it was to provide choice for individual students to meet individual interests and needs, they often didn't have the books they needed. Trade book purchases had to vie with computers or other types of technology for a place in reduced school budgets. When monies were available, few teachers or administrators had a broad enough knowledge of children's literature to choose appropriate works. Since few California schools have librarians, the identification of resources was left to school site specialists. In the few classrooms where children were provided with high-quality literature, it was often the individual teacher who had personally bought most of the books. In these classrooms children made great strides as readers, but there were so few of these literature-rich classrooms that these individual successes were overlooked in the vast picture of the whole state.

Furthermore, both teachers and administrators were hard pressed to respond to the increasing pressure from those on the far right, who did not trust either the schools or the children with broad choices of literature on topics some considered controversial. By the 1990s the attacks on whole language had roused the fears of parents about whether their children were getting the skills that they needed to compete academically and whether they were being taught traditional values.

Changes in Student Population

Over the past ten years, the tremendous growth in the second language (ESL) population in the state has added another pressure to schools. In the period from 1988 to 1997 the number of Limited English Proficient (LEP) students in California's public schools doubled from 652,000 to nearly 1.4 million students. Preparation of teachers to work with second language students has not kept pace with the increase in the LEP population. In 1994, for example, 322,748 students (26.6 percent of the LEP population) were not receiving any special services despite their lack of English proficiency (California State Department of Education 1995).

Responding to the growing number of diverse students in classrooms has not been easy. For example, the Los Angeles school district has a total population of 639,129 students. Of those, 291,527, or 45.6 percent are LEP students. In the Santa Ana district 69.3 percent of the students are English learners (Hopstock and Bucaro 1993). It is not uncommon for teachers to have classes with as many as five or six different first languages other than English among their students.

During the same period that teachers were asked to change their language arts programs to include literature, they were also expected to find ways to make their curriculum accessible to these increasing numbers of non-English-speaking students. Most teachers lacked the preparation and understanding to engage students who did not speak English in authentic literature or to involve them in a process approach to writing. Many of these teachers responded by reverting to an emphasis on skills. As we wrote earlier, "These teachers believe that second language students need more direct instruction in reading skills and they can find support for this view from The Framework" (Freeman, Freeman, and Fennacy 1993, p. 46).

Limited School Budgets

The 1987 Framework was launched at a time when California schools were experiencing severe budget cuts. Joel Taxel (1993) has referred to "the calamitous fiscal crisis that has resulted in major cuts in the budgets of many school districts that already were threadbare" (p viii). At the time that the original Framework was being implemented, budgets were extremely limited.

As early as 1993 (Freeman, Freeman, and Fennacy 1993) educators in California feared that the reading revolution was beginning to fizzle. Attempts at systemic change always meet resistance, and the four pressures just described were undermining attempts by many teachers to implement the kind of literacy programs envisaged by the Framework. The result was a strong backlash against the Framework and the whole language philosophy with which it had come to be associated.

Attacks on Whole Language

During the meetings of the Reading Task Force and immediately after the September 1995 publication of its report, *Every Child a Reader,* the media in California and across the United States interpreted what was wrong with reading instruction, building on widely distributed disinformation. In most instances the newspaper articles reported that the task force was calling on California schools to abandon its "experiment with whole language" and to return to teaching phonics and skills.

Actually, the task force report does not attack whole language at all. As we have explained elsewhere (Freeman, Freeman, and Fennacy 1996), whole language is not mentioned in this document; if anything, it criticizes the 1987 English–Language Arts Framework. Yet newspaper stories and television programs are highlighting not the report but whole language. Headlines are often inflammatory and sources of quotes are consistently omitted. A *Los Angeles Times* (September 3, 1996) article entitled "Teacher Training Lags Behind as State Shifts Strategy on Reading" has this summary statement printed in large, bold letters: "Whole language method recommended eight years ago falters on basic skills, task force found." The article explains how inadequately the Framework had been implemented but concludes that whole language is the culprit causing low test scores.

At the same time that articles bashing whole language and California students' reading abilities grab headlines, positive stories are given little space. Papers that reported the government report of how well American kids did in an international reading study buried the story on inside pages (Binkley and Williams 1996). The article reported that U.S. students scored second only to Finnish children in reading proficiency. However, a source from the Department of Education voiced concern that reports of this success "might draw attention away from problems that continue to pervade the nation's classrooms." Even good news is given a negative spin.

Two Views of Reading Research

The 1987 Framework was not a whole language document, but its emphasis on literature was consistent with whole language. Even though the vision of the Framework was not widely implemented, whole language was blamed for the low reading test scores of California students. The pendulum had swung toward literature; now it is swinging sharply back toward a basic skills approach.

The attack on whole language includes a rejection of both the classroom practices many whole language teachers use and the theory that underlies their practice. Whole language approaches to teaching and learning are supported by an extensive body of research, but supporters of the new reading initiatives claim these approaches are superior because they are based on empirical research. The accompanying table lists key differences between these two kinds of research.

This empirical research is based on a word recognition view of reading. Researchers attempt to identify and isolate skills, such as phonemic awareness, that they believe readers need to identify words. The effectiveness of teaching each skill is tested by having students read lists of isolated words or nonsense syllables under pre- and post-test conditions. Comprehension is kept separate from skill acquisition; if comprehension is measured at all, it is usually through tests containing a series of detailed questions.

Two Views of Reading Research

Reading as Word Recognition	Reading as Meaning Construction
Researchers use an empirical approach with control and experimental groups.	Researchers use naturalistic studies of children reading.
Research focuses on identifying the skills readers need to recognize words.	Research focuses on the strategies readers use to construct meaning.
Testing is based on children's ability to recode words or nonsense syllables from a list.	Testing is based on observation of children reading complete texts, using tools such as miscue analysis.
Testing for comprehension is kept separate from testing for fluent recoding.	Testing includes both comprehending and comprehension.
Researchers assume that reading is an unnatural process that children can learn only through direct instruction and that many children will not learn to read successfully without intervention.	Researchers assume that learning to read is a natural process that children acquire through being read to and read with and that most children will acquire literacy without need for intervention.
Can be replicated—focuses on a method.	Not replicable—focuses on a reader in a certain context.

In contrast, the naturalistic research is based on a sociopsycholinguistic view of reading. Reading is seen as constructing meaning, not just recognizing words. Researchers have students read whole texts. They assess students' abilities in comprehending (what strategies readers use as they read) and comprehension (what they have understood once they have finished reading). Comprehending is often evaluated through miscue analysis, which looks at how readers use all cueing systems. Comprehension is usually evaluated through a retelling of what was read.

Perhaps the biggest difference between the two approaches is that empirical researchers generally assume that reading is not naturally acquired, that children have to be explicitly taught how to read, and that teacher intervention is essential. Many of their studies focus on students with reading difficulties and are published in journals dealing with reading disabilities. Naturalistic researchers, in contrast, assume that reading is acquired naturally and that most children will learn to read if teachers find ways to engage them with interesting books.

These two views of reading research have resulted in two different bodies of literature. Here is a brief list of representative publications that support each view:

Word Recognition Focus

Stanovich, Keith. Matthew Effects in Reading: Some Consequences of Individual Differences in the Acquisition of Literacy. *Reading Research Quarterly* 21 (1986): 360–407. A summary of research on reading. Focuses on phonemic awareness as the key for reading. Argues for reciprocal causation—the rich get richer.

Adams, Marilyn. *Beginning to Read: Thinking and Learning About Print*. Cambridge, MA: MIT Press, 1990. A comprehensive summary of research on word recognition.

Juel, Connie. *Learning to Read and Write in One Elementary School*. New York: Springer Verlag, 1994. The report on a study done in Texas. Shows that poor readers in first grade are still poor readers in fourth grade. Argues that the poor readers are those that lack phonemic awareness.

Yopp, Hallie Kay. Developing Phonemic Awareness in Young Children. *The Reading Teacher* 45, 9 (1992): 12–19. Yopp's work includes many practical ideas for teaching phonemic awareness.

Foorman, Barbara, et al. Early Interventions for Children with Reading Problems: Study Designs and Preliminary Findings. *Learning Disabilities: A Multidisciplinary Journal* 8, 1 (1997): 63–71. A controversial study that compares kids in treatments labeled whole language and direct instruction and finds that kids with more phonics do better on tests of word recognition.

Reading as Meaning Construction

Basic theory: Miscue research and psycholinguistic studies that lead to a coherent sociopsycholinguistic theory of reading

Goodman, Kenneth S. Cues and Miscues in Reading: A Linguistic Study. *Elementary English* 42, 6 (1965): 635–42. The first published report of miscue analysis. It shows that words were easier to read in context than on lists.

Goodman, Kenneth S. *On Reading.* Portsmouth, NH: Heinemann, 1996. A complete and up-to-date presentation of Goodman's constructivist model.

Smith, Frank. *Understanding Reading.* New York: Holt, Rinehart and Winston, 1971. Presents Smith's view of reading.

Smith, Frank. *Psycholinguistics and Reading.* New York: Holt, Rhinehart, and Winston, 1973. A synthesis of psycholinguistic studies of reading.

Early literacy: Piagetian and ethnographic research that provides important insights into natural reading development in English and Spanish

Teale, William, and Elizabeth Sulzby, eds. *Emergent Literacy: Writing and Reading.* Norwood, NJ: Ablex, 1986. The authors bring together research on how literacy develops.

Harste, Jerome, Virginia Woodward, and Carolyn Burke. *Language Stories and Literacy Lessons.* Portsmouth, NH: Heinemann, 1984. Presents a research-based view of literacy development.

Ferreiro, Emilia, and Anna Teberosky. *Literacy Before Schooling.* Translated by Karen Goodman Castro. Portsmouth, NH: Heinemann, 1982. Piagetian research on how young children come to control literacy.

Large-scale studies: studies showing the benefits of free, voluntary reading that leads to the acquisition of literacy in first and second languages

Elley, Warwick. Acquiring Literacy in a Second Language: The Effect of Book-Based Programs. *Language Learning* 41, 2 (1991): 403–39. Reports results of programs in developing nations that emphasize use of real books.

Krashen, Stephen. *Every Person a Reader: An Alternative to the California Task Force Report on Reading.* Culver City, CA: Language Education Associates, 1996. A response to the Task Force report that offers an alternative to its proposals.

California's 1987 Framework was based on a sociopsycholinguistic view of reading and was supported by naturalistic research. The new Framework is based on a word recognition view of reading and on experimental research. The 1987 document stressed learning to read by reading significant literary works. The new document contends that there is an important difference between learning to read and reading to learn. Learning to read primarily involves recognizing words rather than constructing meaning. Further, the key to word recognition is believed to be explicit, systematic instruction in phonics. And the key to phonics is phonemic awareness.

In California, reading has been redefined. The view of reading, the research base for that view, and the resulting classroom practices look quite different from the way they did ten years ago.

Implementing the New Framework

In California, the revolution in reading instruction that was implemented in 1987 has come full circle, at least on an official level. Then, Bill Honig and other officials called for a literature-based program that would engage students in reading significant literary works and discussing the substantive human issues raised in these works. Now state Department of Education documents based on new state laws reflect a very different view. Although the documents call for a "balanced approach," using real literature to teach early literacy is out. Direct instruction in intensive, systematic phonics is in.

The 1987 Framework was not a legal mandate, and it was not widely implemented because of the pressures discussed earlier. The new Framework is legally mandated. State officials are required to ensure that the elements of the new Framework will be put into practice. Paradigm police are in place to ensure that the letter of the Framework and the laws are followed.

The greatest pressure against implementation of the 1987 Framework came from testing requirements. Test results for the new initiative will be available soon. Because standardized reading tests for the early grades are geared toward identification of words or word parts with little emphasis on comprehension, the results may be positive, at least initially. By fourth grade (the first one tested on NAEP), however, older learners will show how little they can understand of what they read.

Another pressure against the 1987 Framework came from limited school budgets. In recent years, increased state monies are being used to decrease class size to twenty students in the early grades. A great deal of the money is being provided to be sure that all teachers of early literacy in all schools receive highly controlled training on exactly how to teach phonemic awareness and phonics to all children. To be certain that the training will then be implemented in schools, all administrators and school board members are being in-serviced so that they also understand clearly what is expected. Universities also are being forced by new tests to prepare prospective teachers to teach reading through a phonics approach. In smaller classes, professional teachers can provide more personal attention for students, so test scores will probably go up even if the focus of reading instruction is not on comprehension. But in classes with nonprofessional teachers the results will be dismal and the schools will be declared unfixable.

All these measures are designed to enforce implementation of the new initiative by administrators, parents, and teachers. Some administrators and parents have already responded favorably to this back-to-basics approach. Some teachers who were not prepared to teach reading through literature may be more comfortable with a prescribed, structured curriculum. Whole language teachers who are convinced of the value of using authentic literature will undoubtedly resist.

Teachers will face pressure to use the new approach with second language learners. These students will be taught phonemic awareness in English as soon as they are able to function minimally in English. Little attention will be given to research in the fields of bilingual education and second language acquisition that shows the importance of teaching reading in students' primary languages (Freeman and Freeman 1997).

Conclusion

Some of the pressures that impeded implementation of the 1987 Framework will apparently not apply to the new reading initiatives in California. There is legal pressure to assure that California's children will be taught to read through a narrow methodology that emphasizes phonics and word recognition and minimizes comprehension, literature, and values. What will the results mean for California's teachers and children?

Ten years ago, the California Department of Education initiated a new kind of language arts program, one that featured powerful literature. As whole language educators know, authentic literature has the potential to liberate. The present pendulum swing back toward a sterile monolithic curriculum with a strong dose of phonics may have little to do with what we know about how to help kids become good readers. It may have a great deal to do with the fear of the kind of real revolution that could result within educational systems if all children were able to use literacy to confront "the real dilemmas faced by all human beings" (Honig 1988, p. 239).

References

Binkley, M., and T. Williams. 1996. *Reading Literacy in the United States.* Washington, DC: U.S. Department of Education, National Center for Educational Statistics.

California Reading Task Force. 1995. *Every Child a Reader.* Sacramento: California Department of Education.

California State Department of Education. 1995. *Languages from Around the World Are Found in California.* Sacramento: California State Department of Education.

Eastin, D. 1996. *Teaching Reading: A Balanced Comprehensive Approach to Teaching Reading in Prekindergarten Through Grade Three.* Sacramento: California Department of Education (May 10).

English–Language Arts Curriculum Framework and Criteria Committee. 1987. *English–Language Arts Framework.* Sacramento: California State Department of Education.

Freeman, D. 1996. Who Decides How We Teach Our Children to Read? *California English* 1, 3: 22.

Freeman, D. E., Y. S. Freeman, and J. Fennacy. 1993. California's Reading Revolution: A Review and Analysis. *New Advocate* 6, 1: 41–60.

Freeman, Y. S., and D. E. Freeman. 1997. *Teaching Reading and Writing in Spanish in the Bilingual Classroom.* Portsmouth, NH: Heinemann.

Freeman, Y. S., D. E. Freeman, and J. Fennacy. 1996. The California Reading Task Force and Whole Language: Does Anyone Understand? *Talking Points* 7, 3: 25.

Goodman, K. 1995. The Report of the California Reading Task Force: Forced Choices in a Non-Crisis. *California English* 1, 3: 8–10.

Honig, B. 1988. The California Reading Initiative. *New Advocate* 1, 4: 235–40.

———. 1996. *How Should We Teach Our Children to Read?* San Francisco: Far West Laboratory.

Hopstock, P., and B. Bucaro. 1993. *A Review and Analysis of Estimates of LEP Student Population.* Arlington, VA: Development Associates.

McQuillan, J. 1995. Did Whole Language Fail in California? *CommuniCATE Newsletter* (October).

Routman, R. 1996. *Literacy at the Crossroads: Crucial Talk About Reading, Writing, and Other Teaching Dilemmas.* Portsmouth, NH: Heinemann.

Taxel, J. 1993. Notes from the Editor. *New Advocate* 6, 1: viii–x.

In Texas, unlike California, the legislature is on record as leaving curriculum and methodology to the Texas Education Agency and the districts. Further, unlike those in California, state board members are elected in Texas. Though the results of the political shift are similar in these two states, the ways they have been achieved in Texas are very different. Linda Ellis has been directly involved in the battles in Texas as observer, participant, and elected leader of professional groups. The role of the far right is much more visible in Texas than in California. The use of the governor's office is similar in both states. But Ellis details a development in Texas that has also occurred in other states, though not in California: the creation of the Governor's Business Council, an organization representing CEOs of major corporations (who are major political contributors). This self-appointed group, with no official status, can exert enormous influence on decision-making groups and politicians. In Texas, you get a sense of what the professional groups, who are much better organized and focused than in California, are up against.

5

We'll Eat the Elephant One Bite at a Time: The Continuing Battle for Control of Literacy Education in Texas

Linda Ellis

After the heated last-ditch effort to overhaul the Texas curriculum, Donna Ballard, a state board member, said to newspaper reporters, "I have nothing left to do but quote scripture. 'Hell hath no fury like a woman scorned.'" Who scorned Ballard? Was it the other board members who wouldn't let her and her radical-right friends have their isolated skills curriculum? Was it the educators in the state? The professional organizations? This day of defeat in July 1997, ended a long and heated battle over the Texas Essential Knowledge and Skills (TEKS) curriculum, but it did not end the radical right attempts in the state to control public education.

Becoming Political

My involvement in the politics of literacy began in a small way when I was a teacher in my small-town school. I had become empowered through the university courses I took, by the books and articles I was reading, and through the success I was experiencing in my classroom with students.

I was encouraged to take action through the words of Patrick Shannon in talks I heard at conferences and through his books *Broken Promises: Reading Instruction in Twentieth-Century America* (1989) and *The Struggle to Continue: Progressive Reading Instruction in the United States* (1990), and a book he edited entitled *Becoming Political: Readings and Writings in the Politics of Literacy Education* (1992). Later I was influenced by the writings of Paulo Freire (Freire and Macedo 1987).

Ken Goodman's words also made me think when I read what he wrote in the December 1992–January 1993 issue of *Reading Today*:

> Education, including literacy education, is political. Some of the irrational arguments used against whole language come from peo-

ple who are afraid it will work too well. They don't want people to be too widely literate, to have easy access to information that may empower them. Others find it good politics to trade on rural and working-class parents' fears that schools are up to no good for their children. (p. 10)

My involvement in Texas politics began in 1995, when someone faxed me a copy of the state Board of Education (SBOE) agenda for the May meeting. I was appalled that one of the newly elected board members was attempting to add references throughout the document to intensive, systematic phonics. Within two hours a colleague and I were in my car on our way to Austin, Texas, for the board meeting . We sat through that meeting, shocked by the inaccurate statements and proposed changes by people who were not even educators. The next month we took action, arranging testimony by other educators before the Long-Range Planning Committee. In June, I became chair of the Governmental Relations Committee of the Texas State Reading Association and began to present testimony each month. I also arranged testimony for the Texas Association for the Improvement of Reading and the Texas Council of Teachers of English.

The Texas Board of Education has fifteen members. In May 1995, four of those members had open affiliations with the radical right. Since that time, voters have added two more radical-right members to the board. If the radical right had won two more seats on the state board, they would have held sway over the curriculum.

The fight is not over in Texas. And the struggle goes on in other states. So I will attempt here to outline the major battles we have fought in Texas during the last two years and the ones we know are yet to come.

The Long-Range Plan for Public Education

The attempt by the radical right to take control of the Texas curriculum began in May 1995 when a dentist from San Antonio, Bob Offutt, who was chair of the Long-Range Planning Committee, introduced his revisions to the long-range goals with the statement "Just look these over. I think you'll see that we've only made some minor changes." Offutt's changes, however, provoked much debate from five of the committee members. The proposed revisions included the following:

- All students should know how to read and write, including how to pronounce and spell words by understanding the letter/sound association of individual letters, letter groups, and syllables as well as the principles governing the associations.
- Students should be able to pronounce and spell words by understanding the letter/sound associations of individual letters, letter groups, and

syllables and principles governing these associations as well as the relationships of words taken together to form sentences that fully express thoughts.

- Effective reading and writing programs integrate explicit knowledge of the sound-symbol relationships, a study of the structures of words and an understanding of the sentence syntax within a language- and literature-rich learning environment.

Board members questioned why reading was the only content being addressed in the long-range goals, which had never addressed content in the past. Jack Christie, chair of the state Board of Education, asked, "Why aren't we telling teachers how to teach history?" The board, he said, should not be prescriptive. "It is not our job to tell teachers how to teach reading." Three members of the committee, however, showed support for Offutt's revisions and supported intensive, systematic phonics instruction in the schools. They contended that for several hundred years people have learned to read through phonics, and now that phonics is not emphasized in Texas schools we have a literacy problem. They asserted that in 1928 Texas had its highest literacy rate and that kids then learned to read through phonics. Their theme was "We need to go back to what works. We know that phonics works." After much debate the committee voted 5 to 4 to stay with the long-range goals as they were written and work at revising them instead of adopting Offutt's revisions.

At the June meeting I arranged for four members of the Texas State Reading Association to testify in support of Christie's statement that reading education should be left to the professional reading teachers in the state. Our speakers stressed the following:

- Teachers are educated to make instructional decisions. Having the board make these decisions instead would be similar to educators sitting on boards that made decisions about the practice of doctors or dentists.
- It takes trained teachers who understand the reading process and who can assess students' strengths and weaknesses to work effectively with students, by using specific strategies to address individual needs.
- The emphasis in reading instruction should be to develop readers who can understand the meaning of what they read, not just isolated words.

I expressed doubt that we had our highest literacy rate in 1928 and that students have learned to read successfully through phonics for several hundred years in our country, reminding the board that: (1) the definition of literacy has changed over the years; (2) we do not have comparative data from 1928 or earlier; and (3) public education only came into existence around the turn of the century.

Several board members referred to whole language or phonics as separate approaches, even though testimony and one board member repeatedly reminded the committee that whole language includes phonics. References were made to "whole word" as if it meant whole language. One board member attempted to take out Offutt's phrase "literature-rich learning environment" and replace it with "linguistics," stating that linguistics meant the same thing.

At the July board meeting, an organizer from the Texas Task Force who is head of the Texas Reading Institute and an antiques dealer from Houston, with the help of the National Right to Read Foundation, organized thirteen people to testify in support of direct, systematic phonemic awareness and phonics instruction. Marilyn Adams and Michael Pressley were among six presenters who came from out of state. Both Adams and Pressley emphasized that phonemic awareness must be taught, but stated that it needs to be done within the context of literature-rich environments. The other eleven presenters, some of whom were producers of phonics materials and staff development programs in phonics, criticized the existing programs in the schools and called for more direct, intensive phonics programs or code-emphasis phonics. At the Committee of the Whole meeting at the end of the day, Offutt pointed out that six "experts" came "at their own expense" to testify and stated that "history was made today at the board."

At the Long-Range Planning Committee in September a new draft was presented related to phonics:

> Phonological skills and meaningful connected texts are the cornerstones of effective reading programs. Such programs promote comprehension and integrate explicit knowledge of the sounds and structures of words and understanding of the sound-symbol relationships of the alphabet within language- and literature-rich learning environments. They result in increased comprehension and enhance student ability to speak and write clearly.

Another statement read:

> The board Policy Statement on Early Childhood and Elementary Education emphasizes the importance of reading instruction that integrates explicit knowledge of the sounds and structures of words and understanding of the sound-symbol relationships within language- and literature-rich learning environments.

An initiative related to that statement recommended providing teachers with

> training to teach reading through structured, systematic, and multisensory approaches to phonemic and alphabetic awareness within language- and literature-rich learning environments.

At that meeting, several members of the Texas State Reading Association again provided testimony requesting the board to rethink the emphasis on phonics, emphasizing that the ability to call words did not ensure comprehension. Barbara Foorman, a professor in the psychology department at the University of Houston, and Pat Lindamood of Lindamood-Bell Learning Processes of California also provided testimony. Foorman argued that reading problems occur primarily at the level of the single word and that decoding problems in reading are primarily associated with problems segmenting words and syllables into phonemes. Lindamood, a speech pathologist, stated that phonics does not work for all learners and emphasized the need for an intensive speech program to develop phonemic awareness.

On October 13 radical-right board members announced more than fifty revisions to the long-range goals that would be presented to the Long-Range Planning Committee the next day. They proposed to delete all references throughout the document to "developmentally appropriate." They also proposed:

- Omitting statements that all students can learn.
- Omitting references to adult and family literacy programs, including, parent, early childhood, preschool, and pre-kindergarten programs.
- De-emphasizing professional development for teachers, except for adding a statement calling for educator training in reading that would emphasize reading instruction that integrates explicit knowledge of the sounds and structures of words and understanding of the sound-symbol relationships.
- Encouraging implementation of preliminary identification programs for pre-kindergarten and kindergarten students with potential phonemic awareness problems.

All the revisions provoked much discussion and with the exception of two were voted down with a 5-to-4 vote. Eight people testified in opposition, including representatives from People for the American Way, the Children's Mental Health Association, and the Texas State Reading Association.

In November, one radical-right board member presented a letter "signed by over forty psychologists and linguists" to the Commissioner of Education in Massachusetts calling for more intensive phonics instruction. Another board member proposed a surprise alternative paragraph that would have taken out references to "cultural diversity," "individual differences," and "developmentally appropriate," but the committee voted against the revision. Another proposed change was to remove the goal that 98 percent of Texas teachers be certified in the areas in which they teach. The only other major change was the proposed addition of the words "listen" and "spell" to "read, speak, and write clearly." Some board members didn't feel that "write clearly" included spelling. The committee voted to include "listen" and "spell."

The committee then approved the long-range goals with a 5-to-4 vote. This brought an end to a seven-month heated battle and gave us an incentive to keep fighting. We realized the importance of opposing radical-right board members who were attempting to take control of the elections and the board. In November, Christie, a Republican, narrowly defeated a radical right opponent in the primaries, though the radical right had spread vicious propaganda against him in the fight to win the seat.

Offutt continued to sponsor "reading experts" every month before the Long-Range Planning Committee. Bill Honig was invited as an expert speaker. He had also spoken at a dinner in his honor the night before. Before the Long-Range Planning Committee he spoke against whole language and emphasized a need for early systematic instruction in phonemic awareness and phonics.

In the following months Offutt introduced other speakers, including a brain surgeon who attempted to show through brain patterns that repetition is important to learning and a former assistant to Honig who attempted to show that the supposed declining state of reading in California resulted from a "whole language curriculum."

In the February 28, 1996, *Houston Chronicle,* board member Donna Ballard stated,

> It won't be long before reading is taught again in Texas schools the way it should be taught. The board is pushing for an intensive, systematic phonetic approach to reading with direct connections to literature. What a refreshing change from the silliness of guessing at words by sight, rather than teaching our children the necessary decoding skills.

A brave quote, since a Senate bill stated that "the board may not adopt rules that designate the methodology used by a teacher" (Senate Bill 1, p. 87).

In May the Texas State Reading Association sponsored Constance Weaver to speak before the Long-Range Planning Committee. In her one-hour testimony, entitled "Toward a Balanced Reading Approach," Weaver emphasized the need for a comprehensive research-based definition and model of proficient reading to guide reading instruction. She expressed concern about much of the testimony and research that had been presented before the Long-Range Planning Committee by Bill Honig, Barbara Foorman, and others; statements to the press by Governor George W. Bush; and summit meetings by the Governor's Business Council. Weaver stated, "By itself this research base focuses too narrowly on word identification, without regard for how readers actually process coherent text."

The next planned battle was over the Texas Essential Knowledge and Skills (TEKS) curriculum. The locus shifted to the Student Committee, which was controlled by members of the radical right. During the debate over the long-range plan, they had been successful at pushing through proposals for separate textbooks for spelling and grammar. Jack Christie and other board members who were aware of the radical-right plans to control curriculum voted to bring TEKS out of the Student Committee and to hear the testimony before the Committee of the Whole.

Spelling and Grammar Textbooks

Years of research and testimony by teachers had guided the decision to move to an integrated textbook for language arts, one that included both spelling and grammar. This decision was reversed in three months.

In October 1989 Dr. Bergin, Executive Deputy Commissioner for Curriculum, explained the decision for adopting an integrated textbook:

> [T]here will be no special spelling textbooks. This reflects five years of curriculum review and the best judgment of professionals in reading and language arts that the best way to teach spelling is to integrate it into the teaching of language arts and that descriptions of textbooks in future proclamations will include spelling rules and exercises. (SBOE minutes, October 1989)

In June 1995, however, Offutt recommended that the board look at adopting separate spelling and grammar books and that this be taken up by the Student Committee. The Student Committee voted unanimously for an action vote in November on a proposal to spend $26 million on spelling books even though Commissioner of Education Mike Moses had asked that the decision be postponed until after the TEKS issue was resolved. There was no testimony in favor of spelling textbooks. In fact, letters were delivered from fifteen literacy organizations in the state in opposition.

Those of us who attended the November 1995 meetings were shocked that the amendment was pushed through so fast. The agenda for the Student Committee in November showed no action to be taken. However, the Student Committee, in a joint meeting with the Finance Committee, presented proposed amendments to Proclamation 1995 to include spelling books. The radical right chair of the Student Committee chaired the joint meeting. Professional organizations again provided testimony, all in opposition. Four options, all including spelling books, were presented by a representative of the Texas Education Agency. Ballard then proposed that the joint committee vote on the options.

There was much discussion about whether this was proper procedure. The chair of the Finance Committee questioned whether this was the right time to take such a vote, since the TEKS were in the process of being written. The Commissioner of Education supported his concern, but felt that separate spelling books were needed. A recommendation was made that the decision be postponed until January but this proposal was voted down 7 to 1. The joint committee then voted unanimously on the option, which included an allocation of $26 million for spelling books, the money to be taken from funds for art programs.

I attempted to get on the agenda of the Committee of the Whole on the day the final vote was to be taken, but was unsuccessful. I contacted the presidents of the Texas Council of Teachers of English, the Texas Association for the Improvement of Reading, and the Texas State Reading Association. That evening I received letters from the first two organizations, composed a letter for the third, and delivered them to all board members the next day. One board member held up the three letters at the committee meeting and said, "I don't think you are listening to teachers in this state. They don't want your spelling books. Within twenty-four hours of what happened yesterday, I had letters from the three organizations in the state representing all language arts teachers. These people aren't very happy, folks. There are representatives in the audience who would love to talk to you, but the chair won't let them on the agenda." He and another board member expressed opposition to the inclusion of spelling books in Proclamation 1995 and attempted to withhold the vote until January. Members of the Student Committee tried hard to rush the vote, but opposition continued. Another board member held up the letters and stated, "I think these organizations see this as an attempt to isolate the skills and destroy the integration of the language arts. If that is the case, then I'm opposed." Another board member asked for clarification, stating that she hadn't heard any of her teachers saying that they didn't have spelling books. A Texas Education Agency (TEA) representative explained that the last adoption decision was to use an integrated language arts text, which included spelling, and that those books were still in the schools. Commissioner Moses said that if teachers wanted to use spelling books, they had to use outdated ones.

A motion to withhold the decision until January was defeated with a 5-to-9 vote. Then a motion that spelling books be withdrawn from the Proclamation and the money be given back to art was also voted down, 3 to 11. The final vote was 10 to 4 in favor of the addition of spelling books to the Proclamation.

In my notes to the Texas State Reading Association board after this meeting I wrote, "Isn't this more than a spelling issue? Isn't it an issue of control of literacy education? Isn't it an attempt to move back to isolated skills instruction? What kind of spelling books do state board members have in mind? Will their control end with spelling? . . . The decisions being made now will have far-reaching effects on literacy instruction in this state and in the nation."

The Finance Committee also met in November to decide whether or not to re-adopt books for which no allowance had been made in Proclamation 1995 (that included grammar books). I again provided testimony for the Texas State Reading Association, the Texas Council of Teachers of English, and the Texas Association for the Improvement of Reading. In fact, the chair of the Finance Committee said he had letters from fifteen literacy organizations in opposition to having separate grammar books. In the end, however, the vote in favor of separate books was unanimous.

Texas Essential Knowledge and Skills (TEKS)

The most heated battle was over the Texas Essential Knowledge and Skills (TEKS), formerly the Texas curriculum framework document called the Essential Elements. The TEKS writing team completed its first draft in March 1996. It was then examined by the Review Committee, public school educators, and members of literacy organizations. Regional service centers throughout the state held public hearings during July and August of 1996.

Members of the Quality English language arts and reading Standards of Texas (QUEST) Writing Team had been selected from over 300 nominations received from school districts, state Board of Education members, and professional organizations. This list was then narrowed based on the nominee's years of experience, professional activity and role, and written statements. Geographic, ethnic, racial, and gender considerations were also criteria for the composition of the team. Names of the top nominees were submitted to the boards of ten professional literacy organizations. Sharon O'Neal, Director of Language Arts and Reading at the Texas Education Agency; Cathy Davis, Assistant Director of Reading at the TEA; Lanny van Allen, Assistant Director of Language Arts at the TEA; and Nancy Roser, professor of education at the University of Texas, directed the process. When Governor George Bush took office, he added additional team members. Ultimately the Writing Team was composed of 43 members, including teachers, administrators/supervisors, educational consultants, teacher educators, and community members (parents, business people).

A Review Committee, selected from recommendations made by state Board of Education members and appointed by the commissioner, was to review each draft and make suggestions, which were to be considered by the Writing Team in developing the next draft. I sat on the Review Committee; we met three times. A national panel of experts also served as

Writing Team consultants, including Marilyn J. Adams, Edmund J. Farrell, Philip B. Gough, James V. Hoffman, Barbara Kapinus, Angela Medearis, Bertha Perez, Linda Rief, Ramsay Selden, and Dorothy S. Strickland. In addition, thousands of copies of the first and second drafts were distributed to school districts and professional organizations with requests for feedback. Approximately 2,000 responses to the first draft and 1,400 responses to the second draft were returned: approximately 88 percent and 89 percent, respectively, were from teachers.

The satisfaction rate of those around the state who reviewed the draft was high. Of over 40,641 separate ratings from the total set of returned forms for the first draft, approximately half (48 percent) said they were "extremely satisfied" with the draft. The overall satisfaction rating for the top two categories, "extremely satisfied" and "moderately satisfied," was 66 percent, while the overall dissatisfaction rate (combining the bottom two ratings) was 14 percent. The second draft showed even better ratings: an overall satisfaction rate of 71 percent; an overall dissatisfaction rate of 9 percent.

In spite of this, an alternative document written by a small group of committee members appeared at the October state Board of Education meeting. It was released to the press on October 10. The introduction stated:

> All of us involved in the writing of this Alternative Document believe in the importance of direct, systematic instruction of explicit skills. We believe that the Texas Legislature in Senate Bill 1 means for the Texas Essential Knowledge and Skills to be an explicit list of the skills which teachers should teach and which students should master before they move to the next grade level. We also believe that teachers should be held accountable to teach all the elements in the Teacher Elements section and that students should then be held accountable on the TAAS [Texas Assessment of Academic Skills] and in the classroom for the elements which are listed in the Student Elements section . . . Whereas the TEKS have followed a format which breaks ELAR [English Language Arts and Reading] into Reading, Writing, Listening/Speaking, and Viewing, our group has decided to break the strands into Reading/Literature, Grammar, Composition, Vocabulary, Spelling, and Listening/Speaking. We acknowledge that the English language is interconnected, but we believe that the strands must be kept separate so that valuable academic content is not lost. (Texas Essential Knowledge and Skills Alternative Draft, October 7, 1996, p. 1)

Sharon O'Neal, Director of the QUEST project, urged the writing team to inspect the alternate document. She said:

You have taught us that individuals with widely differing views can hear one another out, defend points vigorously, and work to reach consensus. As one reviewer wrote in response to the last draft, "This document is a testament to democracy in action." No one's ideas have ever intentionally been taken lightly within our meetings, or turned aside quickly. Each of us has dealt seriously with both the major ideas and with the minutia.

In February 1997 the six radical-right board members, backed by the Eagle Forum, accused Commissioner Moses and the Texas Education Agency of being involved in an international conspiracy with the National Center for Education and the Economy headed by Mark Tucker to bring outcome-based education into Texas.

In March a special meeting was called for airing of complaints. One radical-right board member led the discussion by presenting "evidence" of the conspiracy. A busload of people lined the boardroom, carrying signs displaying quotes from the Bible in an attempt to stop the TEKS process. In April the Eagle Forum brought in three more busloads of protesters to stop the TEKS process. Some board members and the Eagle Forum in a press release that same day charged that the TEKS were a "dumbed-down curriculum" tied to the School to Work reforms, which they saw as an attempt to socialize education and prepare children to enter the workforce.

In a letter dated March 24 to Review Committee members, Commissioner Moses thanked us for our service. He wrote, "It is imperative that the TEKS be rigorous, specific, and measurable." In a letter of April 3, he stated that he had consulted with several experts in the field of reading and language arts, including Barbara Foorman, Isabel Beck, JoAnna Williams, Edward Kameenui, and Sarah Freedman, and that changes that had been made were based on the comments of these educators and reviewers in the governor's office.

Commissioner Moses introduced the revised TEKS, which was different from the Writing Team's third draft, to the state Board of Education Committee of the Whole at a public hearing in April, three days after it was made public. Prior to testimony, all six radical-right board members spoke up in opposition to the TEKS document because of what they saw as its lack of specificity. Thirty-two people provided testimony before the Committee of the Whole; twenty-nine supported the Writing Team's effort and the third draft of the TEKS. The Texas State Reading Association, the Texas Association for the Improvement of Reading, the Texas Council of the Teachers of English, and the Coalition of Reading Education Supervisors of Texas all provided testimony in favor of the document, in spite of its changes. However, only eight of the fifteen board members remained to hear the testimony.

Even though testimony overwhelmingly supported adoption of the draft, some reservations were expressed. Several testimonies expressed concern with the commissioner's appointment of the final review committee. It had not been made clear in the document who these people were, how they were selected, what their qualifications were, or whether or not the Writing Team would have a chance to make a final review and revisions. It was clear that the public would not have a chance to see the revisions again prior to adoption. Testimonies expressed concerns that significant changes had been made and that the public would not have a chance to see the draft again prior to adoption. Concerns addressed the specificity added to the wording in the reading K–3 section related to phonemic awareness and phonics and to the addition of the words "decodable texts."

As the Governmental Relations Chair for the Texas State Reading Association, I presented the testimony in favor of the TEKS each month that testimony was allowed. A major concern was the addition of the phrase "decodable texts" (texts in which all words and/or spelling patterns have been introduced). Even after testimony at the April public hearing and a May Board of Education meeting questioning the added wording referring to "decodable texts," (TEKS, June 1997 draft, pp. 10, 7G) that wording had not been eliminated in the June draft.

In May and June I gave board members copies of the International Reading Association's Proposed Resolution on Beginning Reading Materials and encouraged them to let that resolution influence the wording of the final draft. However, they chose not to change the wording; the July draft, which was adopted by the state Board of Education, still mentioned "decodable texts."

In June, the Texas State Reading Association also expressed opposition to the alternative document that was being promoted by seven of the fifteen board members. The Association stated that the document was too limiting, did not focus on real reading, writing, and comprehension, and would limit children to a one-size-fits-all curriculum.

On July 11, the state Board of Education voted 9 to 6 to adopt the Texas Essential Knowledge and Skills (TEKS) curriculum for English Language Arts and Reading. This vote brought an end to the three-year process. The six radical-right board members attempted to stall the vote. Arguments continued until Jack Christie called for an end to the debate, saying that the six opposing board members were being "dilatory" and were using "delaying tactics." Christie stated later in a press interview that over 400 individuals had testified in public hearings and more than 18,000 faxes, letters, and other written comments had been offered on TEKS, and "to wait until the last hour to challenge three years of work is political." After the vote, board members who supported an alternative document threatened to get a court injunction to block the implementation.

The Governor's Business Council and the Texas Business and Education Coalition

Those of us involved in fighting the political battles became more and more overwhelmed as the control shifted to the business community and to the governor. The state Board of Education seemed like an easy victory compared to these communities.

The shift of locale began in April 1996, when the Governor's Business Council sponsored a Pre-Summit Workshop in Houston entitled "Picking a Research-Based Reading Program." The Governor's Business Council is a voluntary, unofficial, informal organization started under Ann Richards, the former governor, and is made up of around eighty CEOs from around the state. Charles Miller, the chairman, opened the meeting by telling the invited guests that they had been carefully selected to represent a broad spectrum of the leadership of Texas and that the records of the meeting would be recorded and disseminated at the summit in Austin in April. "We need the best advice on how to improve the reading skills of Texas school children we can find," he said (Governor's Business Council 1996, p. 2).

Miller expressed concern about both the number of students who were not passing the Texas Assessment of Academic Skills (TAAS) reading test and the overall literacy rate, which he said had gradually eroded from 97 percent in 1950 to less than 80 percent in 1996. "We should try to build a record today that can be used to start discussions across the state."

Invited guests who attended the meeting were the founder of the John Cooper School in Houston; the president of the O'Donnell Foundation in Dallas; a member of the O'Donnell Foundation who also serves as chair of the Telecommunication Infrastructure Network; a member of the board of regents of Texas Southern University who is also a trustee for the Houston Endowment; the chairman of the Board of Regents for Texas State Technical College and president of Texans for Education; editors of the *Dallas Morning News* and *Texas Monthly;* the chair of the state Board of Educator Certification; a member of the Higher Education Coordinating Board; the retired chairman of Tenneco; Houston mayor's assistant on educational issues; several representatives of the Governor's Business Council; a representative from IBM; a member of the special projects counsel for Governor Bush; a senior advisor to Governor Bush; three principals from Houston, Dallas, and LaJoya school districts; the Director of the Neuhaus Education Center in Houston; a consultant in reading and curriculum alignment in the state of Texas; the president of the Dallas School Board and consultant for the Governor's Business Council; one teacher; a Tyler businessperson; and Mike Moses, Commissioner of Education.

After Miller came the "reading experts"—Doug Carnine, a Distar author and professor and director of the National Center for Improving the

Tools of Educators; Jean Osborne, another Distar author who was introduced as being from the Center for Study of Reading at the University of Illinois; and Barbara Foorman, professor of educational psychology at the University of Houston—who spoke for thirty minutes each. All the speakers supported the teaching of phonemic awareness and phonics through direct, systematic, intensive approaches. The three "reading experts" criticized whole language, the lack of intensive phonemic awareness and phonics (decoding) instruction, and "inadequate" teacher-training programs. They attempted to prove that early skills development is essential, and that it can only happen through intensive, systematic phonemic awareness and phonics instruction.

At the end of the day, Miller stated in his concluding remarks:

> I'd like the group to know that we didn't, let's say, cherry-pick the experts to lean one way or the other. We did look for research or substantial backing for people's opinions or concepts, in other words, that there was scientific, quantitative, or research backing of their opinions . . . The encouraging part is we know what needs to be done. There's good research and good success stories. You heard the success stories today, and I'm sure there are others available. So schools can start improving now. That's the good news. But it's easier said than done. The discouraging part is that our school system seems to resist proven practices and ignore the lack of achievement. Most energies are not directed toward improvement. So that's a big problem. Challenges that we can hear out of this meeting today is that it's important to build awareness and acceptance. The governor's initiative seems to be going well, but it's very important that we keep momentum. One of the challenges is overcoming institutional inertia. Any of us that have worked in the area of changing education, education reform, whatever you want to call it, know that entrenched interests make that difficult. So we need to move to a research-based, accountability-driven system. That's the way to do it. (Governor's Business Council 1996, pp. 68–69)

At the Houston Reading Summit held on June 28, 1996, at the Wheeler Baptist Church, a representative of the Governor's Business Council opened the meeting by stating that the Governor's Business Council and the Texas Business and Education Coalition were concerned about reading scores in the state and that they would not listen to debate on how reading should be taught because debate was not productive.

Barbara Foorman, who had spoken at the pre-summit meeting, and Jack Fletcher, a professor of Pediatrics from the University of Houston Medical School who worked with Foorman on her study, again presented research in support of direct, intensive, systematic decoding instruction. About one hundred invited guests attended the summit. Governor Bush also spoke, emphasizing that schools would not be told how to teach reading, but they would be held accountable and, if children were not reading by the end of third grade, would be told to do something different. Copies of the Houston independent school district curriculum and a transcript of the Houston pre-summit meeting were distributed. The Texas Business and Education Coalition distributed a letter addressed to the state Board of Education recommending "that Texas school districts measure the reading skills of all students in kindergarten through second grade" and that measures of K–2 reading progress be included in the state accountability system.

Literacy organizations were never invited to join in this dialogue. The Governor's Business Council and the Texas Business and Education Coalition are hearing only selective research studies, those that support one methodology, those coming out of the National Institute of Health studies led by Reid Lyon.

The Governor's Reading Initiative

After the defeat of the radical right with the TEKS, many educators who banded together through that process have decided to turn our attention to the Governor's Reading Initiative. In January 1996, Governor George Bush outlined his hopes for the future of education in Texas in a press release at the TEA midwinter conference in Austin, Texas. He said,

> Now is the time to do something really revolutionary. Do something about it. Get back to the shore where the footing is solid. Back to the basics—the building blocks of knowledge that were the same yesterday and will be the same tomorrow. We do not need trendy new theories . . . experiments or feel-good curriculums. The basics work.

Since that time Bush has set up the Governor's Reading Initiative. In September Robin Gilchrist, Assistant Commissioner for the Statewide Reading Initiative and a former lobbyist for an attorney in Austin, was hired to oversee the governor's initiative. Distar author Jean Osborne from the Center for the Study of Reading was hired as a consultant. The Texas Education Agency released *Beginning Reading Instruction: Components and Features of a Research-Based Reading Program* (1996), which was widely believed to be written by Osborne. It outlines twelve essential components of research-based programs for beginning reading instruction.

Curriculum directors, regional center personnel, and teachers from around the state have been called to Austin for training. In February 1997, university, public school, and regional service-center educators were invited to Austin for a full-day conference to hear "reading experts" Reid Lyon, Barbara Foorman, and Joe Torgesen present their research studies, which were sponsored by the National Institute for Child Health and Human Development (NICHD). Jean Osborne presided. Nancy Roser, director of the Texas Center for Reading and Language Arts at the University of Texas at Austin, sat in the audience and was never introduced; neither were Sharon O'Neal and Cathy Davis who were also in attendance. Participants received a handout entitled "A Scientific Approach to Reading Instruction" (1994). The opening quote read,

> The good news is that we have had a scientific breakthrough in our knowledge about the development of literacy. We know a great deal about how to address reading problems—even before they begin . . . The tragedy is that we are not exploiting what we know about reducing the incidence of reading failure. Specifically, the instruction currently being provided to our children does not reflect what we know from research . . . Direct, systematic instruction about the alphabetic code is not routinely provided in kindergarten and first grade, in spite of the fact that at the moment this might be our most powerful weapon in the fight against illiteracy. (Foorman, Fletcher, and Francis 1997, p. 1)

The Texas Center for Reading and Language Arts at the University of Texas at Austin is to direct future professional development for teachers in the state. The training to date has been under the direction of Robin Gilchrist and Jean Osborne and has involved only isolated, intensive, systematic phonemic awareness and phonics instruction. A new Director for the Reading Initiative has recently been named: Sharon Vaughn, a new member of the faculty in the Special Education Department at the University of Texas at Austin.

The Battle Continues

My colleagues and I feel that we won a major battle in Texas over the curriculum. Even though the radical-right board members threatened to file a lawsuit and/or injunction to stop the implementation of the TEKS curriculum, that has not yet happened. Changes are still being made to the document, however, by the five-member committee that was appointed by the commissioner after the final review. The radical right also seems to be very much in control through other avenues, such as the Governor's Reading Initiative, the Governor's Business Council, and the newly formed State Board for Educator Certification, whose members were appointed by the governor.

The realization of the scope of this battle began to hit hard in March 1997, when Leslie Patterson of the University of Houston, Jackie Gerla of the University of Texas-Tyler, and I met after a Governmental Relations session at the Texas State Reading Association state conference in Fort Worth. Feeling overwhelmed by the power shift from the state board to the governor and by the narrow research base that was driving attempted changes in instruction in the state, we wondered how we could continue to fight. Someone asked, "Do you know how you eat an elephant? One bite at a time." We laughed and began to brainstorm what part of the elephant to eat first. We decided that day to host our own conference to get media attention, present a broader research base for early reading instruction, and open up the dialogue. We met once more to plan the day. Within two weeks of advertising the April conference, entitled "Critical Balances: Early Instruction for Life-Long Reading," registration was filled to capacity, then extended to accommodate an overflow audience, and finally cut off at 600 people. Connie Weaver, Richard Allington, Taffy Raphael, P. David Pearson, and Phil Gough presented keynote addresses. Attendance and feedback have shown that the conference was a tremendous success. Yet efforts to get media attention failed. Not one newspaper or television station covered the conference. However, the National Council of Teachers of English and the International Reading Association have reserved rights to the transcript and are in the process of publishing it. In addition, my colleagues and I are in the process of planning a future conference to continue the dialogue.

I still serve as the Governmental Relations Chair of the Texas State Reading Association, and I still monitor the state Board of Education meetings. I still send reports of those meetings to the Texas State Reading Association board, to its Governmental Relations Committee members and council presidents, to its general membership through The Texas Reading Report, and to presidents of other literacy organizations in the state. I continue to write and present testimony for the Texas State Reading Association and the Texas Association for the Improvement of Reading as the incoming president at state Board of Education meetings. I have also asked the Texas State Reading Association to fund a legislative workshop in Austin next year to bring in governmental relations representatives and/or presidents from the International Reading Association councils in Texas for training, to attend the state Board of Education meetings, and to visit key players in Austin who are working with the Texas Reading Initiative and the Texas Board for Educator Certification.

We will be monitoring closely the Texas Board for Educator Certification as they revise the standards for future teachers. No university professors sit on that board as voting members; yet the board has appointed a reading committee to develop the knowledge and skills that future teachers of reading need. Reading organizations were not consulted. This board and its reading committee will be making some major decisions about education in the near future, decisions that will influence the state certification test for teachers.

Those of us who have been fighting so hard for control of the curriculum through the TEKS realize the battle is not over in Texas. The critical test will be how those TEKS are interpreted through staff-development efforts directed by the Texas Center for Reading and Language Arts and through state assessments. The struggle over assessments—both the Texas Assessment of Academic Skills (TAAS) for children and the state certification test for teachers—will be important, since assessment tends to drive instruction. Universities and schools (even individual teachers) are already being highly scrutinized. The Educator Certification Board is recommending that teachers be recertified every five years. The pressure is increasing tremendously, and accountability threatens to drive instruction even more than in the past, since both accreditation of universities and schools and teacher appraisals are being tied to exam scores. The overemphasis on TAAS scores is killing innovation in our public schools as administrators are grabbing for quick fixes—programs that will raise the scores. So, even though my colleagues and I feel that we won a real victory in the curriculum fight, we know the real battle is yet ahead of us. We'll eat the elephant one bite at a time.

References

Attachment I: Long-Range Plan for Public Education, 1996–2000 and Attachment II: Proposed Amendments Submitted by Board Members. *Agenda State Board of Education V3–V15*. Austin, TX: Texas Education Agency (October 13, 1995).

Ballard, D. 1996. Curriculum Changes Will Improve Texas Schools. *Houston Chronicle* (February 28).

Bush, G. W. 1996. Press release TEA mid-winter conference. Austin, TX (January 31).

Foorman, B., J. Fletcher, and D. Francis. 1997. A Scientific Approach to Reading Instruction. Center for Academic and Reading Skills (CARS). Paper presented at the Texas Reading Initiative meeting (February 18).

Friere, P., and D. Macedo. 1987. *Literacy: Reading the Word and the World*. South Hadley, MA: Bergin and Garvey.

Goodman, K. S. 1992. Gurus, Professors, and the Politics of Phonics. *Reading Today* 10, 3: 8–10.

Governor's Business Council. 1996. Pre-summit workshop, partial transcript—draft. *Picking a Research-Based Reading Program* (April).

Honig, B. 1995. The Role of Skills in a Comprehensive Reading Program: The Necessity for a Balanced Approach. Paper presented at the Long-Range Planning Committee Meeting at the state Board of Education in Austin, TX (December 27).

Offutt, R. H. 1995. May 12 revisions of side-by-side comparison of goals 1 and 3 of the May 12 draft of the long-range plan and Dr. Offutt's substitute for these goals. Austin, TX: Texas Education Agency (May 12).

O'Neal, S. 1997. Letter addressed to TEKS writing and review team members (October 15).

Osburn, J. 1996. *Beginning Reading Instruction: Components and Features of a Research-Based Reading Program.* Austin, TX: Texas Education Agency.

Pesetsky, D., and J. McIvoid. 1995. A letter from forty Massachusetts specialists in linguistics and psycholinguistics addressed to Dr. Robert V. Antonucci, Commissioner of Education, Commonwealth of Massachusetts (July 12).

Senate Bill I. State of Texas: 87.

Shannon, P. 1989. *Broken Promises: Reading Instruction in Twentieth-Century America.* South Hadley, MA: Bergin and Garvey.

———. 1990. *The Struggle to Continue: Progressive Reading Instruction in the United States.* Portsmouth, NH: Heinemann.

———, ed. 1992. *Becoming Political: Readings and Writings in the Politics of Literacy Education.* Portsmouth, NH: Heinemann.

State Board of Education. 1989. Minutes of meeting, 15 (October 14).

———. 1995. Long-Range Plan for Public Education 1996–2000. Austin, TX: *Texas Education Agency* (November 10).

Texas Alternative Document Draft (TADD) English, Language Arts, and Reading. 1997. Waco, TX: Kinko's (June 12).

Texas Essential Knowledge and Skills Alternative Document Draft. 1996. A paper presented to the Texas State Board of Education, 1–2 (October 7).

Texas Essential Knowledge and Skills for English Language Arts and Reading. 1997. Austin, TX: Texas Education Agency (June 12).

———. 1997. Austin, TX: Texas Education Agency (September).

Weaver, C. 1996. Toward a Balanced Reading Program. Paper presented to the Long-Range Planning Committee of the state Board of Education Austin, TX (May 12).

There has been a sharp increase in attempts, many of them successful, to use the legislatures to settle paradigm disputes in how to teach reading and the other language arts. What could not be won in the free marketplace of ideas is being seized through acts of legislation. In this chapter, Frances Paterson uses her legal background to research the introduction of these laws and identify who the players are. Efforts are highly coordinated; often one sees identical wording in bills in states far apart geographically. Far-right groups are playing key roles in getting support for state phonics laws.

6

Mandating Methodology: Promoting the Use of Phonics Through State Statute

FRANCES R. A. PATERSON

In March 1996, *Education Week* reported that "policymakers across the country are making laws and writing rules that mandate the use of explicit phonics instruction" (Diegmueller 1996, p. 14). The article briefly described the passage of "the ABC law" in California, attempts to pass legislation in Ohio and North Carolina, and the Nebraska state Board of Education's adoption of a "balanced approach" policy. Barbara Fox, Professor of Curriculum at North Carolina State University, was quoted as saying, "It is not so much the substance of the bill that is discomfiting, but rather the move toward mandating methodology. In the broadest sense there is a real possibility that such legislative actions will strip curricular and instructional decision making from educators" (p. 14).

The use of state statutes to require phonics as a method of teaching reading is a departure from typical legislative concerns related to educational curriculum. This chapter explores the extent to which the Christian Right is a force in the pro-phonics movement and how the movement's advocacy of phonics is being translated into legislative action.

Most Christian Right leaders see themselves as combatants in a cultural war that includes public education. Repeatedly, key players in the evangelical and fundamentalist movements criticize the content of American public education. "The public schools are the battleground on which the holy war is being fought. Textbooks and the curriculum are the tools of social change that must be opposed at all costs" (Provenzo 1990, p. 49). The legislative effort to require and/or encourage the use of phonics represents a shift in orientation for the Christian Right, a move toward attempting to influence how students are taught as well as what they are taught.

Accelerating Phonics Legislation, 1990–96

Since 1990 there has been a sharp increase in state-level phonics-related legislation. Breaking down phonics-related state legislation by the year that these bills were introduced reveals a sharp increase in these legislative initiatives from 1994 to 1996. In 1990, only one phonics bill (in Maine) was introduced. In 1991, three phonics bills were introduced: two in Iowa and one in South Carolina. In 1992, three bills were introduced: two in Hawaii and one in Louisiana. In 1993, four bills were introduced: one in Iowa, two in Mississippi, and one in South Carolina. In 1994, five bills were introduced in three state legislatures: two in Alabama, one in Mississippi, and two in Missouri. In 1995, nineteen bills were introduced in twelve state legislatures with multiple bills in six of the twelve states. By the middle of 1996, eighteen bills had been introduced into eleven state legislatures;[1] 36 percent of these states had multiple bills.

The Language of Phonics Bills

There has also been a significant change in the language of such bills.[2] Recent bills are more likely to employ highly descriptive and detailed language as well as rhetoric similar to or directly from religio-political conservative literature. A smaller number of these later bills includes language either directly or indirectly critical of whole language approaches to reading instruction. Prior to 1992, the language in phonics bills was relatively mild and nonspecific—for example, the term "phonics" was used without modifiers or descriptive phrases. The first use of the term "phonics" with one or more descriptors occurred in a Louisiana bill introduced in 1992.[3] In 1993, when four bills were introduced, three of these bills used the term "phonics" without any descriptors. In 1994, "phonics" with one or more descriptors was used in three of the five bills introduced. Seventy-seven percent of the 1995 bills used "phonics" with one or more descriptors. In 1996, 89 percent used "phonics" with one or more descriptors.

Twenty-eight bills introduced since 1990 include a provision related to the use of phonics as an instructional methodology. Overwhelmingly, the bills are directive ("shall be used") rather than permissive ("may be used"). The second most frequently included provision (in twenty bills) is for staff development or in-service training. A smaller number of bills (thirteen) address the issue of pre-service training and/or certification. Typically, provisions related to teacher education or certification specify that this component applies only to those seeking elementary or reading certification. One bill set out administrative or legal remedies for failure to comply with provisions relating to phonics as a method or instruction or for a college or university's failure to offer pre-service phonics instruction. In addition, eight bills include requirements for parental notification, typically specifying that schools must communicate the method of reading instruction and test results. Eight also require testing. Of these, six require retention, typically of students scoring below the twenty-fifth percentile on a standardized test.

In 1995 Mississippi, North Carolina, and Oklahoma bills made reference to whole language; in 1996 Mississippi, New York, and Tennessee bills included such references. Typically, they are critical of whole language. A number of miscellaneous provisions exist in the bills, including mandates for the use of phonics with incarcerated juveniles (Oklahoma, H.B. 2755, 1996) or in adult education (all three New York bills); a provision for "opting-out" (two bills); requests for studies or demonstration projects (four bills); and a provision for housing the reading curriculum in the school library (one bill).

Religio-Political Conservative Pro-Phonics Activities

In analyzing what fundamentalists do as opposed to what they say we should consider how fundamentalist Christian schools teach reading. Fundamentalist school curricula reflect "the Religious Right's definition of good education" (Holderer 1995, p. 82). In addition to pressing for vouchers and tuition tax credits, religio-political conservatives also seek to shape public schools to conform more closely to their pedagogical philosophies. We may also examine how Christian Right leaders and activists translate their instructional methodologies for reading into action.

Reading Instruction in Christian Schools

Although Christian school advocates are likely to cite the high scores students receive on standardized tests, little research has been done regarding the instructional methodologies employed. Some research focuses on the phenomenon of Christian schooling generally (Rose 1988; Parsons 1987). When studies address curricular matters, the discussion tends to concentrate on the content of secondary instruction (Peshkin 1986; Menendez 1992). Researchers appear to assume that phonics is the preferred method of reading instruction. For example, when Parsons refers to reading lessons he uses the term "phonics lessons" or to students beginning the day with "math or phonics or social studies" (Parsons 1987, pp. 7, 54).

Thogmartin (1994) provides more explicit confirmation of the prevalence of phonics in Christian school reading education, noting that "some form of phonics instruction is the method chosen by the vast majority of Christian educators in their schools" (p. 7). Thogmartin also reports that the majority of fundamentalists who home-school their children use phonics-based instruction. This perception was confirmed during the June 1995 Oklahoma Home School Convention and in interviews with both home-schooling and fundamentalist Christian school parents (Paterson 1995, 1996a, 1996b). At the convention there were no vendors offering non-phonics-based reading materials. Of the 55 workshops offered at the 1995 Oklahoma home schooling conference, only one, "Phonics Forum," concerned reading methodology. Though there is little apparent interest in whole language methods or even "balanced approaches" in Christian schools, religio-political conservatives appear to be increasingly active in efforts to encourage or require the use of phonics in public schools.

State Affiliates of Religio-Political Conservative Groups

Although both the national Christian Coalition and the Oklahoma state chapter deny any active involvement in pro-phonics activities, the Wisconsin state chapter and at least one county chapter of the Christian Coalition in Wisconsin appear to be engaged in pro-phonics political activities (K. Sweet, personal communication, August 7, 1996). A 1995 Wisconsin Christian Coalition voters' guide included the responses of candidates for Board of Education to two questions about reading instructional methodology: "(1) Should the phonics method (systematic decoding of sound-symbols/letters) be the primary method used to teach reading? and (2) Should the 'sight' or 'look say' method (memorizing whole words) be the primary method to teach reading?" (Christian Coalition 1995, p. 1).

In February 1995, Leah Vukmir of Parents Raising Educational Standards in Schools (PRESS), a strongly conservative pro-phonics and "back-to-basics" group, addressed the Walworth County (Wisconsin) Christian Coalition (Walworth County Christian Coalition 1995a). In September 1995, the organization's newsletter advertised the second annual PRESS convention, whose keynote speaker was to be Robert Sweet of the National Right to Read Foundation (Walworth County Christian Coalition 1995c). In December 1995, the organization urged its members to contact their state senators in support of Wisconsin Assembly Bill 237, which would "require all licensed teachers who teach reading to be able to teach intensive phonics" (Walworth County Christian Coalition 1995c, n.p.). The organization distributed a flyer claiming that a government study called What Works stated that reading "must be taught by direct, systematic, intensive phonics" that "must be completed by the end of the first grade" (Walworth County Christian Coalition 1995c, n.p.).

Although involvement of Beverly LaHaye's Concerned Women for America in the pro-phonics movement appears to be minimal, a November 1995 recruitment meeting of the Appleton, Wisconsin, chapter was organized around the theme of "'phonics only' reading instruction" (Planned

Parenthood 1995, n.p.). The group showed a videotape, *Reading, Writing and Ripped Off* (distributed by Robert Sweet's National Right to Read Foundation), which alleges that progressive education and non-phonics-based reading instruction are responsible for virtually all the problems in contemporary American education (Planned Parenthood 1995; S. Robertson 1993). At the meeting a "Petition to Local and State Elected Officials to Restore Literacy Through Intensive, Systematic Phonics" was distributed to participants, who were instructed to send completed copies to Concerned Women of Wisconsin (Concerned Women of Wisconsin 1994). The petition stated that it was a "fundamental and inconvertible fact that written English is based on the alphabetic principle and that the public schools have abandoned systematic phonics for the 'whole word' method" (Concerned Women of Wisconsin 1994, n.p.).

National Phonics-Based Literacy Campaigns

The Eagle Forum has long advocated phonics as the only acceptable method for teaching reading. In 1981, Phyllis Schlafly announced her Headstart Project, citing her testimony before a Subcommittee of the House of Representatives Education and Labor Committee. The Headstart Project was designed to teach children to read by using "the correct method (phonics first) before the school confuses the child with any wrong methods" (Eagle Forum 1981, p. 1). In the 1980s, conservative Christian minister Pat Robertson founded Operation Heads Up, which employed Robertson's Sing, Spell, Read, and Write curriculum (Hertzke 1993, pp. 87–88, 102, 251; P. Robertson 1990, p. 171).[4]

Absent from both Robertson's and Schlafly's 1980s literacy campaigns is the overt political component of the Eagle Forum's 1996 campaign, the Literacy Project, which includes "massive distributions of [the] First Reading Test by mail, radio spots, and the Internet" (Eagle Forum 1996a, n.p.). In addition, the organization planned to provide "packets about the Literacy Workshops to churches and civic groups," increase staff, and establish a Hot Line (Eagle Forum 1996a, n.p.). Like her earlier project, Schlafly urges her supporters to teach their children to read by purchasing her First Reader and attending or sponsoring Literacy Workshops; but, unlike her earlier campaign, the Literacy Project "urg[es] state legislatures to mandate phonics instruction in the public schools" (Eagle Forum 1996a, n.p.). However, Eagle Forum's involvement in urging state legislatures to require the teaching of phonics predates the launching of Schlafly's national campaign. The Ohio Eagle Forum was active in the passage of a 1989 statute requiring the use of phonics in primary classrooms. Local Eagle Forum groups in Tennessee and Alabama have also been active in encouraging state legislators to introduce phonics bills.

Disproportionate Republican Involvement in
Pro-Phonics Legislation

The first formal Republican involvement in the pro-phonics movement occurred in 1989 with the publication of the report of the U.S. Senate Republican Policy Committee, *Illiteracy: An Incurable Disease or Education Malpractice?* (Armstrong 1989). Like both religio-political conservative and secular pro-phonics literature, the report equates whole language and whole word approaches. Much of the material appears to be a greatly compacted summary of the arguments that have appeared over the years in Samuel Blumenfeld's books and newsletter. The term "guessing" is used several times, and "dumbed down" appears once (see also Blumenfeld 1987; Schlafly 1994; Eagle Forum 1996b, p. 5). The report uses the term "intensive, systematic phonics" (sometimes accompanied by the terms "direct" and/or "early"), which appears frequently in pro-phonics legislation (Armstrong 1989, pp. 4, 5, 8, 10, 11, 13). This white paper lays the blame for American illiteracy squarely on college and university scholars in the field of reading instruction, a charge also leveled by many religio-political conservatives. Among other "obstacles to reading reform," the report cites "lack of legal redress for malpractice in reading instruction" (some contemporary phonics bills provide remedies for failure to teach phonics) and the "establishment of public schools and teacher education as a monopoly" (related to Republican support for tuition tax credits and vouchers for private school education) (p. 9). The report ends with a call to "propose legislation requiring teachers to be taught intensive systematic phonics as part of their training to teach in the public schools" and cites with approval an Ohio statute enacted in 1989 that requires the use of phonics in grades K–3 and provides for in-service training in phonics (Ohio Rev. Code Ann. §3301.07(M) 1989, p. 13). With the exception of South Carolina's Senator Michael Rose, few Republican legislators immediately heeded the call to propose legislation. Nevertheless, examining the party affiliations of phonics legislation sponsors shows that Republicans are disproportionately represented when compared with their overall membership in state legislatures.

Thirty-five phonics bills with known party affiliation of sponsors were introduced between 1990 and 1996. Of these, twenty-two, or 63 percent, were introduced by Republican legislators.[5] According to the Conference of State Legislatures, as of July 12, 1996, 48 percent of all state legislators were Republicans (B. Erikson, personal communication, July 23, 1996). Looking solely at legislation introduced in 1996, 89 percent were introduced by Republicans.

Of twenty-five state Republican platforms examined, six (California, Iowa, Kansas, Oklahoma, South Carolina, and Texas) mention phonics. The Christian Right is dominant in the Republican party in 83 percent of the states with platform inclusion of phonics, as opposed to 38 percent of all states. Republican party platform statements range from Kansas's "schools should return to a curriculum that stresses basic skills, such as phonics" to Oklahoma's "the primary goal of our public education system should be to teach the basic subjects of reading (emphasizing the intensive systematic phonics method)" (Kansas State Republican Party 1996, p. 62; Republican State Committee of Oklahoma 1996, p. 16). Of the six states with phonics included in the Republican party platform, five have had multiple phonics bills and/or phonics bills that employed moderately or highly detailed language.

Christian Right Dominance of State Republican Parties and Pro-Phonics Legislation

Excluding the District of Columbia, the Christian Right is dominant in 38 percent of all state Republican parties (Persinos 1994, p. 22). The Christian Right dominates the Republican party in 55 percent of states with phonics bills. Of those states with multiple phonics bills, the Christian Right is dominant in 64 percent; and the Republican party is dominated by the Christian Right in 53 percent of states with moderate or highly detailed bill language. Combining both states with multiple bills and those with moderate or highly detailed language, the percentage rises to 55 percent. Comparing these figures with the number of states where the Christian Right is dominant leads to the conclusion that legislators in states where the Christian Right dominates the Republican party are significantly more likely to introduce one or more phonics bills and/or bills with moderately or highly detailed language.

Including data for states where the Christian Right has moderate influence in the state Republican party changes the percentages to 62 percent for all states, 80 percent for states with phonics bills, 64 percent for states with multiple bills, 73 percent for states with bills containing moderately or highly detailed language, and 78 percent for states with either multiple bills or moderate or highly detailed language. Thus, states where the Republican party is dominated or substantially influenced by the Christian Right are much more likely to have one or more phonics bills with moderately or highly detailed language.[6]

Organizations and Individuals Involved in Pro-Phonics Legislation

Despite the report of the U.S. Senate Republican Policy Committee in 1989, the upsurge in pro-phonics legislation did not begin until 1994 and is most apparent in 1995 and 1996. However, though states influenced by the Christian Right are more likely to have seen an increase in pro-phonics bills introduced in their state legislatures, this increase cannot be attributed solely or even primarily to religio-political conservative groups, no matter how intense their interest in this issue. Rather, the increase in legislative initiatives appears to be more closely related to various secular groups, particularly Robert Sweet's National Right to Read Foundation, founded in January 1993, and Cal Thomas's nationally syndicated columns (R. Sweet, personal communication, July 16, 1996). The establishment of Sweet's organization coincides chronologically with the doubling of phonics bills between 1993 and 1994 and the more than quadrupling of such bills between 1993 and 1994 (a 475 percent increase from 1993 to 1995).

Although the National Right to Read Foundation is a secular rather than a religio-political organization, it has connections to the Christian Right and provides support for at least one state level religio-political conservative group, the Alabama Eagle Forum (B. Hanson, personal communication, September 9, 1996).[7] In addition, the foundation is connected to groups with moderately strong ties to religio-political conservative organizations. It has been endorsed by James Dobson of Focus on the Family (National Right to Read Foundation 1994, n.p.). Many statements made by the National Right to Read Foundation echo those of religio-political conservatives, particularly Samuel Blumenfeld who, together with Mel and Norma Gabler, was named to the organization's "keepers of the flame" honor roll (Sweet 1993). Such statements include the following:

- Non-phonics teaching methods "constitute an unprecedented form of child abuse—education [sic] child abuse accomplished through the technique of deliberate education [sic] malpractice" (Sweet 1994b, p. 7).
- Phonics has been successfully used to teach reading for 3,500 years.
- Whole word methods treat English as if it were Chinese pictographs.[8]
- Non-phonics methods result in illiteracy, juvenile delinquency, and learning disabilities, particularly dyslexia, and are promulgated by "educrats" (Baughman 1993; Wood 1994).[9] A Fairfax, Virginia, school's adoption of an "Integrated Language Arts" program is termed "a Trojan horse for the Whole Language reading methodology . . . which experts say is academically unsound and creates between two and three million new illiterates a year" (Jacobson 1993, p. 3).

Like overtly religio-political conservative organizations, the National Right to Read Foundation is unequivocally opposed to outcome-based education, Goals 2000, and the National Education Association. Sweet argues that "Charles Darwin's theory of education, John Maynard Keynes' 'spend yourself rich' economic theories, Sigmund Freud's sexual revolution, Karl Marx's failed communism, [and] John Dewey's progressive education" are "aberrant philosophies" that stand in opposition to Noah Webster's

American spelling book and the Holy Bible (Sweet 1993). Direct references to Christianity are rare, although not altogether absent, from the organization's *Right to Read Report*. In January 1995, the newsletter noted that a Republican school board in Michigan had adopted "a mission statement proclaiming they are 'grateful to God for the blessings of freedom' and 'believe that to teach a child created by God is a noble calling'" (Michigan School Board Puts God 1995, p. 2). In May 1995, the newsletter reported that in Michigan "a single student, who found a portrait [of Jesus Christ] offensive," had brought suit and that Justice Stevens, by refusing certiorari, "had refused to let a Bloomingdale, Michigan, school re-hang [the] picture" which "had been on display for more than three decades" (U.S. Supreme Court Justice Says "No" to Portrait of Christ 1995, p. 5).

Robert Sweet, the president of the organization, has been a guest on several Christian Right radio programs: the Cal Thomas radio program, Paul Weyrich's *Ways and Means,* and Marlin Maddox's *Point of View.* The Hooked on Phonics program is often mentioned with approval in the *Right to Read Report,* and the Federal Trade Commission's investigation and subsequent consent decree against its producers was characterized as the result of "an unholy alliance" between the FTC, the U.S. Department of Education, and the NEA (Sweet 1995, p. 7).[10] *Right to Read Report* readers were exhorted to "win one more for the Gipper!" (p. 7).[11]

In July 1993, the newsletter stated that a copy of the May issue had been sent to "every legislator in Ohio by a concerned Ohioan" (News Report 1993, p. 3). In 1994, Sweet urged readers of the *Right to Read Report* to use the "Western Union ProPhonics Hotline" to send telegrams to U.S. senators. At issue was language in the Improving America's Schools Act of 1993. Sweet claimed the bill was anti-phonics because it prohibited "emphasis on repetitive drill and practice" in Chapter I programs (Sweet 1994b, p. 7). A few months later Sweet reported that the offending language had been removed. In November 1994, the newsletter reported state-level activity on the issue of phonics instruction for the first time. By 1996, the reporting of state-level developments appeared to be becoming a more frequent feature (Special Report 1996; Uprising Continues 1996).

Religio-Political Conservative Influences in State-Level Secular Political Groups

As with groups challenging Holt, Rinehart and Winston's *Impressions* reading series, some pro-phonics activists emphatically assert that their religious views have nothing to do with their advocacy of phonics. For example, Al Moehr, president of Parents for Systematic Intensive Phonics in the Classroom, stated that he had no religious motivation for his successful campaign in support of Wisconsin's bill requiring pre-service teachers to be trained in phonics. Moehr stated that the initial impetus for his involvement in this issue was the recommendation of the local school district that his son be "labeled L.D." (A. Moehr, personal communication, July 10, 1996).[12] Notwithstanding Moehr's disavowal and the fact that his organization, which appears to be a key player in the pro-phonics movement in Wisconsin, is secular, there are connections between local secular conservative groups and the religio-political conservative movement. Moehr endorsed both David Shimmels, a member of the National Right to Read Foundation who advocated "a heavy emphasis on phonics," and Jaime Shutes, who subsequently founded a Christian Coalition chapter, as candidates for the West Bend Board of Education in 1994 (Vote Shutes 1994; Davis 1994; Seibel 1995).

Like the publications of the National Right to Read Foundation, Moehr's explanation of his pro-phonics activism echoes much of the material in Blumenfeld and Schlafly. For example, Moehr uses the terms "phony phonics" and "educrats" and makes a connection between illiteracy and juvenile crime (A. Moehr, personal communication, July 10, 1996; Moehr, n.d.). Like both the religio-political conservative literature and some of the bills in other states, Moehr equates whole language and whole word approaches. "With systematic sequential phonics a child at 4th grade level can read and understand at least 24,000 words. With the whole language method the same child should be able to memorize 1554 words" (Moehr 1994, n.p.). Moehr distributed flyers, gathered 8,000 signatures on four hundred petitions, and testified in support of the Wisconsin bill (A. Moehr, personal communication, July 10, 1996). Robert Sweet also testified in support of this bill (*Testimony* 1995).

Marc Duff, the state representative who introduced Wisconsin House Bill 237, identified both Moehr's Parents for Systematic Intensive Phonics in the Classroom and Parents Raising Educational Standards in Schools (PRESS) as influential in his decision to sponsor pro-phonics legislation (M. Duff, personal communication, June 12, 1996). PRESS's links to the state and local affiliates of the Christian Coalition are confirmed by Ruth Schmitt, a member of the Kewaskum Board of Education, and Susan Matulis of the Wisconsin Research Center (Huettl 1995; S. Matulls, personal communication, August 8, 1996). In an article reporting the November 1995 PRESS convention (see previous discussion), *The Christian Interpreter* described PRESS organizers and participants as "ecstatic about the electricity of the conference" (Dykema 1995).[13]

A request to the Oklahoma Family Policy Council, which has been active in opposing that state's implementation of the school-to-work program, resulted in the organization's sending a chapter of Blumenfeld's *NEA: Trojan Horse in American Education* (1984). The Oklahoma Council for Public Affairs has also been active in opposing outcome-based education and school-to-work programs. A 1995 issue of the Oklahoma Council for Public Affairs newsletter was devoted to educational issues. Its lead article, titled "Partners in Crime" (Dutcher 1995b), claims a link between illiteracy and crime. The article cites studies by the conservative Heritage Foundation and a white paper by Floyd Coppedge, Dean of Education at Oklahoma Christian University of Arts and Sciences, who states that "whole language is a political movement with a left-leaning agenda which attracts many education professors" (p. 3).[14] As in much religio-political conservative literature, which uses religious terms to describe ideological opponents, "Partners in Crime" describes whole language as the "current incarnation" of "faulty" whole word methods and Ken Goodman as "one of America's whole language evangelists" (p. 2). Like the 1995 and 1996 legislation introduced in Oklahoma and other states, the article uses the term "guessing" to describe whole language. Echoing much of the thinking of religio-political conservatives generally and quoting Blumenfeld (identified as an "education writer") specifically, Dutcher calls for the implementation of "intensive, systematic phonics" in the public schools and for "schools of education in Oklahoma's colleges and universities [to] start offering their students instruction in teaching phonics" (pp. 2–4).

In May 1996, Dutcher wrote a letter to the editor of the *Sunday Oklahoman,* supporting the actions of an Oklahoma high school student whose graduation address was a statement of her Christian faith (Dutcher and Dutcher 1996, p. A8). To the Dutchers "the coercive power of the state [is used] to expose youngsters to 12 years of government-approved ideas and compelling taxpayers to pay for it" (p. A8). Such "government approved ideas . . . deny that God is an objective reality, that in Christ all things consist and in Him are all the treasures of wisdom and knowledge from anthropology to zoology" (p. A8). Schools "cannot mention" "the architect of history," "the one on whose shoulders government rests (civics)," and "the designer of our orderly universe (science and math)" (p. A8).

The Oklahoma Council for Public Affairs' 1996 publication "The Dumbbell Curve" repeats many of the secular arguments of pro-phonics advocates by tying increasing illiteracy to the introduction of the whole word method (Wood 1996).[15] "American grade schools (in the 1930s) suddenly and amazingly began to lose their capacity to produce literate citizens" (p. 11). "The new 'see and say' whole word repetition [had] terrible consequences" (p. 13). Like Dutcher, Wood sees illiteracy as the root cause of a variety of social ills besetting America: a "ballooning number of violent citizens," "[a doubling] in the numbers of fatherless children and unmarried mothers," "the increasing attract[ion of drugs to] bored, illiterate teens forced by state laws to stay in school until age sixteen," even "defaults on college and trade school loans—now totaling $22 billion" (pp. 10, 12, 14). Contemporary illiteracy is contrasted with the allegedly successful system of education in Puritan New England (a recurring theme in Blumenfeld's writings): "Historians say that 95% of the Massachusetts men could read in 1700" (p. 12; Thomas 1993, p. A15).

State Eagle Forum Leaders and Pro-Phonics Legislation

Prior to the initiation of its Literacy Project in July 1996, activism by local chapters of the Eagle Forum was scattered. A national Eagle Forum representative identified "Eagle Leaders" in Ohio and Alabama who "had been able to influence legislation" (K. Lovelace, personal communication, June 27, July 9, 1996). In addition, Bobbie Patray, president of the Tennessee Eagle Forum, testified before the K–12 subcommittee of the Tennessee House Education Committee on March 27, 1996 (J. Winters, personal communication, July 1, 1996).[16] Each of these states had multiple introductions of phonics legislation (Alabama had three bills, two of which contained highly detailed language; Ohio also had three, two with moderately detailed language and one with highly detailed language; and Tennessee had two, both with moderately detailed language). Phonics bills were ultimately enacted in both Alabama and Ohio.

Stephanie Cicil of the Texas Eagle Forum disseminated pro-phonics material to members of the Texas legislature, particularly Representative Charlie Howard. Bobbie Patray of the Tennessee Eagle Forum and Eunie Smith of the Alabama Eagle Forum were actively involved in promoting the pro-phonics bills in their respective states. Bobbie Patray says she wrote the draft for the identical Tennessee House and Senate bills with the assistance of Jeanne Chall, retired Harvard professor of reading and the author of *Learning to Read: The Great Debate;* Patrick Groff, a retired professor at San Diego State University; and Robert Sweet. Patray also "lined up" sponsors for the bills. Representative Callicott was asked to sponsor the House bill because he was not running for re-election. The Tennessee Eagle Forum formed "a working coalition" for the proposed legislation with other state-level religio-political conservative organizations: Concerned Women for America, the Christian Coalition, and "right to life people." The state Eagle Forum endorsed the legislation, and members were asked to write to their legislators "to offer their personal stories and support" (B. Patray, personal communication, August 1, 1996).

Eunie Smith, president of the Alabama Eagle Forum and a registered lobbyist, advised Sharman Ramsey, the leader of the Committee to Correct Core Problems of Education. Ramsey's husband, Joel, drafted the Alabama bills. Like Al Moehr's Parents for Systematic Intensive Phonics in the

Classroom, the Committee to Correct Education's Core Problem circulated a petition (Committee to Correct 1995). Sharman Ramsey testified with a group of Eagle Forum members at a hearing before the Alabama House Education Committee in 1994. In addition, the Eagle Forum paid the travel expenses of John Winston, a Louisiana principal who had successfully used the Spalding "Writing Road to Reading" program. Mr. Winston testified before the Alabama House Ways and Means Committee in 1995 in support of the bills.

Other pro-phonics activities included the showing of "a U.S. Justice Department video showing how illiteracy causes crime" (E. Smith, personal communication, August 23, 1996) and distributing a literacy fact sheet. Both Bobbie Patray and Eunie Smith mentioned Samuel Blumenfeld as an important influence. Stephanie Cicil noted an informal relationship between the Texas Eagle Forum and Mel and Norma Gabler, long-term critics of school textbooks, on educational issues. Patray, Smith, and Cicil all mentioned the National Right to Read Foundation as being particularly helpful to them in their cause. Eunie Smith alluded to the religious basis of her successful efforts to require the inclusion of an insert regarding evolution and creation science in biology textbooks used in Alabama.[17]

Patray, Cicil, and Smith all identified opposition to phonics as coming from universities and professors of education within their respective states. Cicil and Smith identified specific universities as primary sources of opposition to phonics instruction. Both Smith and Cicil noted the vehemence of the opposition to their pro-phonics activities. "Reading professors of education" were "extremely hostile" when Stephanie Cicil testified at a hearing before the state textbook commission, and the "educational establishment [was] just as emotional as some people are on the prolife position" (S. Cicil, personal communication, August 24, 1996; E. Smith, personal communication, August 23, 1996). In addition, Bobbie Patray attributed the failure of the Tennessee bills to "the house committee which is owned by the teachers' union" (the Tennessee Education Association). Eunie Smith identified the Alabama Department of Education as active in opposing the proposed legislation. Cicil mentioned the state affiliate of the International Reading Association as actively opposing phonics instruction.

Conclusions

Not only are religio-political conservatives staunch advocates for the use of phonics as a method of reading instruction in public schools; they have also translated that commitment into political action. Religio-political conservative literature clearly discloses a pro-phonics position. As is the case with other religio-political positions held by Christian Right leaders, their pro-phonics arguments are grounded directly in scripture and indirectly in their religious worldview. In addition, religio-political conservative writers make use of secular arguments to increase the viability of their position.

This activism corresponds to a sharp and dramatic increase in both the number of phonics bills and changes in their language. The evidence suggests that secular organizations with fairly strong ties to the Christian Right have led the way in pressing for legislative consideration of this issue. Christian Right penetration of state Republican parties is also tied to an increased willingness on the part of state legislators to introduce pro-phonics legislation. This phenomenon may also reflect an overall turn to the right in state legislatures generally.

It is too early to predict whether pro-phonics legislative initiatives will continue to increase, maintain their 1995 and 1996 levels, or decrease. Certainly, continued or increased involvement, especially on the part of the national Eagle Forum and the Right to Read Foundation, coupled with a similar or increased number of bills would indicate that religio-political conservative activism is a significant factor in legislative attempts to promote the use of phonics as a reading instructional method in public schools.

Endnotes

1 The breakdown was as follows: California, three; Hawaii, Idaho, Illinois, Indiana, Mississippi, and New York, one each; Oklahoma, four; Ohio and Tennessee, two; and Wisconsin, one.

2 For a more complete examination of the language and substance of phonics bills introduced in state legislatures from 1990 to 1996, see Paterson, 1996b, 51–67.

3 "Descriptors" refers to separate adjectives, phrases, and/or clauses modifying the noun "phonics." Typical descriptors include such adjectives as "early," "systematic," "direct," or "intensive." Phrases include such language as "training in letter-sound associations and blending drills" (Washington, H.R. 1172, 1995; Washington, S. 5498, 1995)" or "presentation of phonetic knowledge through techniques and practices which are introduced incremental, logically, systematically such that students are taught to read, enunciate and spell accurately by learning the letter/sound associations of individual letters, letter groups and syllables, as well as the principles governing these associations" (Pennsylvania, H.B. 2105, 1995).

4 *Sing, Spell, Read, and Write* is produced by International Learning Systems. It is not clear if Robertson (unlike Schlafly) ever had a financial interest in the sales of the program he was promoting. *Sing, Spell, Read, and Write* is listed as an approved reading curriculum in bills in Mississippi and (Alabama S. 420, 1994; Alabama H.B. 567, 1994; Mississippi H.B. 567, 1995; Mississippi H.B. 971, 1996).

5 Taking figures for only the 1995 legislative sessions does not appreciably alter the disparity. In 1995, Republicans comprised 48 percent of all state legislators.

6 "Moderately detailed" is defined as three to six descriptors modifying the term "phonics." "Highly detailed" bill language has seven or more descriptors.

7 Billie Hanson is the Alabama director of the National Right to Read Foundation. Hanson's written testimony before the Alabama House Education Committee stated, "When a man cannot read . . . he must depend on someone else to find spiritual satisfaction" (Hanson 1994, n.p.).

8 Both assertions, that phonics-based instruction has been used successfully since the ancient Phoenicians invented alphabetic writing and that non-phonics-based approaches employ techniques more suitable to an ideographic system, have been repeatedly made by Blumenfeld and other religio-political conservative commentators.

9 The term "educrats" is used frequently by religio-political conservative writers to describe a somewhat vaguely defined educational establishment. "Educrats" include professors of education and state and federal department of education personnel. It can also include school district administrators. The use of the term in National Right to Read Foundation materials appears to mark its first appearance in ostensibly secular literature.

10 Blumenfeld is another commentator who argues that Hooked on Phonics was unfairly treated by the FTC. For Blumenfeld the FTC, the International Reading Association, *Newsweek,* and NBC "ganged up" on the program (Blumenfeld 1995, n.p.).

11 The Sweet article portrays the National Right to Read Foundation as an opponent of the U.S. Department of Education, "a many-headed hydra" whose agencies "spew their venomous, innovative, and intrusive policies," which are responsible for such things as "revisionist history," "condom distribution [in schools]," "inclusion," "report cards which tell parents nothing," "inventive-spelling," "suicide," and naturally the "abandonment of phonics" (Sweet 1995, p. 7).

12 Other key players in state-level pro-phonics organizations have cited their own child's difficulty in learning to read as the original impetus for their involvement. Moehr, however, was the most vehement on this subject.

13 A November 1994 article in the *Christian Interpreter* described the use of phonics at Jubilee Christian School in Franklin, Wisconsin, and a petition drive initiated by a West Bend parent to have the "state legislature pass a law that all public schools teach K–3rd grade students 'Intensive, Systematic Phonics'" (Dykema 1994). Unlike whole language ("invented spelling and sight memorization of whole words"), Dykema asserts that phonics was highly successful in teaching kindergartners to read at Jubilee (p. 12). The phonics article appeared on the same page as a report of a lecture on plant physiology sponsored by the Creation Science Society of Milwaukee.

14 An article in the *Sunday Oklahoman,* which was virtually identical to "Partners in Crime," repeated Coppedge's concerns about the connection between illiteracy and crime. Coppedge was identified as a Democrat and also as the governor's education secretary. No mention was made of Coppedge's affiliation with Oklahoma's Christian University of Arts and Sciences, nor was Blumenfeld quoted or cited in the article. In the article, Dutcher stated that "low God-esteem" rather than poverty or low self-esteem is "the root cause of crime" (Dutcher 1995a, n.p.).

15 Regna Wood, the author of this report, is a research consultant for the National Right to Read Foundation; see Wood 1994.

16 Both Bobbie Patray and Eunie Smith, president of the Alabama Eagle Forum, are registered lobbyists for their respective organizations.

17 "The courts would not allow Genesis in the classroom. That's not something that could be debated *right now*" (emphasis added) (E. Smith, personal communication, August 23, 1996).

References

Armstrong, W. 1989. *Illiteracy: An Incurable Disease or Education Malpractice?* Washington, DC: U.S. Senate Republican Policy Committee.

Baughman, F. 1993. Dyslexia: A Second Opinion! *Right to Read Foundation* 1, 3: 1–2.

Blumenfeld, S. L. 1984. *NEA: Trojan Horse in American Education.* Boise, ID: Paradigm.

———. 1987. Dumbing Down America. *Blumenfeld Education Letter* 2, 11: [n.p.].

———. 1995. The International Reading Association, Newsweek, NBC, and the Federal Trade Commission Gang up on "Hooked On Phonics." *Blumenfeld Education Letter* 10, 2: [n.p.].

Chall, J. 1967. *Learning to Read: The Great Debate.* New York: McGraw Hill.

Christian Coalition. 1995. Wisconsin Christian Coalition Voters Guide. Milwaukee: Wisconsin Christian Coalition; Wisconsin Research Center (dist.).

Claggett, D. 1995. Simple Guidelines for Early Reading Instruction. *The Teaching Home* (November–December): 49.

Committee to Correct Education's Core Problem. 1995. Giving Every Child the Right to Read: Phonics. Flyer. Birmingham: Eagle Forum of Alabama (dist.).

Concerned Women of Wisconsin. 1994. Petition to Local and State Elected Officials to Restore Literacy Through Intensive, Systematic Phonics. Flyer. Milwaukee: Wisconsin Research Center (dist.).

Davis, A. 1994. Six of Seven Candidates for Two Board Seats Are Newcomers. *Milwaukee Journal* (February 9).

Diegmueller, K. 1996. A War of Words: Whole Language Under Siege. *Education Week* (March 3): 1, 14, 15.

Dutcher, B. T. 1995a. Is Reading Just a Guessing Game? *Sunday Oklahoman* (August 20).

———. 1995b. Partners in Crime. *OCPA Perspective* 2, 7: 1–4.

Dutcher, B., and S. Dutcher. 1996. Speech Was Free. Letter to the editor, *Sunday Oklahoman* (June 9): A8.

Dykema, K. 1994. PRESS Conference Attracts Electric Crowd. *Christian Interpreter* (December): 12.

Eagle Forum. 1981. How and Why I Taught My Children to Read. *Phyllis Schlafly Reports* 14, 11: 1–4.

———. 1996a. Help Eagle Forum's Literacy Project. Flyer. Alton, IL: Eagle Forum.

———. 1996b. A Proposal to Train and Equip Parents to Teach Their Children How to Read in Order to Reduce Illiteracy and Reduce Delinquency Among Minors. Brochure. Alton, IL: Eagle Forum.

Hanson, B. 1994. *Phonics Is the Answer to Illiteracy.* Flyer. Birmingham: Eagle Forum of Alabama.

Hertzke, A. D. 1993. Echoes of Discontent: Jesse Jackson, Pat Robertson, and the Resurgence of Populism. *Congressional Quarterly.*

Holderer, R. W. 1995. The Religious Right: Who Are They and Why Are We the Enemy? *English Journal* 84, 5: 75–83.

Huettl, M. L. 1995. Is the Christian Coalition Part of School Politics? *Cudahy* (Wisconsin) *Reminder* (November 22).

Iowa Code Ann. §294.14 (West 1993).

Jacobson, J. B. 1993. Examining the Evidence: Is Your School Telling You the Truth? *Right to Read Report* 1, 3: 3–4.

Kansas State Republican Party. 1996. Kansas Republican Party 1996 Handbook. Brochure. Topeka: Kansas Republican Party.

Menendez, A. J. 1992. *Visions of Reality: What Fundamentalist Schools Teach.* Buffalo, NY: Prometheus.

Michigan School Board Puts God at the Heart of Its Mission. 1995. *Right to Read Report* 2, 8: 5.

Moehr, A. n.d. Top Ten Reasons for Voting Against AB237, the Bill Requiring Teacher Training in Phonics. Flyer. West Bend, WI: Parents for Systematic, Intensive Phonics.

———. 1994. The Time Is Now for Phonics!!!!! Flyer. West Bend, WI: Parents for Systematic, Intensive Phonics.

National Right to Read Foundation. 1994. A Guide to Understanding the Issues: An Educational Resource Guide for Parents, Teachers and Policy-Makers. Brochure. Washington, DC: National Right to Read Foundation.

News Report. 1993. *Right to Read Report* 1, 4: 3.

Ohio Rev. Code Ann. §3301.7(M). 1989. Baldwin.

Parsons, P. F. 1987. *Inside America's Christian Schools.* Macon, GA: Mercer University Press.

Paterson, F. R. A. 1995. Reading Instructional Methodologies Employed by Home Schooling Parents. Unpublished raw data.

———. 1996a. Challenges to Public School Reading Textbooks. *West's Education Law Reporter* 106 (March 7): 1–20.

———. 1996b. From Outside the Schoolhouse Gates: Christian School Parents Look at Public School Curriculum. Unpublished manuscript.

———. 1996c. Mandating Methodology: Promoting the Use of Phonics Through State Statutes. Department of Educational Leadership and Policy Studies, University of Oklahoma.

Persinos, J. F. 1994. Has the Christian Right Taken Over the Republican Party? *Campaigns and Elections* 15, 9: 21–24.

Peshkin, A. 1986. *God's Choice: The Total World of a Fundamentalist School.* Chicago: University of Chicago Press.

Phonics Hopes to Catch on in Schools. 1996. *Memphis Commercial Appeal* (March 5): B2.

Planned Parenthood. 1995. CWA Recruits in Appleton. Flyer. Milwaukee: Wisconsin Research Center (dist.).

Provenzo, E. F., Jr. 1990. *Religious Fundamentalism and American Education: The Battle for the Public Schools.* Albany: State University of New York Press.

Republican State Committee of Oklahoma. 1996. Oklahoma Republican State Convention. Brochure. Oklahoma City: Republican State Committee of Oklahoma.

Robertson, P. 1990. *The New Millennium: Ten Trends that Will Impact You and Your Family by the Year 2000.* Dallas, TX: Word.

Robertson, S. 1993. *Reading, Writing, and Ripped Off: The Incredible Tragedy of Whole Language and the Progressive Philosophy in Public Education Today.* Videotape. Humble, TX: Higher Knowledge (dist.).

Rose, S. D. 1988. *Keeping Them Out of the Hands of Satan: Evangelical Schooling in America.* New York: Routledge.

Schlafly, P. 1994. Illiteracy: Its Consequences and Cure. Cassette recording of speech presented at the Texas Education Summit (October 8). Alton, IL: Eagle Forum.

Seibel, J. 1995. Man's Mission: Zap Power of Teachers' Union in Elections. *West Bend Daily News* (November 8).

Special Report on Prophonics State Legislative Activity, 1994–1995. 1996. *Right to Read Report* 3, 1: 6.

Sweet, R. W., Jr. 1993. Keepers of the Flame. *Right to Read Report* 1, 4: 8.

———. 1994a. Outlaw Phonics? What Is Going on in Washington? *Right to Read Report* 7.

———. 1994b. Who Is the Anti-Phonics Movement? *Right to Read Report* 2, 5: 7.

———. 1995. The Unholy Alliance. *Right to Read Report* 2, 6: 7.

Testimony Presented to the Wisconsin Senate Education Committee. 92d Legislative session. 1995. Testimony of Robert W. Sweet, Jr.

Thogmartin, M. B. 1994. The Prevalence of Phonics Instruction in Fundamentalist Christian Schools. *Journal of Research on Christian Education* 3: 103–30.

Thomas, C. 1993. It's a Crime Education Is No Longer Hooked on Phonics. *Seattle Post-Intelligencer* (September 17): A15.

U.S. Supreme Court Justice Says "No" to Portrait of Christ. 1995. *Right to Read Report* 2, 8: 5.

Uprising Continues. 1996. *Right to Read Report* 3, 2: 3.

Vote Shutes for School Board. 1994. Flyer. Milwaukee: Wisconsin Research Center (dist.).

Walworth County Christian Coalition. 1995a. Agenda. Milwaukee: Wisconsin Research Center (dist.).

———. 1995b. Things to Tune Into. Sandtree 1, 2: n.p. Milwaukee: Wisconsin Research Center (dist.).

————. 1995c. Flyer. Milwaukee: Wisconsin Research Center (dist.).

Wood, R. L. 1994. A Closer Look: Special Education, in the Name of Helping the Disadvantaged Are We Consigning Them to Permanent Illiteracy? *Right to Read Report* 1, 8: 1–3.

————. 1996. *OCPA Policy Analysis: The Dumbbell Curve.* Oklahoma City: Oklahoma Council of Public Affairs.

In this chapter, Constance Weaver and Ellen Brinkley explore the subtle differences and commonalities between the political right and the religious right and their advocacy of phonics and opposition to whole language. For some, the notion of teaching reading through phonics comes directly from God. To them, phonics is divinely good and, by the same logic, whole language is the devil's work, because it teaches children to question the written word and to interpret both reading and the world for themselves. Disinformation—deliberate misrepresentation—is common in far-right literature. Weaver and Brinkley suggest ways to help others see the intentions of the political right and to deal with the disinformation.

7

Phonics, Whole Language, and the Religious and Political Right

Constance Weaver and Ellen H. Brinkley

[Learning to read can be] a breeze . . . if reading is taught the way God made us to talk—by syllables, by what is called phonics, not by the "look say" method forced on the schools by the behaviorist models.
—Pat Robertson, 1990

I've often mused that we Christian educators treat phonics instruction as though it were mandated by Scriptures.
—Mark Thogmartin, 1994

The quotes above from Pat Robertson and Mark Thogmartin make us wonder: Why is phonics so attractive to the religious right? Why, in contrast, is whole language sometimes considered undesirable, even when phonics is taught in the context of reading and writing whole texts? Why is literacy education, especially when associated with whole language, being attacked? And how can we help administrators, parents, community members, and politicians understand the benefits of good literacy education and whole language rather than teaching phonics intensively and systematically, in isolation, prior to engaging children in reading and writing experiences?

Understanding the Concerns

In 1989, a U.S. Senate Republican Policy Committee document claimed that "the overwhelming evidence from research and classroom results indicates that the cure for the 'disease of illiteracy' is the restoration of the instructional practice of intensive, systematic phonics in every primary

An earlier version of this chapter was originally published as part of an article in the *Peabody Journal of Education*, March 1998.

school in America!" (Armstrong 1989, p. 13). The attempt to get the federal government to mandate the teaching of phonics and the training of teachers to teach phonics failed, but some states have enacted such bills, and pro-phonics bills have been introduced in more than 40 percent of the states. Furthermore, the introduction of such bills has increased significantly in 1995 and 1996 (as detailed in Chapter 6). Sometimes the demands of such proposed legislation can be quite extreme. For instance, legislation proposed in the New York State Assembly demanded that students with limited English proficiency be taught by the "direct, systematic, and intensive, phonetic instruction," allegedly "a method of teaching students to read, write, spell and speak by learning the sound associations of individual letters, letter groups and syllables and the alphabetic principles governing these associations." Teachers and teacher aides would be trained "on the use of direct systematic, intensive phonetic teaching of reading, writing, spelling and speaking the English language" (State of New York, "An act to amend," 6637A, March 28, 1995).

Certainly anyone with a background in linguistics and language acquisition would understand the absurdity of expecting to teach people to read, write, spell, and speak, all by a "phonetic" method. Likewise, most parents can understand that such an edict is nonsense. They know from having observed their own young children's oral language acquisition that language learning happens most effectively when child and parent focus first on meaning. They understand that language learning begins without formal instruction. Too often, however, a lack of background knowledge and professional expertise does not stop legislators from proposing laws to dictate how reading will be taught. How has this come about?

The primary push for intensive, systematic phonics comes originally—especially—from the religious right (see, for example, Simonds 1984) and more generally the far right, which currently wields considerable influence and power in our national and state governments. Phyllis Schlafly, for instance, is urging members of her Eagle Forum to get elected officials to propose pro-phonics legislation (1996). Schlafly and other proponents of intensive phonics, of "phonics first," refer to research, but they tend to cite summaries that ignore research that does not support phonics or skills as the best approach to teaching reading (Smith and Elley 1995; Shapiro 1990; Weaver 1994) and instead make claims for the effectiveness of phonics that go far beyond what the research actually demonstrates (Groff 1993, 1995, n.d.; Grossen, n.d.; but see critique of Grossen's document by Allington and Woodside-Jiron in Chapter 8). The purpose of this chapter is not to contest the claims made by pro-phonics advocates; that has been done elsewhere (see, for example, Weaver 1997b; Weaver, Gillmeister-Krause, and Vento-Zogby 1996). Rather, we wish to explore the question of why phonics has such an appeal for the religious right and to consider whether, or to what extent, phonics is the real issue. In this discussion, it should be kept in mind that the majority of Christians do not identify themselves as fundamentalists; in addition, some fundamentalists do not agree with the educational views of the religious right. However, the educational views attributed to fundamentalists—and especially to members of the religious right—have been widely disseminated, so that they have influenced others who do not necessarily share their religious views.

"God Believes in the Beauty of Phonics"

Why would anyone claim that "God believes in the beauty of phonics" (quoted in Moffett 1988, p. 31)? Perhaps a hint is provided in the advertisement for a grammar series that appeared in a home schooling catalog from a major Christian fundamentalist publisher of educational materials: "Grammar is taught with the purpose of making clear to the students the orderly structure of their language, a picture of God's orderly plan for the world and for their lives" (*Home School Catalog* 1996). There is some evidence that phonics is viewed in much the same way. For example, in an article in *The Teaching Home* titled "Is There a Best Way to Teach Beginning Reading?" the author cites 1 Corinthians 14:40 as a guide in deciding how best to teach reading: "Let all things be done decently and in order." He also cites Isaiah 28:10—"For precept must be upon precept"—as a principle to guide the style of the beginning reading curriculum (Winters 1995). These and other biblical quotes seem designed to lead readers of such pieces to the conclusion that systematic phonics is the best way to teach reading.

A related issue is authority and control. Just as fundamentalists commonly emphasize the authority of God and the authority and control of parents, so they emphasize authority in the teaching of phonics. Winters (1995) writes: "Throughout Scripture, God raised up leaders to teach His principles to others. Christ personally taught His disciples and led them to understand God's plan. One of Paul's primary tasks was to instruct new believers. The parent-educator should lead the learner in beginning reading" (p. 48). Winters implies that teaching phonics directly is better than having students develop phonics knowledge indirectly through other methods. Having attempted to convince readers of the greater appropriateness of teaching phonics directly, Winters concludes his article with a section promoting systematic, multisensory phonics.

In investigating why phonics is so attractive to Christian fundamentalists, Mark Thogmartin—himself a fundamentalist educator—discovered that authority, control, and tradition were all important reasons. Many fundamentalist parents associate phonics with the McGuffey readers, which used a very basic phonics approach and included texts that had a moral point: Bible stories, stories from literature, and some stories written by McGuffey himself (Thogmartin 1994, p. 112). The phonics instruction in these readers "was compatible in spirit and implementation with the classroom atmosphere most desired by the teachers and parents of the time: whole group, drill-oriented instruction, and authoritarian management. Virtue in the form of hard work was its own reward—or would be rewarded later; learning was not to be associated with pleasure" (Alongi 1984, p. 16, as cited in Thogmartin 1994, p. 113). Thus phonics is associated with tradition, with morality and ethics, with order and structure, and with the assumption that what is taught is automatically learned—the transmission model of education.

Belief in the authority of texts themselves offers another reason for promoting phonics. Fundamentalist Christians believe in Biblical inerrancy, in the idea that the Bible is literally "the word and the Words of God" (Averill 1990, p. 57; see also Brinkley 1994, 1995; Holderer 1995). Therefore, they reason, a Christian's task is to unlock the meanings God embodied in the scriptures. It is assumed that to do that, one must read every word correctly, and phonics logically seems to be a way of "getting" all the words. For example, James A. Chapman insists that

> the emphasis upon individual words has always been of paramount importance to [fundamentalist] Christian educators . . . If one uses the whole-word method, which treats phonetic words as if they were ideographs, one can get away from stability, from standards, from restraint, from traditional pronunciation, from traditional spelling, and from correct and incorrect forms of speech. (Chapman 1986, pp. 13–15)

Thus intensive phonics is believed to be more than a way of teaching reading or a means of getting the words right: it is thought to be a means of preserving standards in education and in life.

The idea of preserving standards is related to fundamentalists' belief in absolutes and consequently in dualism, a sharp division between the godly and the ungodly, the saved and the lost. Since phonics can be laid out neatly in sequenced lessons, it fits nicely into the worldview that there are standards that must be maintained and taught by appropriate authority figures. Robert W. Holderer, who taught for many years in fundamentalist schools, explains this viewpoint as follows: Just as "God established an orderly universe (Genesis) and gave humanity language as part of that order, traditional 'rules only' methods [such] as phonics, spelling drill, diagraming sentences, and so on are God's law for teaching the young"

(Holderer 1995, p. 77). Many fundamentalists believe that rules and standards get lost when skills are taught in context, as in whole language classrooms.

In any case, it seems clear that standards, rules, authority, and control are key issues for religious fundamentalists, who may easily gravitate toward intensive, systematic phonics because it fits their worldview.

Is Phonics the Real Issue?

Certainly phonics is a real issue. Many parents, not necessarily fundamentalists, can easily be roused to concern when confronted with some of the polemics that allege the superiority of teaching children to read by phonics. They may not realize that phonics is taught as effectively in the context of reading and writing (Stahl, McKenna, and Pagnucco 1994; Weaver 1994), and they themselves may have had phonics instruction in school. For these reasons such parents may easily be enlisted in the crusade for teaching phonics intensively and systematically. Not familiar with any of the contrary research, they buy into the demand for intensive phonics because they are concerned for their children. For these parents, phonics is the issue.

Fundamentalists may also advocate phonics because many home-schooling parents rely heavily on educational materials produced by publishers of fundamentalist textbooks. Not trained as teachers, they naturally are drawn to reading materials that promote their own theological worldview through explicit references to God (Sleeth 1995) and to materials that are—let's face it—easier to teach. Some parent-teachers, in fact, seem not to be familiar with other methods for teaching reading, or even with other methods for teaching phonics. Furthermore, systematic phonics programs are used in parochial schools where children are seen as succeeding (Thogmartin 1994). No wonder, then, that teaching phonics systematically is seen as sensible and necessary—even "right."

But for many fundamentalist parents, phonics is only part of the issue. A substantial amount of literature and information disseminated by far-right conservatives calls not only for teaching phonics intensively and systematically, but also for ousting whole language teaching from the schools. (See, for example, literature from the National Right to Read Foundation; Phyllis Schlafly's Eagle Forum; Norma and Mel Gabler's Educational Research Analysis; the Christian Coalition; the National Association for Christian Education's activist arm, Citizens for Excellence in Education; and views expressed on the radio talk shows of Marlin Maddoux, G. Gordon Liddy, and others.) In other words, they insist on teaching beginning reading through intensive phonics in part because they believe in it (though their belief is based on a superficial understanding), but also in part because it's a way of getting rid of whole language.

It's much easier for opponents to oust whole language by insisting that only phonics is supported by "scientific" research than to focus on the concerns some fundamentalists have with some of the values inherent or implicit in whole language education. What is it about whole language that these fundamentalists object to? In part, of course, it's the perceived abandonment of rules, the teaching of phonics in the context of reading and writing rather than "by the book," and the research-based view that reading is not a process of identifying every word so much as a process of constructing meaning from texts (Goodman 1967; Rosenblatt 1978; Pearson and Stephens 1992). Samuel Blumenfeld, for instance, claims that the whole language concept of reading is "an attack on the notion of absolute truth and literal comprehension of a written text" (1982, p. 6). Although psycholinguistic research has demonstrated beyond reasonable doubt that the reading of *any* text is determined or affected by prior knowledge, experiences, and beliefs, this fact is not acceptable to those who believe that texts have one literal and absolute meaning for all readers, whose task is to discover the "truth" of texts. Given this belief, many religious conservatives view phonics as the route to accurate word identification, and accurate word identification as the route to uniform understanding of texts. They simply ignore, or remain comfortably ignorant of, convincing research and classroom practice that demonstrate that reading doesn't work that way.

Given such beliefs, these people may view whole language with suspicion because whole language teachers engage children in literature discussions wherein students formulate and discuss their own interpretations of texts. Uncomfortable with any move away from standardization, many fundamentalist parents similarly disapprove of giving students choice in what they read, of engaging in critical and creative thinking, and of accepting the whole language view of learning as constructing meaning— all perceived as contrary to a worldview that favors memorizing facts and focusing on questions with single right or wrong answers. Indeed, Holderer reports that teachers who encourage independent thinking are by that act alone seen as attempting to discredit biblical absolutes through relativism (Holderer 1995, p. 78). This belief may underlie the many— often successful—attempts to oust critical thinking programs from the schools (Gaddy, Hall, and Marzano 1996; Marzano 1993–94; Jones 1993).

No wonder, then, that religious conservatives try to instill intensive, systematic phonics in place of whole language. Whole language is considered dangerous. By some twist or abandonment of logic, whole language is even claimed to be "a devilish means to keep children illiterate" (Holderer 1995,

p. 78—a view he has heard expressed on Marlin Maddoux's talk show; see also Blumenfeld 1984, 1996; Spohn 1995). White (1994) and Miller (1984) have both "documented how Fundamentalist leadership has twisted facts carelessly (although some are deliberate) and has often refused to recant falsehoods when proven wrong" (Holderer 1995, p. 81). Such is the case in terms of what has been said about phonics and whole language. For example, the "Illiteracy" paper (Armstrong 1989) prepared as a U.S. Senate Republican Policy Committee document is riddled with problems: irrelevant statistics from which inaccurate cause-effect relationships are drawn; research from only one perspective, despite contrary research evidence; and misinformation, such as the claim that a psycholinguistic view of reading and whole language education are the same as a "whole word" approach. Patient attempts by leading whole language advocates to correct some opponents in these misconceptions have been ignored by these individuals, who continue to make the same misstatements in the public arena, and whose claims are given credence by the far right's distribution of their work.

Some fundamentalist critics sincerely fear that whole language may inhibit their children's learning, subvert their minds, and even endanger their very souls (Brinkley 1995, p. 92). Teachers need to work patiently with such parents to demonstrate the validity of whole language learning through their children's actual performance. Less willing to listen, of course, are religious-right lobbyists and politicians, whose primary motivation and agenda are political (Brinkley 1995, p. 97). They rarely try to determine whether the scholarship that others feed them is balanced, fair, or even accurate. They worry not about logical argument, nor inquire about research evidence that might be contrary to what they are given by those who promote phonics legislation.

Unfortunately, this is the reality of politics, wherein the end is all too often seen as justifying the means. Thus, whole language educators need to take on the additional task of informing legislators about the limitations of intensive, systematic phonics and about the validity and benefits of whole language education.

Working and Communicating with Others

Given the current promotion of intensive phonics, literacy educators need to help parents, legislators, and the public understand and appreciate whole language and good literacy education. Possibilities for working with others occur in three overlapping contexts: the personal and professional, the professional and political, and the political and public (see also Chapter 3 for suggestions for addressing religious issues).

Working with Parents: Personal and Professional Contexts

Among the various ways literacy educators might help parents better understand and appreciate whole language teaching are the following, some of which are specifically targeted to religious conservative parents who are concerned about the effects of whole language teaching on their children. (See also Weaver, Gillmeister-Krause, and Vento-Zogby 1996 for other suggestions.)

1. Literacy educators can draw analogies with other kinds of learning: learning to ride a bicycle, for instance, or learning one's native language as a baby and toddler. Parents usually understand that learners generally try the whole of a thing with adult support (perhaps including training wheels for the bicycle) and then gradually refine the parts.

2. Educators can explain some of the ways phonics is and can be taught in the context of authentic reading and writing within whole language classrooms. (Detailed descriptions are offered by Mills, O'Keefe, and Stephens 1992; Routman and Butler 1995; Powell and Hornsby 1993.)

3. Educators can help parents, especially religious conservative parents, understand the constructive nature of the reading process: the fact that meaning is not in the text, but rather in the head of the author and the reader, who transacts with the text to construct meaning. This is an important issue, for most people probably believe that the meaning resides in the text and that the reader's job is to extract, not construct, the meaning. In order to understand that it's not critical for readers to identify every word of a text, they need to understand that the meaning is not exactly in the text anyway. Reading and discussing together a short article from a newspaper may be sufficient to encourage people to realize that meaning is a product of readers' transactions with a text. Parents who participate in Bible study groups know that the meanings of biblical passages are discussed and interpreted within a faith tradition, not simply dispensed (see Chapter 3). One of the basic tenets of Protestantism in fact is the idea that each person should read and interpret the Bible independently of the authority of the church. Indeed, it is this aspect of Protestantism that has promoted literacy and the teaching of reading in many countries.

4. Educators can help parents reconsider their notions of how reading was acquired in the early days of America. It is true that the widely used hornbook, a piece of wood resembling a ping-pong paddle, typically contained the upper- and lowercase letters and some simple syllables: for example, *ab, eb, ib, ob, ub; ba, be, bi, bo, bu.* Children who were taught from the typical hornbook first learned the names of the letters and then learned to spell and pronounce such vowel-consonant and consonant-vowel combinations and syllables. In colonial America, learning letters and the syllabary (remember, this was less than one page, not a whole phonics

program) was typically followed by learning to read the Lord's Prayer, which was also commonly printed on the hornbook. After this came a primer with familiar texts such as the Lord's Prayer, the Ten Commandments, and the Apostles' Creed. Reading of the Bible commonly followed. While it is true that children were made to read by spelling and then pronouncing each word in sequence, it is also true that oral familiarity with such texts would have promoted learning to read by reading and rereading familiar texts (Mathews 1966; Smith 1965).Teachers might share with parents the picture book *Least of All* by Carol Purdy (1987). In this story a little girl, Raven Hannah, is the youngest and least strong member of her family. Bored because she cannot do the work of the others, Raven Hannah teaches herself to read by matching the printed words to the lines in the Bible that she has memorized at Sunday school. When her family discovers that she can read the Bible, Grandmamma points out, "People can be strong in differing ways; by learning to read the good book you have proved yourself strong in mind and spirit." Raven Hannah's method of teaching herself to read is similar to the whole-to-part teaching that occurs in whole language classrooms.

Professional and Political Contexts

Nowadays, the contexts in which we are called upon to share our professional expertise are increasingly political: local and state school boards, for instance, and politically influenced task forces. Meanwhile, policymakers and politicians have been inundated with misinformation about phonics and whole language. The minds of many of them are made up; their attitude is "Don't confuse me with the facts." They have listened to those who insist that good readers read most words accurately, that phonemic awareness (awareness of separate sounds) correlates highly with reading achievement, that there is no scientific evidence to support whole language, and that whole language educators have nothing useful to say about the nature of reading (Adams 1990; Adams and Bruck 1995; Beck and Juel 1995). Since such scholarly opinions have been promoted by the far right and the media, we must consider ways of regaining credibility as professionals in the public and political arenas. The following are some possibilities that can help accomplish this goal.

1. Educators must not only research and develop but also promote an alternative theory of how readers acquire knowledge of letter/sound patterns through reading—knowledge that they can then use to "unlock" more and more words. For example, Margaret Moustafa's research supports the hypothesis that children develop phonics knowledge by noticing onset and rime patterns ("chunks" of letters) in their reading; that is, it suggests a mechanism by which "learning to read by reading" takes place

(Moustafa 1993, 1995, 1997a, 1997b). Thus we have a research-supported theory to counteract the currently popular idea that children must develop phonemic awareness before they learn to read. This theory also offers an alternative to the popular misconception that children learn to read words letter by letter, correlating letters with individual phonemes as they read. (See, for instance, the California Department of Education document *Teaching Reading: A Balanced, Comprehensive Approach to Teaching Reading in Prekindergarten Through Grade Three,* Eastin 1996.)

2. Educators should not just ignore opponents' research or belittle it because of its limitations. Instead, answer it with scholarship and research, including experimental research that fits their paradigm for research. When researchers have compared children's learning in whole language classrooms with their learning in skills-intensive and phonics-intensive classrooms, they have found that those in the whole language classrooms typically do as well or better on standardized tests and subtests, including tests of phonics (letter or letter/sound identification). In addition, however, the children in whole language classrooms—including "at risk" children—typically do *better* on a considerable range of other measures, including the ability to use phonics knowledge effectively, to use a variety of strategies to handle problems in reading, and to read for meaning rather than just for word identification (see, for example, Weaver 1997a and the fact sheets in Weaver, Gillmeister-Krause, and Vento-Zogby 1996; Smith and Elley 1995; Shapiro 1990; Tunnel and Jacobs 1989). Educators need to make people aware of the various lines of research that support whole language teaching and learning (Stephens 1991), including, but of course not limited to, experimental research.

3. Educators should admit to the validity of scholarly opponents' views whenever possible. Recognizing other views is more reasonable and responsible than simply rejecting, or seeming to reject, everything that differing scholars say. For example, in making a presentation before the long-range planning committee of the Texas State Board of Education, Connie chose not to say that Marilyn Adams and others are wrong in claiming that proficient readers read most words correctly. Rather, she incorporated Adams's view—derived from very different kinds of research—into a more comprehensive model of reading, with comprehension at the core. Thus she defined reading as "processing symbols and texts to derive meaning," but then noted that in attending to meaning, readers: (1) predict by using prior knowledge, context, word knowledge and letter/sound knowledge all together; (2) monitor comprehension and use fix-it strategies when meaning has gone awry; and (3) identify words readily, which makes it easier to attend to meaning. By incorporating other research-based conclusions into an essentially psycholinguistic model of reading, she managed to defuse some arguments of the religious right while giving moderate board mem-

bers something they could offer in place of others' more limited concepts of reading—and, by implication, reading instruction (see also Weaver's introduction and introductory article in Weaver 1997b).

4. Educators can help people understand that even most of those who advocate intensive and/or early teaching of phonics and phonemic awareness do not advocate phonics first. For example, Marilyn Adams makes clear in her 1990 book *Beginning to Read: Thinking and Learning About Print* that children should have numerous and rich experiences with books before phonics is introduced. This is abundantly clear also from her 1995 article with Maggie Bruck in the *American Educator,* and from the Beck and Juel article in the same issue. People need to know that hardly any researcher advocates phonics first—not even most phonics advocates.

5. Educators can decide where to compromise with others who see reading and the teaching of reading differently, and where to stand firm. For example, some whole language educators have suggested teaching some aspects of phonics explicitly (Mills, O'Keefe, and Stephens 1992; Routman and Butler 1995; Powell and Hornsby 1993; Weaver 1994). However, this does not mean that they have abandoned constructivist learning theory or, more specifically, the belief that language and literacy are learned best from whole texts; it means simply that they are trying to make sure they provide guidance for those children who need it in order to make more comprehensible what there is to be learned about letter/sound relationships from reading and composing texts (Weaver, Gillmeister-Krause, and Vento-Zogby 1996). But while more and more whole language educators might be willing to compromise in the direction of teaching some phonics more explicitly, or admitting that they do so— and there's plenty of evidence that this is happening—surely all whole language educators will continue to promote and act on their research-based conviction that reading is fundamentally a meaning-driven, meaning-seeking process.

Influencing Others in the Public and Political Arena

Today's political climate requires that educators make their voices heard not only in personal and professional contexts but also more broadly as informed citizens in the public and political arena. There are many things literacy educators can do to help others understand whole language, the research supporting it, and the relationship of phonics to whole language. They can, for example, contact organizations such as the International Reading Association and the National Council of Teachers of English to find out how to become part of networks that provide information about legislation being introduced in support of good literacy education. As knowledgeable professionals and as citizens, educators can serve on committees that formulate educational policy; write letters to the editor and opinion pieces; call in to radio talk shows; participate in panels dealing with educational issues; and so forth. These individual actions can have an impact, but often they are not enough. Many educators also recognize that they must learn to work with concerned colleagues and citizens and take political action. Paradoxically, and ironically, it may be through such political and group means that literacy educators' voices as professionals can best be heard.

Our concerns about political influences on pedagogy and about threats to public education in Michigan led us to join with other educators, librarians, and citizens to form a statewide nonprofit organization, Michigan for Public Education (Brinkley et al. 1997; also see www.ashay.com/mpe). Other literacy educators may find, as we did, that information is one of the more important ways we can influence the public and that networking is one of the best means to distribute information about education—including, but not limited to, curricular and pedagogical matters. By joining coalitions and being willing to take on broader educational and even societal issues, we have gained credibility with, and the support of, those who share our vision of an educated, informed citizenry in a democratic society.

References

Adams, M. J. 1990. *Beginning to Read: Thinking and Learning About Print.* Cambridge, MA: Harvard University Press.

Adams, M. J., and M. Bruck. 1995. Resolving the "Great Debate." *American Educator* 19, 2: 7, 10–20.

Allington, R. I., and H. Woodside-Jiron. 1997. *Thirty Years of Research on Reading . . . Adequacy and Use of a "Research Summary" in Shaping Educational Policy.* Albany, NY: National Research Center on English Learning and Achievement. <http://cela.albany.edu/allington/index.html>.

Alongi, C. V. 1984. Phonics Battle in Perspective. *The School Administrator* 14, 2: 16–19.

Armstrong, W. 1989. *Illiteracy: An Incurable Disease or Education Malpractice?* Washington, DC: U.S. Senate Republican Policy Committee.

Averill, L. J. 1990. *Religious Right, Religious Wrong: A Critique of the Fundamentalist Phenomenon.* New York: Pilgrim Press.

Beck, I. L., and C. Juel. 1995. The Role of Decoding in Learning to Read. *American Educator* 19, 2: 8, 21–25, 39–42.

Blumenfeld, S. L. 1982. The "Whole Language" Fraud. *The New American* 8, 16: 6–8.

———. 1984. *NEA: Trojan Horse in American Education.* Boise, ID: Paradigm.

———. 1996. *The Whole Language/OBE Fraud.* Boise, ID: Paradigm.

Brinkley, E. H. 1994. Intellectual Freedom and the Theological Dimensions of Whole Language. In J. Brown, ed., *Preserving Intellectual Freedom: Fighting*

Censorship in Our Schools, pp. 111–22. Urbana, IL: National Council of Teachers of English.

———. 1995. Faith in the Word: Examining Religious Right Attitudes About Texts. *English Journal* 84: 91–98.

Brinkley, E. H., et al. 1997. Believing in What's Possible, Taking Action to Make a Difference. *Language Arts* 74: 537–44.

Chapman, J. 1986. *Why Not Teach Intensive Phonics?* Pensacola, FL: A Beka Book.

Eastin, D. 1996. *Teaching Reading: A Balanced Comprehensive Approach to Teaching Reading in Prekindergarten Through Grade 3.* Sacramento: California Department of Education (May 10).

Gaddy, B. B., T. W. Hall, and R. J. Marzano. 1996. *School Wars: Resolving Our Conflicts over Religion and Values.* San Francisco: Jossey-Bass.

Goodman, K. S. 1967. Reading: A Psycholinguistic Guessing Game. *Journal of the Reading Specialist* 6: 126–35.

Groff, P. 1993. Research Supports Phonics: A Summary of Research Findings on Reading Instruction. Appendix to M. Brunner, *Retarding America: The Imprisonment of Potential.* Portland, OR: Halcyon House, a division of Educational Research Associates.

———. 1995. Focus: Whole Language Versus Phonics. *Education Reporter* 108 (January): 3–4.

———. n.d. *Whole Language Versus Phonics.* Burke, VA: National Right to Read Foundation.

Grossen, B. n.d. *Thirty Years of Research: What We Now Know About How Children Learn to Read.* Santa Cruz, CA: Center for the Future of Teaching and Learning. <http://www.cftl.org/30 years/30 years.html>.

Holderer, R. W. 1995. The Religious Right: Who Are They and Why Are We the Enemy? *English Journal* 84 (September): 75–83.

Home School Catalog. 1996. Pensacola, FL: A Beka Book.

Jones, J. L. 1993. *No Right Turn: Assuring the Forward Progress of Education.* Federal Way, WA: Washington Education Association.

Marzano, R. J. 1993–94. When Two Worldviews Collide. *Educational Leadership* 51, 4: 6–11.

Mathews, M. M. 1966. *Teaching to Read, Historically Considered.* Chicago: University of Chicago Press.

Miller, W. E. 1984. The New Christian Right and the News Media. In D. G. Bromley and A. Shupe, eds., *New Christian Politics,* pp. 139–49. Macon, GA: Mercer University Press.

Mills, H., T. O'Keefe, and D. Stephens. 1992. *Looking Closely: Exploring the Role of Phonics in One Whole Language Classroom.* Urbana, IL: National Council of Teachers of English.

Moffett, J. 1988. *Storm in the Mountains: A Case Study of Censorship, Conflict, and Consciousness.* Carbondale, IL: University of Illinois Press.

Moustafa, M. 1993. Recoding in Whole Language Reading Instruction. *Language Arts* 70: 483–87.

———. 1995. Children's Productive Phonological Recoding. *Reading Research Quarterly* 30: 464–76.

———. 1997a. *Beyond Traditional Phonics: Research Discoveries and Reading Instruction.* Portsmouth, NH: Heinemann.

———. 1997b. Reconceptualizing Phonics Instruction. In C. Weaver, ed., *Reconsidering a Balanced Approach to Reading,* pp. 135–57. Urbana, IL: National Council of Teachers of English.

Pearson, P. D., and D. Stephens. 1992. Learning About Literacy: A Thirty-Year Journey. In C. Gordon, G. D. Labercane, and W. R. McEachem, eds., *Elementary Reading Instruction: Process and Practice.* New York: Ginn.

Powell, D., and D. Hornsby. 1993. *Learning Phonics and Spelling in a Whole Language Classroom.* New York: Scholastic.

Purdy, C. 1987. *Least of All.* Illus. Tim Arnold. New York: Macmillan.

Robertson, P. 1990. *The New Millennium: Ten Trends that Will Impact You and Your Family by the Year 2000.* Dallas: Word.

Rosenblatt, L. 1978. *The Reader, the Text, the Poem: The Transactional Theory of the Literary Work.* Carbondale, IL: Southern Illinois University Press.

Routman, R., and A. Butler. 1995. Why Talk About Phonics? *School Talk* 1, 2: [n.p.].

Schlafly, P. 1996. Unpublished letter to members of the Eagle Forum. July.

Shapiro, J. 1990. Research Perspectives on Whole Language. In V. Froese, ed., *Whole Language: Practice and Theory,* pp. 313–56. Boston: Allyn & Bacon.

Simonds, R. L. 1984. *How to Start Your Citizens for Excellence in Education Committee.* Costa Mesa, CA: National Association of Christian Educators.

Sleeth, N. 1995. *A Handbook for Reading: Phonics Textbook.* Pensacola, FL: A Beka Book.

Smith, J. W. A., and W. B. Elley. 1995. *Learning to Read in New Zealand.* Katonah, NY: Richard C. Owen.

Smith, N. B. 1965. *American Reading Instruction.* 2nd ed. Newark, DE: International Reading Association.

Spohn, L. 1995. *An Analysis of Whole Language.* Pittsburg, PA: Public Education Network.

Stahl, S. A., M. C. McKenna, and J. R. Pagnucco. 1994. The Effects of Whole-Language Instruction: An Update and a Reappraisal. *Educational Psychologist* 29: 175–85.

State of New York. 1995. An Act to Amend the Education Law, in Relation to Phonetic Instruction and Bilingual Education. 6637-A (March 28).

Stephens, D. 1991. *Research on Whole Language: Support for a New Curriculum.* Katonah, NY: Richard C. Owen.

Thogmartin, M. B. 1994. The Prevalence of Phonics Instruction in Fundamentalist Christian Schools. *Journal of Research on Christian Education* 3, 1: 103–30.

Tunnel, M. O., and J. S. Jacobs. 1989. Using "Real" Books: Research Findings on Literature-Based Reading Instruction. *The Reading Teacher* 42: 470–77.

Weaver, C. 1994. *Reading Process and Practice: From Socio-Psycholinguistics to Whole Language.* 2nd ed. Portsmouth, NH: Heinemann.

———. 1997a. Experimental Research: On Phonemic Awareness and on Whole Language. In C. Weaver, ed., *Reconsidering a Balanced Approach to Reading,* pp. 321–71. Urbana, IL: National Council of Teachers of English.

———, ed. 1997b. *Reconsidering a Balanced Approach to Reading.* Urbana, IL: National Council of Teachers of English.

Weaver, C., L. Gillmeister-Krause, and G. Vento-Zogby. 1996. *Creating Support for Effective Literacy Education.* Portsmouth, NH: Heinemann. Some fact sheets in this book were published by the National Council of Teachers of English as SLATE starter sheets; all are available on the World Wide Web page of Heinemann publishers: <http://www.heinemann.com>.

White, M. 1994. *Stranger at the Gate: To Be Gay and Christian in America.* New York: Simon & Schuster.

Winters, D. 1995. Is There a Best Way to Teach Beginning Reading? *The Teaching Home* (November–December): 48.

One of the articles most widely circulated by the forces attacking whole language and pushing direct instruction of phonics is Bonnie Grossen's "Thirty Years of Research," which purports to be a summary of research funded by the National Institute of Child Health and Development (NICHD). With funding from the U.S. Department of Education and the Office of Educational Research and Investigation, Richard Allington and Haley Woodside-Jiron have systematically read all of the studies funded by the NICHD and checked the other research cited. They had a hard time doing so, because much of it was not reported in refereed professional journals. They conclude that the commonly disseminated "findings" that Grossen summarizes are not in fact supported by the actual studies. Curiously, much of the wording of Grossen's article is the same as the wording of promotional materials for the McGraw-Hill Mastery Reading Program (formerly Distar).

8

Thirty Years of Research in Reading: When Is a Research Summary Not a Research Summary?

Richard I. Allington and Haley Woodside-Jiron

We have been tracking the process of educational policymaking in several states for the past two years. During the course of this activity we have identified one particular document that has been widely distributed in several forms and has been influential in shaping educational policy both nationally and in at least two of the states we have been studying.

This document, "Thirty Years of Research: What We Now Know About How Children Learn to Read—A Synthesis of Research on Reading from the National Institute of Child Health and Development," which we will refer to in this chapter as the "Thirty Years . . ." report, has appeared as a journal article, as a hard-copy report, and on various web pages. It has appeared variously with no author identified, with the Center for the Future of Teaching and Learning (CFTL) as the author, and with Bonita Grossen of the National Center to Improve the Tools of Educators (NCITE) as the author. Authorship varies depending on the location of the document. When it appeared in the journal of the Association for Direct Instruction (ADI), *Effective School Practices* (vol. 15, pp. 33–46), where Grossen is the journal editor, the CFTL was listed as author. On the CFTL web page, Grossen is listed as author. But in the accompanying materials on the web page, one of the CFTL "accomplishments" is noted as follows:

> We convened a group of reading experts and organizations that affect the performance of teachers. Their job was to produce a consensus on what teachers need to know and be able to do to teach reading well. The report, Thirty Years of Research: What We Now Know About How Children Learn to Read, has been widely distributed through printed copies and on the Internet's World Wide Web. (p. 1)

The fact that two different authors—and no author—are credited in three different sources of this article poses a small problem of attribution, not to mention a puzzling breach of the conventions of scholarly writing. We cannot be sure who actually authored this report. We have not located any information on just who the "reading experts and organizations" mentioned in the CFTL background document (this "fact sheet" accompanies the Grossen version on the Internet but no author, title, or date is listed) are or whether they actually view the "Thirty Years . . ." report as a consensus document. We do know this: The International Reading Association, the National Council of Teachers of English, and the National Reading Conference were not among the organizations that were convened.

In this chapter we examine the adequacy of the "Thirty Years . . ." document as a research summary. We have elected to focus on the version available on the CFTL web page—the version listing Bonita Grossen as author—primarily because we have also located this version on other web sites, including those of state board members and those of various organizations critical of public education, and because several thousand copies of this version were distributed to state policymakers by the CFTL.

Who Are the Actors?

It appears to us that there are three organizations and one person that can be associated with the development and/or dissemination of the "Thirty Years . . ." document.

The Center for the Future of Teaching and Learning (CFTL)

According to information available on the CFTL web site, the Center for the Future of Teaching and Learning was founded in 1995 as a private, nonprofit organization. The purpose of the CFTL is "to increase the capacity of California's teachers for delivering . . . rigorous, well-rounded curriculum" (p. 1). The CFTL identifies its primary work as "bridging the gap" between educational research, policy, and practice. The "Thirty Years . . ." document is said to be funded by the Pacific Bell Foundation.

The National Center to Improve the Tools of Educators (NCITE)

Located at the University of Oregon in Eugene, the National Center to Improve the Tools of Educators is funded, at least in part, by the U.S.

Department of Education's Office of Special Education Programs. The NCITE has a cooperative agreement with the federal office for the Learning to Read/Reading to Learn initiative, which is targeted at "helping children with learning disabilities succeed" (promotional flyer, n.d.). Documents disseminated as part of this initiative report that

> the relatively recent swing away from phonics instruction to a singular whole language approach is making it more difficult to lift children with learning disabilities out of the downward spiral and, in fact, may impede the progress of many students in learning to read with ease. (NCITE n.d., p. 3)

The Association for Direct Instruction (ADI)

The nonprofit Association for Direct Instruction is headquartered in Eugene, Oregon. The mission of the ADI is "to improve education . . . a major obstacle to improved education is old fads recycled as new reforms." The ADI publishes *Effective School Practices,* described as a "quarterly magazine" in an informational box in a recent issue of the *American Teacher* (1994, vol. 18, p. 12). The articles in *Effective School Practices* seem not to be peer reviewed, and the publication is listed in neither the ERIC *Current Issues of Journals in Education* nor in *Education Index.* The magazine reprints materials from other sources, including other journals, publishers' promotional materials, and reports of the implementation of commercial curriculum materials, primarily those published by SRA/McGraw-Hill (see the Spring 1994 issue for a particularly rich example).

Bonita Grossen

Bonita Grossen is the only person whose name is directly associated with the "Thirty Years . . ." document. On the CFTL version Grossen is simply listed as a "Research Associate with the National Center to Improve the Tools of Educators." She is, however, as previously noted, also listed as editor of *Effective School Practices.*

There is a fourth organization implicated in the "Thirty Years . . ." document: the National Institute of Child Health and Development (NICHD), which is part of the National Institutes of Health. The CFTL version of the "Thirty Years . . ." document begins with a short preface, which notes that the report is "a synthesis of research on reading from the National Institute of Child Health and Human Development (NICHD)." Other versions of "Thirty Years . . ." include the mention of NICHD research in the title of the paper.

G. Reid Lyon directs the NICHD research branch that is charged with studying dyslexia and learning disabilities. This branch funds research at a dozen or so centers across the United States; most of these centers are affiliated with a medical school. The NICHD research program is broad-based but has a long history of investigating the etiology of dyslexia and learning disabilities. Much of the research in the past decade has focused on two themes: learning disability incidence/definitional issues; and phonological core deficits as the locus of the problems of children exhibiting severe reading difficulties (Lyon 1995a).

It is important to note that the "Thirty Years . . ." report was not sponsored by NICHD, and NICHD officials have stated that the report does not reliably represent the findings of NICHD research efforts. Yet G. Reid Lyon is listed in the NCITE materials as one of "three leading researchers in the field of reading instruction" who produced a review of the research that identified "what they believe are the most important strategies for improving reading instruction" (NCITE n.d., p. 4). The other two were Marilyn Adams, of Bolt, Beranek, and Newman, and Edward Kameenui, who serves as the associate director of the NCITE.

The "Thirty Years . . ." Report

The eighteen-page "Thirty Years . . ." report opens with background information on the NICHD research program. It describes the "scientific rigor" of the funded studies and contrasts these studies with "other educational research." The next sections offer a "plain language" discussion of phonological awareness and explicit, systematic instruction in sound-spelling correspondences. In these sections a dozen NICHD-funded research team reports are cited, although two are listed as "in press." Three of these reports are studies of learning disability incidence and definitions. Four are general summaries with little or no original data. Three are on studies that employed dyslexic subjects. One of the unpublished papers, summarizing three separate studies, is quoted extensively, though none of the original reports of this research is cited.

The second half of "Thirty Years . . ." is devoted largely to "seven key principles of effective reading instruction identified in the research" (Grossen 1997, p. 9). For us to review each of the seven principles here would produce a long and redundant chapter. Instead, we have chosen to examine just three of the principles, numbers 1, 3, and 5 in the report. It would be an easier task to assess the accuracy and adequacy of the research support for these principles had the author directly cited the research she felt supported each principle. Unfortunately, no research citations are provided in the section of text that follows each principle. Thus, we were forced to review each of the NICHD-funded studies cited at the beginning of "Thirty Years . . ." Each was reviewed for evidence supporting any of the three report principles, as described below.

Principle 1

The first of the "Thirty Years . . ." report's seven principles is: *Begin teaching phonemic awareness directly at an early age (kindergarten)*. This principle is followed by examples of recommended phonemic awareness tasks for teachers to use in their classrooms. Each of the eight tasks offers isolated word work. For instance:

- What word would be left if the /k/ sound were taken away from *cat*?
- What sound do you hear in *meat* that is missing in *eat*?
- What word would we have if we put these sounds together: /s/, /a/, /t/?
- Is there a /k/ in *bike*?

These tasks are similar to those that researchers have used in studying the development of phonemic awareness and in some of the NICHD intervention studies. But the NICHD studies have typically targeted children identified as dyslexic, learning disabled, or with phonological processing problems; the research reports have typically noted gains only on similar isolated phonemic awareness tasks and on pseudo-word pronunciation tasks (Lyon and Moats 1997). At the same time, improvement in reading of real words, in reading fluency, or in text comprehension have not been reported in the majority of NICHD studies.

In contrast, Scanlon and Vellutino (1997), reporting on their NICHD-funded research, note that the most successful kindergarten classrooms for at-risk children were those that offered more opportunities to engage in meaningful writing activities supported by teacher scaffolding during invented spelling (basically modeling sound-stretching). Beyond this study, there are few published NICHD kindergarten studies, and none that Grossen cites reports significant effects on later text reading achievement from the sort of decontextualized "direct teaching" tasks specified in the document.

Principle 3

The third principle in the "Thirty Years . . ." document is: *Teach frequent, highly regular sound-spelling relationships systematically*. There are actually several potential principles embedded here. There is the *frequency* of the sound-spelling patterns, the *regularity* of the sound-spelling relationships, and the nature and effects of *systematically* teaching sound-spelling relationships. Thus, it is difficult to know where to begin. It is especially difficult because there are no data in any of the cited NICHD-funded studies on just what sound-spelling relationships were taught—frequent or infrequent, regular or irregular. Grossen provides a list of the "48 most regular sound-letter relationships" (which we can only assume would be similar to a list of the 48 sound-spelling relationships). No study is cited as a source for this listing; no NICHD study even investigated the issue. It is difficult to see how this facet of the principle could be derived from the NICHD studies.

According to the "Thirty Years . . ." report, to "teach systematically means to coordinate the introduction of the sound-spellings with the material the children are asked to read . . . all the children must be taught using the same sequence" (p. 11). There are some data in the NICHD-funded studies on teaching letter-sound relationships (Felton 1993; Foorman, Francis, Novy, and Liberman 1991; Lovett et al. 1994; Wagner and Torgeson 1987). But there is little unity across the studies on just how this was done. In some NICHD studies, the research team employed basal reader series and identified them as having either a code emphasis (Lippincott, Economy, Open Court) or a context emphasis (Houghton Mifflin, Scott Foresman). Other studies used supplementary programs, some commercial (Educators Publishing Service, Edmark) and some locally developed, but few details are offered in the published research papers on just how these programs were delivered or whether the sound-spellings taught were coordinated with the material children were reading. Some studies used a replacement design, where the research team controlled all reading instruction offered; other studies offered an add-on design, where targeted children were provided with supplementary instruction. Simply said, there are no specific data in the NICHD studies that could be construed as support for "teaching systematically" as defined in this third principle and no specific research support for teaching the "frequent, highly regular sound-spelling relationships" identified by Grossen.

Principle 5

The fifth principle in "Thirty Years . . ." is: *Use connected, decodable text for children to practice the sound-spelling relationships they learn.* The text following this principle begins,

> The findings of the NICHD research emphasize that the children need extensive practice applying their knowledge of sound spelling relationships to the task of reading as they are learning them. This

integration of phonics and reading can only occur with the use of decodable text. (p. 11)

The document goes on to define "decodable text" as composed of words representing the sound-spelling correspondences the children have been taught. Again, little information is available in the research cited on the sorts of texts children read in the NICHD studies, beyond general references to particular commercial series. Perhaps Grossen completed some sort of content analysis of the named products and could use this information as some sort of support for this principle. But the original research reports offer no such evidence, and Grossen offers no evidence of any other sort. In addition, the NICHD has recently awarded several grants funding the "first objective studies of the decodable/predictable text" issue.

Again, the NICHD-funded research and the other research Grossen cites offers no support for the "principle" advocated.

A Snapshot of NICHD-Funded Research

It might be useful to briefly review several of the NICHD-funded research studies that Grossen claims in support of her principles. The accompanying table (see pages 154–157) provides a brief summary of both NICHD-funded research and other studies of potential relevance to the principles offered in "Thirty Years . . ."

There are two key elements of the NICHD studies that deserve attention. First is the nature and size of the samples. Most NICHD intervention studies have involved populations of students identified as experiencing some severe reading difficulties or as being at risk of such difficulties based on an early school screening. Study findings from such specific, narrow population samples would not seem to be a reasonable basis for developing general education policy or a basis for restructuring early literacy instruction generally. This would seem especially true when the design simply provides an add-on tutoring component. Second, most of the NICHD studies were not successful in improving students' performance in word reading, reading fluency, or passage comprehension. Instead, as Lyon and Moats (1997) have noted, these intervention studies have more often produced improvement on pseudo-word pronunciation tasks but with little reliable or replicable impact on other reading development measures.

Many of the non-NICHD studies included in our table were not cited by Grossen but have been cited by others as supporting her fifth principle, the importance of decodable text. But in fact none of these studies offer support for the recommendation. This lack of evidence in support of decodable text was a key factor in the passage of the recent International Reading Association resolution decrying legislative or regulatory restrictions on the nature of beginning reading materials. Nonetheless, such restrictions have been included in recent actions in at least two states.

Recently Allington (1997) argued that phonics is being oversold. Central to this argument are the exaggerated claims being made about the findings from the research on code-emphasis approaches to beginning reading instruction. The Grossen version of the "Thirty Years . . ." report, in our view, falls well outside the accepted boundaries for a research summary. But if it is not a research summary, what is it?

Personal Preference Versus Research-Based Principles

The "Thirty Years . . ." document is more an offering of personal opinion than a reliable summary of findings drawn from the NICHD-funded research. Interested parties might compare the principles Grossen offers in "Thirty Years . . ." with those she offers in another document: "A Research Base for Reading Mastery SRA" (Grossen n.d.)—in particular the Technical Notes section on pages 3 and 4 of this document with the identical paragraphs on pages 6 and 7 of "Thirty Years . . ." The "Research Base" document was provided by the Association for Direct Instruction; it offers a rationale for the design of a commercial reading series for which Grossen is listed as an author. But the research base and several of the principles developed bear an uncanny similarity to the content of the "Thirty Years . . ." report. (Even more remarkable is the similarity between the wording of the recommendations found in "Thirty Years . . ." and that of the recommendations recently advanced in several state reading initiatives, but that is yet another story; see Chapter 6.)

Summary

We found the "research evidence" offered in support of three of the seven principles in the "Thirty Years . . ." document to be lacking on several counts; yet this document has been influential in several political venues and cited as fact by various proponents of a code-emphasis agenda. But while this disinformation campaign was taking place there was no adequate response from the National Council of Teachers of English, the National Reading Conference, or the International Reading Association. It is true that the IRA developed, passed, and published two resolutions that contradicted many of Grossen's assertions about effective decoding instruction and condemned restrictions on beginning reading materials. These actions occurred largely in response to the advancement of Grossen's principles 2, 3, and 5 in state education agency or legislative actions. But the IRA resolutions had little impact in the states where "Thirty Years . . ." was most widely influential. Neither resolution, unfortunately, had detailed supporting documentation—nothing that offered an examination of the research Grossen cited or the research she elected to ignore. In addition, neither the IRA nor the NRC nor the NCTE has seemed to be able to mount any sort of effective political public relations campaign proffering a reliable interpretation of the research evidence on issues relating to beginning reading instruction. There have been no position papers, no targeted mailings, no telephone campaigns, no media blitz, no glossy flyers, no news conferences, no news releases, no lobbying, no nothing.

Perhaps the lesson to be learned is that learning to read is a political topic. Governors, legislators, and even presidents campaign on reading proficiency agendas. With all the media attention that reading achievement has received in the last few years (Routman 1996), no one should be surprised that politicians of all stripes are willing to listen to "expert solutions" to the "reading crisis" that has been manufactured by education agencies and fellow politicians (Berliner and Biddle 1995). What is surprising, perhaps, is how ill-prepared our professional associations are to deal with this new visibility.

References

Allington, R. L. 1997. Overselling Phonics. *Reading Today* 15, 1: 15–16.

Beck, I., and E. S. McCaslin. 1978. An Analysis of Dimensions that Affect Development of Code-Breaking Ability in Eight Beginning Reading Programs. No. 1978/6. Pittsburgh: Learning Research and Development Center, University of Pittsburgh.

Berliner, D. C., and B. J. Biddle. 1995. *The Manufactured Crisis: Myths, Fraud, and the Attack on America's Public Schools.* Reading, MA: Addison-Wesley.

Center for the Future of Teaching and Learning. 1996. Thirty Years of NICHD Research: What We Now Know About How Children Learn to Read. *Effective School Practices* 15: 33–46.

Felton, R. H. 1993. Effects of Instruction on the Decoding Skills of Children with Phonological Processing Problems. *Journal of Learning Disabilities* 26: 583–89.

Foorman, B. R., D. J. Francis, T. Beeler, D. Winikates, and J. M. Fletcher. 1997. Early Interventions for Children with Reading Problems: Study Designs and Preliminary Findings. *Learning Disabilities: A Multidisciplinary Journal* 8, 1: 63–71 (Winter).

Foorman, B. R., D. J. Francis, J. M. Fletcher, C. Schatschneider, and P. Mehta. n.d. The Role of Instruction in Learning to Read: Preventing Reading Failure in At-Risk Children. Unpublished paper.

Foorman, B. R., D. J. Francis, D. Novy, and D. Liberman. 1991. How Letter-Sound Instruction Mediates Progress in First-Grade Reading and Spelling. *Journal of Educational Psychology* 83: 456–69

Foorman, B. R., D. J. Francis, D. Winikates, B. Melita, C. Schatschneider, and J. Fletcher. 1997. Early Interventions for Children with Reading Disabilities. *Scientific Studies of Reading* 1: 255–76.

Grossen, B. 1997. "Thirty Years of Research: What We Now Know About How Children Learn to Read—A Synthesis of Research on Reading from the National Institute of Child Health and Development." Santa Cruz, CA: Center for the Future of Teaching and Learning. (www.cftl.org).

———. n.d. "A Research Base for Reading Mastery SRA." Eugene, OR: University of Oregon.

Juel, C. 1994. *Learning to Read and Write in One Elementary School.* New York: Springer Verlag.

Juel, C., and D. Roper-Schneider. 1985. The Influence of Basal Readers on First Grade Reading. *Reading Research Quarterly* 20: 134–52.

Lovett, M., L. Borden, T. DeLuca, L. Lacerenza, N. Benson, and D. Brackstone. 1994. Treating Core Deficits of Developmental Dyslexia: Evidence of Transfer of Learning After Phonological- and Strategy-Based Reading Training Programs. *Developmental Psychology* 30: 805–27.

Lyon, G. R. 1994. *Research in Learning Disabilities at the NICHD.* Bethesda, MD: Human Learning and Behavior Branch, National Institute of Child Health and Human Development, National Institutes of Health.

———. 1995a. Research Initiatives in Learning Disabilities: Contributions from Scientists Supported by the National Institute of Child Health and Development. *Journal of Child Neurology* 10: 120–26.

———. 1995b. Toward a Definition of Dyslexia. *Annals of Dyslexia* 45: 3–77.

———. 1997. Testimony Before the Committee on Education and the Workforce, U.S. Congress, Washington, DC (July).

Lyon, G. R., D. B. Gray, J. F. Kavanagh, and N. A. Krasgegor, eds. 1993. *Better Understanding Learning Disabilities.* Baltimore, MD: Paul Brookes.

Lyon, G. R., and L. C. Moats. 1997. Critical Conceptual and Methodological Considerations in Reading Intervention Research. *Journal of Learning Disabilities* 30: 578–88.

National Center to Improve the Tools of Educators. n.d. *Reading: The First Chapter in Education.* Eugene, OR: University of Oregon.

Olson, R., H. Forsberg, B. Wise, and J. Rack. 1994. Measurement of Word Recognition, Orthographic, and Phonological Processing. In G. R. Lyon, ed., *Frames of Reference for the Assessment of Learning Disabilities,* pp. 243–77. Baltimore, MD: Paul Brookes.

Rack, J. P., M. J. Snowling, and R. Olson. 1992. The Non-Word Reading Deficit in Developmental Dyslexia: A Review. *Reading Research Quarterly* 27: 28–53.

Routman, R. 1996. *Literacy at the Crossroads: Crucial Talk About Reading, Writing, and Other Teaching Dilemmas.* Portsmouth, NH: Heinemann.

Scanlon, D. M., and F. R. Vellutino. 1997. A Comparison of the Instructional Backgrounds and Cognitive Profiles of Poor, Average, and Good Readers Who Were Initially Identified as At Risk for Reading Failure. *Scientific Studies of Reading* 1: 191–216.

Torgeson, J. K., R. K. Wagner, and C. A. Rashotte. 1997. Prevention and Remediation of Severe Reading Disabilities: Keeping the End in Mind. *Scientific Studies of Reading* 1: 217–34.

Wagner, R. K. and J. K. Torgeson. 1987. The Nature of Phonological Processing and Its Causal Role in the Acquisition of Reading Skills. *Psychological Bulletin* 101, 2: 192–212.

Summaries of NICHD-Funded and Other Reading Studies

Study	Subjects	Intervention	Outcomes	Key Quote
NICHD-funded studies				
Felton (1993)	81 Ss: 24 code-emphasis (Lippincott), 24 context-emphasis (HM), 33 controls.	Code and context Ss got classroom intervention from a "research teacher" in gr. 1 and 2.	End of gr. 2. Code Ss sig. greater ach. on non-words when compared to controls; nsd when compared to context Ss. Word reading nsd with 42% of code and 43% of context Ss scoring above gr. level; nsd between code and context Ss on decoding skills test except on polysyllabic words subtest.	
Lyon et al. (1993); Lyon (1994, 1995 a&b, 1997)	No original data.	None.	Overviews of NICHD research incl. genetic, MRI, and epidemiological or papers on LD definitional issues.	"No program is equally effective with all children." (1997, p. 7)
Rack, Snowling, and Olson (1992)	No original data.		Summarizes dyslexia research with an emphasis on establishing pattern of difficulties in pseudo-word pronunciation.	"We have reviewed a large number of studies which compared dyslexics and reading-level matched normal readers . . . Roughly two thirds of the studies found specific phonological reading problems in the dyslexic group, and the remainder did not." (p. 49)

Study	Subjects	Intervention	Outcomes	Key Quote
Olson, Forsberg, Wise, and Rack (1994)	Reading level match twin Ss design: younger twins w/o dyslexia, older with; matched on PIAT writing test.	None.	Older dyslexic twins sig. higher achievement on both reading and listening tests.	"As regard phoneme analysis . . . there is no structural format that enjoys consensual validation . . . There is no extensive or systematic documentation of important properties of these tasks, such as difficulty level developmentally, memory demands, conceptual loading." (pp. 312, 313)
Scanlon and Vellutino (1997)	151 Ss. All had very low letter-name scores at beginning of K, but 38 became good readers at end of gr. 1 while 63 achieved avg. reading and 50 were poor readers.	None; observation of K classroom environments.	Few sig. diff. in K classrooms' instruction; good readers attended K classes where there was more phoneme awareness and more writing activity; nsd on time spent in K on letter-sound, phoneme segmentation, decoding, word ident., text meaning activities.	"Phoneme awareness activities generally occurred in the context of writing, typically as sound analysis in the service of 'figuring out' the spellings of words used in more meaning-based writing activity." (p. 204)
Torgeson, Wagner, and Rashotte (1997)	138 Ss selected on low K letter-name performances; ach. tracked at end of K, 1, 2.	Ss randomly assigned to 1 of 3 add-on tutorial treatments or control (explicit phonemic awareness plus synthetic phonics, implicit phonemic awareness plus phonics embedded in reading and spelling, regular class basal reading support). Four 20-min. sessions wkly, half from trained T, half from trained para.	At end of gr. 2 the p.a. + synthetic phonics Ss achieved s.d on phonetic reading but nsd on word identification and comp.	"We still do not have convincing evidence that the relative differences in growth on phonetic reading skills produced by certain instructional approaches led to corresponding advantages in orthographic reading skills and reading comprehension for children with phonologically-based reading disabilities." (p. 230)

Study	Subjects	Intervention	Outcomes	Key Quote
Foorman, Francis, Winikates, Melita, Schatschneider, and Fletcher (1997)	3 treatments w/114 2nd and 3rd graders w/reading difficulties.	Treatments were: Edmark (n = 39), sight word program; modified Recipe for Reading (46), onset-rime program; Alphabetic Phonics (28), explicit, synthetic phonics. 60 min. daily, by trained Ts in resource rms. for 1 school yr.	When socio-economic status, ethnicity, gender, and IQ were controlled, the only treatment effect that remained significant was the superiority of synthetic phonic treatment compared to sight word treatment on phonological processing tasks; nsd on word reading.	"The results did not support the hypothesized superiority of analytic phonics . . ." (p. 272)
Other studies				
Lovett et al. (1994)	62 dyslexic Ss, ach. below the 25th percentile.	Contrasts SRA Reading Mastery (RM) with Benchmark word identification (WIST) and control. 35 hrs. of training in pairs.	Sd between treatment groups and controls, nsd between treatment groups on spec. trained content. Sd between treatment groups and controls on transfer tasks. Diff. tasks resulted in diff. between treatments (e.g., WIST Ss better on regular and exception real words, strategy use, and metacognitive control; RM better on non-word and phonological tasks).	"The phonological program (RM) resulted in greater generalized gains in the phonological domain and the strategy program (WIST) in broader-based transfer for real words . . . The success of the WIST program can be used as evidence that there are different routes of subsyllabic segmentation [other than letter-sound training and l-to-r letter-sound decoding] possible in the remediation of dyslexia." (pp. 805, 820)

Study	Subjects	Intervention	Outcomes	Key Quote
Juel (1994)	129 Ss in gr. 1, 54 Ss still in school end of gr. 4; focus is on the 54.	Two basals in use (ABC and SF) and a 20–30-min. daily synthetic phonics curriculum; phonics curriculum didn't match either basal.	By 4th gr. most poor readers were both poor decoders and poor comprehenders; gr. 1 poor readers typically still poor at gr. 4; almost half of Ss did not learn phonic elements when taught.	"Children with phonological awareness do not automatically become good readers." (p. 121)
Juel and Roper-Schneider (1985)	11 gr. 1 classes.	Classes used either context (HM) or code-oriented (Economy) basals; all classes used local synthetic phonics curriculum 20–30 min. daily.	Nsd between code and context Ss on non-word test; nsd on Iowa Test of Basic Skills between groups.	"The interpretation of the results of this study do not constitute advocacy of any one specific approach to beginning reading instruction. In particular, the results should not be interpreted as supporting an explicit phonics method." (p. 150)
Beck and McCaslin (1978)	No Ss, content analysis of basal series.	None.	Finds few basals that offer decodable text.	

nsd = No statistically significant differences observed
sd = Statistically significant differences observed
HM = Houghton Mifflin
ABC = American Book Company
SF = Scott Foresman

S = subject
gr. = grade
sig. = significant(ly)
T = teacher
para = paraprofessional

Sharon Murphy is fascinated by the parallels between the saga of the reading wars and the children's folktale, The Sky Is Falling, in which Henny Penny turns a falling acorn into a crisis of immense dimensions. In this chapter, she uses the allegory to explore the role of the press in moving from acorns to literacy crises and the chain of misinformation and disinformation in the major news media. She shows how certain themes, sources, and claims overlap from one news account to another and how the media have thus created a literacy crisis easily attributed to whole language and easily solved through a mandated dose of phonics. In too many of these accounts the distinction between reporting, editorializing, and advocating are blurred.

9

The Sky Is Falling:
Whole Language Meets Henny Penny

SHARON MURPHY

In the classic children's story Henny Penny (Galdone 1968), the title character is sitting under a tree when she is hit on the head by an unseen acorn. Quick to seek out the culprit, but somewhat dazed by the bump on her head, Henny Penny casts her eye about to find something in the vicinity on which she can lay blame. The sky, the only object overhead, seems the logical choice. Panicked but failing to recognize that if the sky remains overhead it cannot be falling, Henny Penny rushes about to inform one and all that the sky is falling. A myth is born.

Over the past several years, whole language has come face-to-face with the Henny Penny experience. Whole language has become the center of a myth about literacy education in the United States. That myth has been propagated by its own Henny Penny: the press. In the misguided literacy education panic, the "failure" of literacy education is attributed to the "failure" of whole language.

The Acorn: The Wake-up Call

For Henny Penny, it started with an acorn. There is an "acorn" in the whole language story as well. The acorn for whole language is the low performance of children in the state of California on national tests of reading. One of the headlines from 1995 seems to tell it all: "State's Reading, Math Reforms Under Review as Scores Fall" (Colvin 1995d). In this, as well as numerous subsequent reports (for example, California Leads 1996; Colvin 1995b, 1996f, 1996h; Goodale 1997; It's Time for California 1996; O'Harrow, Jr. 1995; Progress 1995; Right Direction 1996; Stein 1995; Walters 1996; Welsh 1995), low performance on national tests proved to be the "bump on the head" for politicians in California.

In reality, however, the grounds for the reactivity of California politicians were established long before California's 1994 test scores were reported. These contexts may seem somewhat removed from the particularities of whole language, but they helped to create a climate in which some ideas flourished and others did not. I begin with what may seem an unlikely starting place, but one that seems to be appropriate given other factors: global politics.

In the 1980s, with the dissolution of the Soviet Union, the United States lost its chief competitive enemy. This loss ultimately led to the search for new symbols through which the United States could renew the rhetoric of competitiveness and market rule over the economy.[1] The sluggish economy of the late 1980s added to the development of a sensibility that the United States might lose its competitive edge. Employment became a key political issue, and education was portrayed as the means of obtaining it. The seeds for this shift in the role of education were sown earlier, in the 1960s, when it became common for poverty to be blamed on the failure of the poor to make sufficient use of education to rise above their situation (P. Shannon, personal communication). The wedding of education and employment in the 1980s and 1990s ultimately meant that the corporate sector had effectively shifted the emphasis of schooling away from the liberal arts ideal of educating citizens for participation in democracy and toward a concept of schools as the tools of business.

At the same time, global politics were becoming increasingly conservative. Overspending in countries admired for their social programs and high spending on other priorities (such as defense) resulted in massive deficits throughout the 1980s. Throughout the 1990s balancing the budget and paying down the deficit became chief concerns of these governments. Education was a popular budget-cutting target because it represented a significant portion of expenditures. But actually cutting education budgets was a somewhat daunting task, given the socially beneficial aura surrounding education. If the aura was tarnished, however, the cuts would not be perceived as unjust. Given this context, it should come as no surprise that questions began to be raised over whether education was doing its job. The image of education began to be systematically eroded, and eventually education programs fell victim to budget cuts.

Global political conservatism also tended to result in previously marginal far-right groups being perceived as less extreme. Religious fundamentalists developed political agendas, and ultranationalist groups became more active and visible participants in many different levels of political life. Many of these groups used a rhetoric of traditional values to cloak fairly restrictive goals. In harking back to tradition, however, these groups would conveniently forget the uncertainties that marked the past. As a consequence, the solutions presented under the guise of traditionalism invariably were, and continue to be, overly simplistic and naive. But the call to traditionalism and the feelings of security evoked by solutions based on tradition are quite powerful. As Linda Brodkey (1996) puts it, "The way it never was is the way we wish it were because we long to be, *and to be among,* the blameless subjects of meritocracy, for merit is the secular equivalent of innocence" (p. 177).

In short, the context was set for the sky to fall on a readily identifiable group that could become symbolic of the need to recover from the excesses of the 1980s, return to the competitiveness that had supposedly made the United States great, build on traditional values, and save money while accomplishing all of these goals. In educational circles, whole language became this symbol.

How Did the Press Become So Henny-Penny-ish?

To understand how it was possible for the press to create a myth about whole language, we should consider certain characteristics of the press. First of all, Vietnam and Watergate had a significant effect on reporters' practice. Before these two events, the general consensus was that the worst thing a reporter could do was make false accusations. This encouraged a fastidiousness among reporters. But in the post-Vietnam, post-Watergate world, the worst thing that can happen to reporters now is, as one of them put it, "that you can be 'taken'" (Shaw 1996, p. A11).

Added to this was the need for competitiveness in a burgeoning information-entertainment industry. Negative news sells newspapers, and the press operates to "give people what they need—and while few people say they want or need more cynicism, the cynicism continues to mount" (Shaw 1996, p. A11).[2] Competitiveness means that the press relies not just on Associated Press stories and their own sources. In some cases, they use "reputable advocacy groups that news organizations know they can trust" (Randolph 1996, p. A5). However, the use of these secondary sources leaves newspapers open to influence peddling. But influence peddling does not stop there. Some education reporters judge the newsworthiness of stories by the number of phone calls they get on a subject, and others develop stories simply because the personalities are interesting (see, for example, Routman 1996 for a discussion of a *20/20* program on whole language and Distar).

In sum, the context and operational mode of the press can result in information coverage that is less information than disinformation. Given the climate of conservativism that exists today, the Henny Penny style of press coverage on whole language is probably not surprising. What is surprising is that, like Henny Penny, the press left out some evidence for a competing explanation of events. It is to the coverage of whole language and this alternate evidence that I now turn.

What a Bump on the Head Did to the Henny Penny Press

The performance of schools on standardized tests forced politicians to confront difficult questions asked by constituents. For the press, test performance was the "bump on the head" that created the opportunity for a story. Negative news sells, so the press set out on its journey to create their post-Vietnam, post-Watergate story. Their coverage, which might be considered a textbook Henny-Penny reaction, was marked by a number of fallacies that are reviewed below. Not only did the press raise a false hue and cry, as Henny Penny did, but it also appeared to be suffering all the symptoms of the mild concussion Henny Penny must surely have endured when the acorn hit her.

Dizziness (or Loss of Balance)

For the press, the acorn of testing always has been powerful and, in the United States, rarely questioned. So it should be no surprise that when the press was hit with the acorn of testing, it suffered one of the classic symptoms of concussion: loss of balance. The loss of balance manifested itself in numerous ways, but three are noteworthy.

SOURCES FOR STORIES From December 1994 to May of 1997, more than twenty stories about whole language and phonics appeared in five major U.S. newspapers: the *Christian Science Monitor,* the *Los Angeles Times,* the *New York Times,* the *Wall Street Journal,* and the *Washington Post.*[3] To state that the overall collective tone of these articles was anti–whole language does not begin to reveal the lopsided reporting that characterized the coverage.[4] One way to provide more definition to the slanted reporting is to consider the sources journalists cited in their reports.

An examination of who the spokespeople were for each position in this collection of articles is revealing. As the table on the facing page illustrates, the sources represented a range of positions, from whole language supporters (WL+), to those opposed to whole language and in favor of phonics (WL-), to those who argued for a balanced approach, to those who were eclectic and argued for a mixed approach, to those who were neutral in their comments. What is striking is that the most frequently cited sources against whole language were those with some political motivation (Group A in the table). Those in Group B, the presidents of reading associations, may also have been motivated in part by their political desire to represent the interests of their association. In Group C, consisting of people in various tiers of educational management and bureaucracy, opinion appears more dispersed. However despite allegations of the widespread use of whole language, reporters presented more teachers who were negative than positive toward the movement. This is another sign of imbalance.

Positions of Spokespeople Cited in Newspaper Reports

Category	WL+	WL-	Balance	Mixed	Neutral
Group A					
Politicians/political aides	0	13	0	0	1
Lobbyists	0	9	0	0	0
School board members	0	3	3	0	0
Group B					
President of reading associations	0	3	0	0	0
Group C					
State dept. bureaucrats	0	5	2	1	0
School district officials	1	0	1	1	0
Principals and asst. principals	0	2	0	1	0
Group D					
Teachers	5	9	0	4	0
Parents	1	2	0	0	0
Students	3	1	0	0	0
Group E					
Professors	14	10	1	0	1
Group F					
Directors of institutes	0	1	0	1	0
Publishers	0	1	1	1	0
Consultants	1	0	0	1	0
Tutors	0	1	1	0	0

A more subtle sign of imbalance is hidden by statistics for Group E, professors. Although there appear to be more instances of academics speaking out on behalf of whole language, this hides an imbalance. Of the ten citations credited to professors negative toward whole language, seven different professors were involved. However, in the fourteen citations positive toward whole language, ten came from one source, Ken Goodman. By quoting Goodman almost exclusively in support of whole language, reporters implicitly made the case that there was not widespread academic support for it. This position would have been undercut if these reporters had explored the academic literature on the subject.

Tendency to Keep Falling to One Side The amount of space the press gave to reporting the positions of each side of the whole language–phonics debate highlights their tendency to keep falling toward one side in their reportage. This can be demonstrated quite effectively by counting up the number of words directly or indirectly attributed to those cited as spokespeople in reports.

Of the 5,668 words directly or indirectly attributed to others discussing the whole language and phonics issues, only 24 percent (1,343 words) of the comments are positive toward whole language; 61 percent (3,457 words) are negative toward whole language or are in favor of phonics, 9 percent (509 words) argue for a balanced approach to language instruction, another 4 percent (241 words) support mixed views, and 2 percent (118 words) appear neutral. Again, given the alleged pervasiveness of whole language, the statistics reveal the lopsided position of the press.

WORD CHOICES Sometimes the concussed can come out with unexpected words or phrases that reflect their pain, astonishment, or confusion. Their comments can take on an emotional tone. Here again, the Henny Penny press is no exception. The imagery evoked in the discussions of reading portrayed it as a war (see, for example, Goodale 1997) or a "battle for the souls of children" (Stein 1995, p. 3). In one article, the Superintendent of Public Instruction was portrayed as a "no-nonsense field general, marshalling her troops for an assault," ordering up "a strategic battle plan," giving "marching orders," and awaiting "the attack [that] has yet to be launched . . . against the costly enemy of illiteracy" (Colvin 1996e, p. A3). Either explicitly or implicitly, the enemy to be fought was whole language.

The following are other examples of the imbalance of the press regarding whole language:

- Articles imply that whole language does not include attentiveness to sound-symbol relationships. For example, one article, in describing a move away from whole language, stated, "What's being proposed is not something new but something old, a return to teaching reading by emphasizing phonics and spelling" (Progress by looking 1995, p. B8).
- They imply that children who learn how to read using whole language will not have learned basic skills (an impossibility, since basic skills are what enable reading in the first place). For example, an education advisor was quoted in one article as saying, "You need the foundational skills as well as the applied skills" (Di Marco cited in Stein 1995, p. 3). Another article dubs the ABC bill in California an "unapologetic endorsement of basic skills" (Colvin 1995b, p. A3). (California's ABC bill is a law mandating the teaching of phonics and spelling.)
- They imply that whole language is extreme. For example, an assemblywoman said in one article, "What we're hoping to do is return to the middle and not let the pendulum swing wildly one way or another" (Alpert cited in Stein 1995, p. 3).

These examples suggest just a few of the ways the articles condemned whole language by implication.

Forgetfulness

Another classic symptom that the Henny Penny press exhibited after its bump on the head was that of forgetfulness. The press seemed to treat the coverage of stories as isolated incidents rather than a complex set of inter-relationships.

MINDLESS OVER MONEY In proffering explanations for the performance of children on tests, the press isolated its explanations to those that were convenient to its closest sources (lobbyists such as Marion Joseph, opportunist politicians, right-wing conservatives). For instance, the language arts framework that was adopted in California in 1987 (and that was sometimes mentioned in the articles as synonymous with whole language, even though it wasn't) was deemed to be ineffective. Two issues that clearly were linked to the success of the framework were the amount of in-servicing that teachers had on the framework and the literature available for a curricular framework whose basis was literature. Both of these issues relate to the general financial support of schools.

In a September 13, 1995, report that considered whether whole language was implicated in the performance of young Californians on tests, the reporter noted, as a minor detail, that a California government official attributed the problem with whole language not to whole language per se but to the fact that only 2 percent of teachers were exposed to whole language principles through in-service sessions. This limited amount of in-service over the eight years since the publication of the language arts framework was shameful and probably worthy of investigation, but this issue was forgotten as the press fell under the spell of other explanations and set about to create its own story of war complete with heroes and villains (see, for example, Colvin 1995a).

A story that got slightly more play was that of the impossibility of achieving success with a program dependent on literature when the state drastically underfunded school libraries. Again, I turn to an article by Richard Lee Colvin, this time on the poor state of school libraries in California (Colvin 1996d). In this article he stated that California ranks fiftieth in the nation in librarians per pupil, that its libraries have about thirteen books per pupil, and that 85 percent of these were published thirty years ago. However, Colvin seems to have forgotten this issue when he reported on the reading performance of children in the state. Some reporters in other jurisdictions (for example, Stein 1995) and even the editors of the *Los Angeles Times,* Colvin's own paper, at least began to look at such issues as California's low spending in relation to the move back to phonics. However, it seems that it is left up to the readers of Colvin's paper to remind him that there might be a connection between the lack of resources for libraries and children's reading (see Perez in Steinberger, Ary, Klein, and Perez 1996, p. M4). Colvin conveniently forgot the issue until he reported on the response to the new reading policy announced by the state (Colvin 1996f); even then he cast the information about state underfunding as a response of whole language critics.

AN ABSENCE OF PHONICS FLASHBACKS Another amnesiac response by the press in the articles I examined was in the general area of phonics. Despite its coverage of the Federal Trade Commission's concerns about "Hooked on Phonics," a commercial phonics program (see, for example, Gateway Educational 1994; Nathans 1994; Walsh 1994, 1995), articles that lauded the benefits of phonics made no mention of the overextension of the claims made by the manufacturer of this program. In fact, in an explicit gesture that echoed the title of this commercial product, one newspaper report headline read, "As Reading Scores Plummet, States Get Hooked on Phonics" (Walters 1996). In this case, at least, the forgetting of past reportage was quite dramatic.

Confusion

Another classic symptom of mild concussion is confusion. The mix-ups cited below are not comprehensive, but are merely illustrative.

HOW BIG IS WHOLE LANGUAGE? Numerous reports of the level of use of whole language peppered the news articles surveyed. Many articles contained comments suggesting that whole language was in use on a national scale (Goodale 1997, p. 10; O'Harrow, Jr. 1994, p. B2; 1995, p. 10; Sanchez 1996, p. A20), while other reports restricted their discussion to the pervasiveness of whole language in particular states (for example, Welsh 1995, p. C4). However, in none of these articles were statistics provided to document the implicit or explicit claims. In 1995, whole language advocates estimated that about 20 percent of teachers were using whole language (Hornstein and Murphy 1995). In 1997, the Whole Language Umbrella, an organization of educators using whole language, was surveyed; members' estimates of the proportion of whole language teachers in their schools was approximately 21 percent, not far from the earlier estimate (Murphy and Dudley-Marling 1997).

Why, then, did the reporters overstate the use of whole language? There is an explanation that might justify their confusion. That explanation lies in the opportunistic character of textbook publishers. Many basal reading companies, when confronted with reports critical of their materials in the late 1980s (Goodman, Shannon, Freeman, and Murphy 1988) quickly began to advertise their materials as "whole language" even though they did not fit the description (see, for example, Shannon and Goodman 1994). Given the press's tendency to superficially cover stories, their characterization of national trends might be expected.

However, there is another part of the reportage on incidence level that is much more perplexing. Over and over again, reporters mentioned the numerous teachers who never adopted whole language and who were practicing phonics "underground" (see, for example, California Leads 1996; Colvin 1995a, 1995b; Goodale 1997; O'Harrow, Jr. 1995; Sanchez 1996; Steinberger in Steinberger et al. 1996; Walters 1996; Welsh 1995). What the reporters of these stories never caught on to is the contradiction between their characterization of whole language as a national phenomenon and all of these subversive teachers. Furthermore, most failed to make the link between the maintenance of old-style methods and the student performance on test scores that they, and others, were so quick to blame on whole language.

None of the reporters made the distinction between written policy documents (such as that of California) and the length of time it takes to turn policy into practice, even though, in some instances, these reporters were covering stories about the implementation problems for the phonics initiatives in California (for example, Colvin 1996a, 1996c, 1996e). And only one reporter hinted at the resistance of teachers to having their professional practice dictated:

> But whole language can hardly take the whole rap for reading failures. Clever teachers, adept at finessing the fads administrators foist on them, have taken what was good about whole language—the emphasis on stories that capture a child's interest—and added it to their repertoire. (Welsh 1995, p. C4)

Finally, as the table in this chapter suggests, if there are a lot of whole language teachers out there, they aren't being interviewed by the press. So reporters are either unable to find whole language teachers, or they must admit to lopsided reporting.

How Long Has This Been Going On? Most news reports tied the length of time that whole language has influenced education on the "national scale" to the publication in 1987 of the California literature framework policy document. This conceptualization largely ignored the thorny process of the implementation of policy and gave readers the erroneous impression that the policy was fully implemented immediately. Even more surprising is the reporters' failure to challenge some of the sources they quoted as to the accuracy of the duration of whole language education. For instance, Colvin (1996h) failed to question the statement of a senior official in the governor's office who said, "We've now seen two generations of failure with the old system" (p. A1). This statement could relate to progressive education as a whole, but the focus of the article is on phonics. With the statement neither questioned nor clarified, the result is not only confusing reporting but a misled public. (The fact is, whole language has not existed for the "two generations" mentioned by the governor's spokesperson.)

WHEN IS REPORTING NOT REPORTING? Another source of confusion that appears to have struck the educational press is its partisanship in reporting. Everyone knows that some papers are known to be conservative while others are more liberal. However, even within this context, there seems to be an unspoken protocol about how explicit any partisanship might be. Yet in the case of the reporting on whole language I examined in detail, one reporter so blurred the line between reportage and partisanship that he indulged in writing a feature length human interest piece on Marion Joseph, a phonics lobbyist (Colvin 1995a). In this piece, the reporter glorified Joseph's lobbying of the press, her advance briefing of participants in a California Board of Education meeting (she is now an appointed member), and her positioning of herself as a near prophet, "'a voice crying in the wilderness'" (p. E2).

Blurring of Vision

Associated with loss of balance, forgetfulness, and confusion for those suffering from concussions is the associated symptom of blurring, and occasional loss, of vision. The Henny Penny press exhibited this symptom with respect to several issues.

FINDING ONLY FOORMAN Despite the thousands of reading research articles that are published annually and the many that are published on phonics and whole language in particular, the press's vision was so blurred that it could find only one research study, and that one had not even been published. Barbara Foorman's study generated the headline "Phonics is best aid for reading, study shows" (Colvin 1996b) (see Chapter 1). Studies such as that of Dahl and Freppon (1995), published in a respected journal, *Reading Research Quarterly,* were ignored. Even Foorman rejected that characterization of her study but her rejection has been ignored (letter to *Toronto Globe and Mail,* March 10, 1997).

MISSING CONNECTIONS Not seeing some things at all was another characteristic of the press's blurred vision. Reporters failed to recognize that several of the advocates that they were using as spokespeople in support of phonics programs were authors of commercial phonics-based programs. The second missed connection, again by all reporters, was the opportunism of textbook publishers in the late 1980s when they labeled their programs whole language programs even though researchers demonstrated that the programs fell far short of the mark (Shannon and Goodman 1994).

A third connection was not missed by all reporters (I suppose some have harder heads than others): the connection between the far right and the attack on whole language. Some, like Robert O'Harrow, Jr. (1995), not only quoted from whole language researchers and theorists but also demonstrated evidence of independent reporting, quoting from documents that demonstrated an explicit link between the attack on whole language and the agenda of the far right. In a 1995 article, for instance, O'Harrow identified R. W. Sweet, president of the National Right to Read Foundation, as a former official in both the Reagan and Bush administrations and quoted from an article Sweet published in his group's magazine to demonstrate that their agenda involves controlling schools. Sanchez (1996) also tried to broaden the analysis of the attack on whole language. Other reporters (for example, Stein 1995) quoted whole language researchers and theorists in such a way that they appear to be arguing about reading rather than simply explaining. The quotes often made those who said them sound not only defensive but even a little paranoid.

Where Is a Fox When You Need One?

Henny Penny, with the bump on her head, set about gathering up her friends to tell them that the sky was falling. The Henny Penny press was no different. Goosey Loosey, in the form of the *20/20* television program ("Direct Instruction" October 13, 1995) on Distar and whole language, joined the Henny Penny press, followed by Ducky Lucky, in the guise of *Parents* magazine, with its article "Parents Report on America's Reading Crisis: Why the Whole-Language Approach to Teaching Has Failed Millions of Children" *(Parents* 1996, p. 63). And of course, Turkey Lurkey, also known as *Better Homes and Gardens,* added to the chorus by asking "Whatever Happened to Dick and Jane?" (Berryhill 1997). I could add to this list, but the list itself is not important. What is important is the manner in which the media, in their post-Vietnam, post-Watergate state, jumped onto the bandwagon without doing a deeper investigation of the story.

In the Henny Penny tale, a fox steps out into the path of Henny Penny and friends to tell them that there is a shorter way to the palace of the king and proceeds to lure the mindless troop into a cave. Together with the rest of his family, the fox literally enjoys his new friends for supper. In the whole language tale, there is no fox. Neither does there seem to be a physician standing by to tell the members of the press how they should take care of a concussion. Instead, it is left to those in the educational community to take up the challenge of helping Henny Penny see the acorn for what it is and the symptoms of the concussion for what they are and to take note that the blue sky still hangs overhead. In short, educators must do what they know best—educate. First, we must educate ourselves about how to gain a voice in the press. Cultivating a relationship with reporters, creating news releases that present information in such a way that neither marginalizes the message nor results in the relinquishing of principles, and sustaining contacts are the kinds of strategies that lobbyists use effectively to communicate their message. Beyond this, we must remind ourselves and others of the potential—and the harm—that schooling offers. Linda Brodkey (1996) tells us what is at stake when regulation replaces education: "I was not taught to read in the first grade, but was instead taught to unlearn how I already read by a well-meaning and dedicated teacher authorized by the state to regulate my reading" (p. 40). To avoid a return to the reading classes of Brodkey's childhood, we must work not just with our immediate stakeholders; we must also work with the press so that when it gets bumped on the head the next time, it will pause, look about, and see the acorn for what it is.

Endnotes

1 The United States suffered a similar setback in the 1950s when the Soviets launched Sputnik, except that on that occasion the rhetoric was that the United States was lagging behind the Soviets in the sciences and technology.

2 It seems an ultimate irony here that even the press's coverage of itself has to be negative before it becomes news.

3 The number was obtained by searching the National Newspaper Index on June 30, 1997, using the descriptors "whole language" and "phonics." Over twenty items were listed. These included regular staff, AP, or byline articles; several editorials; one tribute to Marion Joseph; and one op-ed piece written by G. Reid Lyon. I excluded the editorials, tribute, and op-ed pieces from my analysis, since these pieces were not direct reports of the whole language versus phonics debate.

4 There are two notable exceptions to this characterization. One is O'Harrow, Jr. (1995), who, despite momentary lapses, attempts to present a more complex and broad-based analysis than other columnists. The other is Matthews (1996), who

presents a story that whole language, not the computer, is responsible for the academic turnaround of a school in Union City, New Jersey.

References

Berryhill, A. 1997. Whatever Happened to Dick and Jane? The Debate Between Whole Language and Phonics. *Better Homes and Gardens* (February): 50, 52, 54.

Brodkey, L. 1996. *Writing Permitted in Designated Areas Only.* Minneapolis: University of Minnesota Press.

California Leads Revival of Teaching by Phonics. 1996. *New York Times* (May 22): B8.

Colvin, R. L. 1995a. Her Best Subject. *Los Angeles Times* (November 19): E1, E2.

———. 1995b. School Goals Spelled Out in "ABC Bill." *Los Angeles Times* (July 5): A3, A12.

———. 1995c. State Report Urges Return to Basics in Teaching Reading. *Los Angeles Times* (September 13): A1, A24.

———. 1995d. State's Reading, Math Reforms Under Review as Scores Fall. *Los Angeles Times* (March 23): A1, A21.

———. 1996a. Delay on State Reading Policy Provokes Anger. *Los Angeles Times* (May 10): A1, A26, A27.

———. 1996b. Phonics Is Best Aid for Reading, Study Shows. *Los Angeles Times* (May 4): A1, A20.

———. 1996c. Pivotal Skirmish Nears in State Battle over Phonics. *Los Angeles Times* (December 11): A3, A34.

———. 1996d. School Libraries Shelved Amid Neglect. *Los Angeles Times* (April 21): A1, A22, A23.

———. 1996e. School Still Waiting for New Reading Plan. *Los Angeles Times* (January 22): A1, A14.

———. 1996f. State Board OKs Reading Policy Based on Phonics. *Los Angeles Times* (May 11): A20, A21.

———. 1996g. State Embraces Phonics in Approving New Texts. *Los Angeles Times* (December 13): A1, A29.

———. 1996h. Wilson Ties Offer of School Funds to Use of Phonics. *Los Angeles Times* (May 7): A1, A20.

———. 1997. Trouble in the Mecca of Reading. *Los Angeles Times* (May 5): A1, A28.

Dahl, K. L., and P. A. Freppon. 1995. A Comparison of Innercity Children's Interpretations of Reading and Writing Instruction in the Early Grades in Skills-Based and Whole Language Classrooms. *Reading Research Quarterly* 30, 1: 50–74.

Duff, C. 1996. ABCeething: How Whole Language Became a Hot Potato in and out of Academia. *Wall Street Journal* (October 30): A1, A10.

Foorman, B. R., D. J. Francis, T. Beeler, D. Winikates, and J. M. Fletcher. 1997. Early Interventions for Children with Reading Problems: Study Designs and Preliminary Findings. *Learning Disabilities: A Multidisciplinary Journal* 8, 1: 63–71 (Winter).

Galdone, P. 1968. *Henny Penny.* New York: Clarion Books.

Gateway Educational Settles FTC Charges of Misleading Claims. 1994. *Wall Street Journal* (December 15): B6.

Goodale, G. 1997. Word Wars. *Christian Science Monitor* (January 7): 10.

Goodman, K. S., P. Shannon, Y. S. Freeman, and S. Murphy. 1988. *Report Card on Basal Readers.* Katonah, NY: Richard C. Owen.

Hornstein, S., and S. Murphy. 1995. Open Letter to ABC News (October 30). Web site http://130.63.218.180:80/~WLU/ABC_lttr.htm or http:www.edu.yorku.ca/~WLU/.

It's Time for California to Open the Book on Phonics. 1996. *Los Angeles Times* (December 12): B8 (editorial).

Larson, D. E. 1990. *Mayo Clinic Family Healthbook.* New York: Morrow.

Matthews, J. 1996. NJ School's High-Tech Myth. *Washington Post* (June 22): A1, A14.

Murphy, S., and C. Dudley-Marling. 1997. Whole Language: Is There Anybody Out There? *Talking Points* 9, 1: 21–26.

Nathans, A. 1994. Hooked on Phonics Settles with FTC on Advertising Claims. *Los Angeles Times* (December 15): A48.

O'Harrow, Jr., R. 1994. Phonics Getting the Hook in Reading Class. *Washington Post* (June 23): B1, B2.

———. 1995. Wrangling About Reading. *Washington Post Educational Review* (November 5): 10, 19.

Parents Report on America's Reading Crisis: Why the Whole-Language Approach to Teaching Has Failed Millions of Children. 1996. *Parents* (October): 63–68.

Progress by Looking to the Past. 1995. *Los Angeles Times* (September 14): B8 (editorial).

Randolph, E. 1996. News Organizations' Use of Outside Research: The Inside Story. *Los Angeles Times* (April 17): A5.

The Right Direction for Reading. 1996. *Los Angeles Times* (May 9): B8 (editorial).

Routman, R. 1996. *Literacy at the Crossroads: Crucial Talk About Reading, Writing, and Other Teaching Dilemmas.* Portsmouth, NH: Heinemann.

Sanchez, R. 1996. California School Sounds Out Change. *Washington Post* (March 17): A1, A20.

Shannon, P., and K. Goodman, eds. 1994. *Basal Readers: A Second Look.* Katonah, NY: Richard C. Owen.

Shaw, D. 1996. A Negative Spin on the News. *Los Angeles Times* (April 17): A1, A10–A11.

Stein, L. 1995. Reading, Writing, and Phonics Coming Back to California Schools. *Christian Science Monitor* (July 11): 3.

Steinberg, J. 1997. Teaching Children to Read: Politics Colors Debate Over Methods. *New York Times* (May 11): 24.

Steinberger, M., C. Ary, D. Klein, and J. Perez. 1996. Whole Language, Phonics Methods. *Los Angeles Times* (January 28): M4 (letters to the editor).

Walsh, S. 1994. FTC: Phonic Hook Is Misleading. *Washington Post* (December 15): B17, B24.

———. 1995. FTC Seeks to End "Phonics" Fight. *Washington Post* (June 3): C2.

Walters, L. S. 1996. As Reading Scores Plummet, States Get Hooked on Phonics. *Christian Science Monitor* (April 18): 1, 4.

Welsh, P. 1995. Why a 12th-Grader Can't Read: Blame Fads, Fear of Phonics and Frenzied Schedules. *Washington Post* (November 26): C1, C4.

Bess Altwerger brings us back to a central reality: there are no reading wars; this is not a battle for phonics and against whole language. The goal is "to discredit, control, and privatize American public schools." Whole language is a visible and highly successful target, with great support among professionals but without a political base on the local or national scene.

All of the logic, facts, and theoretical soundness professionals can muster are, in the end, essentially irrelevant to the attacks and the attackers. And the arguments about whole language distract the public from the real issues of education in North America. Altwerger summarizes the underlying agenda of the attacks. "Lies, distortions, money, media, and political power" are the means used to promote the agenda. Altwerger writes that whole language educators need to see their fight as part of a much broader political struggle and must find common cause with other groups in society who are involved in the broader issues of child welfare and democracy. She offers a series of actions concerned professionals can take.

10

Whole Language as Decoy: The Real Agenda Behind the Attacks

Bess Altwerger

Our purpose in this book is to discuss, analyze, and critique the most recent attacks on whole language and to develop a strategy for responding in a responsible and assertive manner. Many teachers and other professional educators are drawn to whole language as a pedagogy that best represents state-of-the-art knowledge concerning language and literacy development, so it would seem logical to use this knowledge as a primary resource in constructing our response to these attacks. And it is clearly necessary to do so when attacks against whole language appear in the press and in our school communities. It makes sense that like us, our critics would be swayed by the logic of a whole language framework once they are made aware of the research and theoretical basis of our position. And some of the most respected people in our field (such as Connie Weaver and Ken Goodman) have succeeded in packaging the reasons behind whole language practices in numerous books, articles, and monographs that communicate the message clearly to proponents and opponents alike.

But I argue that this academic approach will have only limited success in countering the attacks against whole language. Though being forced to defend our knowledge base may strengthen our own convictions and enlighten some genuinely concerned and confused parents that what we are doing is right for kids, we will never convince the more organized opposition if we use research and theory as our sole weapons. In fact, a virtual arsenal of conclusive evidence may prove impotent in deterring the attacks on whole language. That's because this is not a battle of reason, fact, or evidence. This is not even a battle over reading instruction, classroom pedagogy, or the literacy development of our children. The American political and religious right is simply using language and literacy as a convenient and convincing cover and whole language as a trendy rallying cry for their true agenda: to discredit, control, and privatize American public schools. They seek to perpetuate their historical role of preserving privilege and class in this country.

We in education have been politically naive to believe that with the right evidence, the definitive study, and the persuasive publication we will convince our opposition and quell the attacks. Clearly, the Right has been much more adept than the whole language community at recognizing and then using literacy as the political tool it is in this country.

While many whole language educators have tried to deny, ignore, or soften the political content and implications of whole language pedagogy, even going so far as suggesting that we try to win over the political and religious right through communication, understanding, and a kinder, gentler political rhetoric, the Right has marched forward in the battle to control schools. But we whole language educators, who believe in the right of all children to learn and participate in a democratic process, can no longer close our eyes to the political realities of our work. My goal here is to begin a dialogue about the not-so-hidden agenda of whole language opponents, and place this agenda within the larger political struggle over race, class, and privilege in this country. I will pose the following questions:

1. Who or what is really behind the reactionary attacks on whole language?
2. Why is whole language an easy target for these attacks?
3. What should the position of the whole language movement be in responding to these attacks?
4. What can whole language educators do to fight the attacks?

Let's begin with the first question: Who or what is really behind the attacks on whole language? Many believe that the instigators are a sincere, if misguided, group of worried and frightened parents reacting to instructional practices that are unfamiliar and alien to their own school experiences and who just want their children to learn to read. If this were the case our mission would be easy. Our strategy would simply be to educate and communicate. But this is not the case. Though there are, of course, a good many people who fit this description and deserve our attention, they do not constitute the true force behind the attacks. Rather, they serve simply as the prey of a highly organized and powerful reactionary movement against public education and the disenfranchised populations of our society who can most benefit from public education. It is a carefully orchestrated and thinly veiled effort to wage an American-style class and ethnic cleansing campaign, beginning with the public schools as the primary and most vulnerable battleground. A willing media effectively uses distorted test data and outright scare tactics to convince the public that America's public schools are rapidly deteriorating and that the problem lies in newfangled teaching practices, incompetent teachers, and liberal, out-of-touch teacher educators. Though there is no evidence that whole language practices have any deleterious effect whatsoever on literacy development, or even that literacy rates are actually on the decline, these efforts have become a highly effective way to deflect focus away from the real problems facing our schools and the real goals of the reactionaries. While we engage in efforts to defend whole language, we must not allow ourselves to lose sight of the real problems facing public education:

- The United States falls far below other industrialized nations in expenditures for public education (Berliner and Biddle 1995).
- There is a huge discrepancy in per-student expenditures among states, and among school districts within states, and this discrepancy is directly linked to income level (Kozol 1991).
- The nation's poorest student population is growing even poorer, with less access to health care and decent living conditions.
- Linguistic and ethnic minorities comprise a disproportionately high percentage of the poorest income group in society.
- The percentage of uncertified teachers is higher in poorer, needier school districts, in states such as California. In Los Angeles in 1996, the percentage of uncertified teachers was up to 60 percent (see Chapter 1).

Though the Right would have us believe that the United States outspends other nations to support public education, this is simply untrue. According to David Berliner and Bruce Biddle (1995), the United States ranks sixteenth among other industrialized nations in per-capita expenditures for public school students. The fact is, education is grossly underfinanced in this, one of the wealthiest countries in the world. And sadly, this doesn't even begin to tell the whole horror story. Jonathan Kozol's book *Savage Inequalities* (1991) confirmed what every teacher in every inner-city school has always known, the most hideous and shameful fact of all: our poorest communities, our neediest schools, are funded at levels far, far below that of more affluent, suburban, and whiter communities. Some school districts in this country are funded at levels comparable to some undeveloped and third-world countries. Mississippi, for example, according to data reported in Berliner and Biddle, is comparable to Jordan in per-student expenditure. And who are the students who attend these schools? The children of the working poor, families living below the poverty line, families that struggle for survival. These are children of the disenfranchised of our country—people of color, ethnic minorities, documented and undocumented immigrants, linguistic minorities. These are the children who need and deserve our greatest educational resources. But as Berliner and Biddle point out, we continue to fail them:

> Rich people in the United States are able to buy some of the world's finest education for their children, either in private academies or in well-financed, suburban, public-school districts. In contrast,

children of the poor are often crowded into miserable rural or inner-city schools whose annual per-student support may be one-fifth or less of that in nearby suburban public schools. (Berliner and Biddle 1995, p. 58)

And the economic picture is becoming increasingly dismal for our nation's poorest; the income gap is growing steadily, and our nation's poor are growing in number. The *New York Times* recently reported that in 1995 about 14.7 million children, or 20.8 percent of all children in America, fell into the "poor" category. Rising expectations in the past are being replaced by hopelessness and despair for many students, as the wealthiest become still wealthier and the poorest become inconceivably poorer. Whereas the poor of the past were convinced that education was the key to the future, the poor of today are more wary of such dreams, especially when their schools reflect the impoverished conditions of their own communities. Their teachers, facing extraordinary challenges, are often uncertified nonprofessionals, working under "temporary" or "emergency" certificates, who have very little pedagogical knowledge or skill.

It is a credit to schools, teachers, and students that the public school system has survived as well as it has in the face of these enormous obstacles. Instead of being scorned and attacked, professional educators should be treated as our nation's heroes for persevering against such odds. It is truly absurd to think that whole language, or any approach for that matter, could possibly be responsible for the failures of public education; the issue of method, of approach, is simply a decoy, a cruel manipulation of a public with hopes and dreams for their children's futures.

What is the real agenda behind these attacks against whole language? When we look beyond our pedagogy to the larger political context, it becomes as clear as red, white, and blue:

- To convince the mainstream public (middle-class America) that public education (especially in poor communities) is beyond salvation and unworthy of federal support.
- To salvage only the wealthier school districts whose tax base adequately supports schools without federal assistance (in other words, create a class of "private" public schools for the well-off).
- To dismantle the public school system as we now know it and replace it with voucher systems (sold as "school choice"), which create an essentially subsidized private school system for the wealthy.
- To ensure the perpetuation and deepening of race and class divisions, which protect privilege and power for wealthy, white, conservative America.
- To create a third-world class of American poor denied government support for adequate health care, housing, and education.

These goals won't be achieved with weapons of destruction such as bombs and tanks, but with lies, distortions, money, media, and political power. The future it would create would mean a slow, inside-out genocide against the poor, minorities, and immigrant populations in this country, through denial of basic human rights such as health care, education, and decent housing. This vision is already becoming a reality in the most rapidly "browning" state in the country, California, through Propositions 187 and 209, and a series of twelve mean-spirited education laws. One of the most vicious attacks against whole language, literature-based instruction, bilingual education, and the "new-new" math is being waged in that state.

A smear campaign against public education is necessary in order to convince the white, middle-class population to turn its back on the American ideal of providing free, quality education for all, citizens and noncitizens alike. The stage has been set for vouchers, privatization, and an overall cutback in funding for education. With an end to racially or ethnically targeted scholarships and financial support, the dream of a college degree has all but disappeared for many marginalized people. And it doesn't stop here. Congress has passed, and President Clinton has signed, a welfare reform bill that drastically reduces subsistence support for women, infants, and children and all aid to noncitizens (even legal residents), including health care. Politicians would have us believe that state block grants would provide a safety net to those in need, but even the press acknowledges that there is no historical precedent for these assurances (*Baltimore Sun*, July 26, 1996).

As with the hysteria over public education, the media, increasingly controlled by corporate interests, have willingly supported the reactionary agenda. They continue to portray welfare recipients as the culprits behind the deficit, crime, and every other social ill in this society instead of focusing on profit-driven layoffs, the unavailability of free child care, and a failing health care system controlled by a greedy private insurance industry.

Those of us in education must see the attacks against whole language and other progressive pedagogies within the context of a much larger political struggle and not simply as a pedagogical disagreement over phonics or skills teaching. Why is the whole language movement the target of these attacks? Perhaps it is because, as a movement, we haven't placed the battle over literacy instruction squarely and directly within its political context. Unlike our political opponents, few in whole language have understood the fact that literacy and literacy instruction is intimately linked to political ideology, and positions on class, race, and gender. Few understand or acknowledge the fact that literacy in the United States has always functioned as a socioeconomic gatekeeper.

Most whole language educators, focusing only on what is best for their students, have been unaware of the political implications of their own pedagogical perspectives. In reality, whole language stands in total contradiction to the ideological position of the reactionary agenda—in its opposition to testing and tracking that systematically privileges particular social-cultural groups over others; in its opposition to authoritarian control over the content and processes of literacy and learning, which imposes particular forms of knowledge and views of the world over others; and, most important, in its theoretical premise that the knowledge, experiences, and sociocultural realities of all learners, rather than a select, privileged few, are valuable educational resources. It is the ideological and political content of whole language more than its classroom practices that the reactionaries find so threatening.

As long as we allow ourselves to engage solely in methodological debates over phonics, skills, and basals without directly addressing the real political struggle behind our pedagogy, we will continue to be vulnerable. Whole language is indeed the most theoretically appealing way to help kids attain literacy, but it is also liberatory, democratizing, and rich in transformative potential. In order to realize this potential, and to face our opponents with a unified political stance, we need to assert the following:

- Whole language educators stand for students' right to learn, and also for the human, social, and political rights of all people in this society.
- Whole language educators stand for democratic classroom communities, but also for a democratic and just national community intolerant of racism, classism, and sexism.
- Whole language educators stand for free, equitable, and high-quality public education for all students living in our nation.

In asserting openly and publicly our political stance, we will then be in the position to take some decisive action. What can whole language educators do to fight these attacks? First, we must consider the question of how we project ourselves as a movement. Do we seem more concerned with attracting teachers and parents to a pedagogical perspective than in stimulating serious dialogue concerning cultural, racial, and political issues facing education and society today? Do we need to grow in our own ability to provide people of diverse political, ethnic, racial, and linguistic backgrounds voice, presence, and influence in the movement? Do our regional and national conference programs reflect and address the diversity of the communities, students, and teachers it serves? If we are united in favor of critical, democratic, and equitable education for all children, this must be reflected in conference programs, initiatives, publications, media coverage.

But we cannot respond effectively to the real agenda behind the attacks without reaching beyond the movement itself. We need to form alliances with parents and community members in order to fight the attacks against high-quality public education. We need to inform others about the current injustices and inequities in education, and those we will face in the future should our opponents succeed.

The following are ten strategies for action that whole language educators should consider in responding to attacks:

1. Form coalitions with parents and community organizations.
2. Use the media to expose inequities and injustices.
3. Offer educational forums to the community.
4. Pressure unions and professional organizations to act.
5. Run support candidates for local school board elections.
6. Address issues in TAWL (Teachers Applying Whole Language) newsletters and distribute such accounts widely.
7. Become active in PTAs and discuss issues of concern.
8. Form coalitions with and join other educational organizations, such as the NCEA (National Coalition of Educational Activists).
9. Stay informed of educational struggles through such publications as *Rethinking Schools*.
10. Demonstrate at board meetings to expose the attacks and defend public education.

Whole language educators can become a formidable movement opposed to a system that perpetuates privilege through testing, tracking, and mandated curriculum and that tolerates inequitable and insufficient funding. If we have the courage and determination to face the politics of our pedagogy we can expose the real agenda behind the reactionary attacks and promote the type of principled leadership this nation needs if we are to create a school system and society that is just, equitable, and humane.

References

Berliner, D. C., and B. J. Biddle. 1995. *The Manufactured Crisis: Myths, Fraud, and the Attack on America's Public Schools.* Reading, MA: Addison-Wesley.

Kozol, J. 1991. *Savage Inequalities: Children in America's Schools.* New York: Crown.

In this final chapter, Ellen Brinkley and Connie Weaver tell the story of their bringing together a group in Michigan to oppose the attacks on education, and offer this story as a model for concerned professionals who wish to organize opposition in their own areas. Based on their experiences, they present a series of issues to consider in forming and shaping such a group.

11

Organizing for Political Action: Suggestions from Experience

Ellen H. Brinkley and Constance Weaver

It didn't seem like a promising beginning. There were just a handful of us—educators, librarians, and friends—who met in Connie's living room on a crisp October night in 1994. We spent a lot of time telling each other disturbing stories about attacks being waged on public education in our state. Some of us were particularly concerned with curricular issues. For example, we knew that while teaching language skills in the context of their use is more effective than teaching them in isolation, in various Michigan communities there was (and is) a push for teaching skills first and in isolation, through phonics programs, spelling books, and grammar books. We were aware of attempts—all too often successful—to oust good literature from classrooms and school libraries. We had heard parents at public hearings say that while all men are created equal, some cultures are, well, better than others, and should form the basis of the school curriculum. We knew that a state legislator had called an emphasis on multicultural diversity "a bunch of garbage." Others of the group had experienced the attempted takeover of a school board by far-right individuals in their community. We knew the chilling effects on teaching and learning that often follow such takeovers. Eventually we talked about how public education is denounced by politicians and the media, despite substantial evidence of the success of public schools. All in all, it was a pretty depressing evening.

But some of us had been involved with state and local education projects and issues or with local politics long enough not to be afraid of rolling up our sleeves and at least trying to do something that might make a positive difference. We live in a state where the governor and the far right routinely bash teachers as being more concerned about paychecks than about kids. We wondered if maybe one reason K–12 teachers feel so under siege is that there hasn't been a broad support group that could articulate the issues without being perceived as having another agenda. Call us naively optimistic if you like, but we were pretty sure that we knew a lot more about real teaching and learning than many of those who have the power to make major decisions about how and what children will be taught. So before we left that night we decided to form a group that would try to support and strengthen public education. Now, three years later, we have Michigan for Public Education (MPE), a tax-exempt, grassroots organization (donations to which are tax deductible) that we think has begun to make a difference for public education. We also have a World Wide Web site.

How did we get from there to here? We would like to share some of our steps and missteps with you, in the form of suggestions. All of what we've accomplished, and probably more, could be accomplished in a year by a small group of dedicated individuals who have full-time jobs and more obligations besides! (It took us a year and a half, but you could avoid some of our floundering.) We know that every group has to think through the issues and purposes for themselves, but we hope these suggestions, based on our experience, can be adapted to help you too become a politically active force in your state and/or community.

1. *Don't think you need a cast of thousands to begin.* Start with a handful of people and coffee and cookies in someone's living room. We discovered that big isn't always better. We tried at first to enlist friends and acquaintances in an effort to involve as many community members as we could in our meetings. That was a mistake. Although many people care and are concerned about public education, few can or will devote their time, talents, and passion to supporting it. (Don't be disheartened; instead, think of all the good causes that you yourself are able to support in spirit only.) Then too, every time new people came to a meeting, we had to start all over explaining what we were trying to do. Fortunately, after a few months of inviting a variety of people and (wisely) soliciting advice from locally prominent leaders, we evolved into a small active, committed group that could get down to the business of doing the work that needed to be done.

2. *Work together to decide your purpose, and develop a mission statement.* In our case, the process was every bit as important as the product. It gave us the chance to better understand our own and each other's concerns, to get to know and trust one another, and to determine what we as a group cared about the most. After venting our feelings about what we were against, we worked to frame our mission statement in terms of what we are for. At some point in our deliberations we discovered, for example, that our concerns were primarily focused on issues across the state rather than just in our local area. A local corporate public relations director advised us to think big in choosing a name and to create a one-sentence version of the mission statement that could be quoted to reporters and others. Thus we boldly decided to call our group Michigan for Public Education and to describe it as a citizens' organization "advocating educational equality and excellence." (See our web page: <http://www.ashay.com/mpe>.)

3. *Don't be afraid to speak out about controversial topics; indeed, speak up boldly in public and get noticed, because the stakes are high.* Our

first public statements on behalf of Michigan for Public Education were made in the form of testimony at state Board of Education meetings, a forum in which both of us felt relatively comfortable. We have sometimes gone to testify at such meetings alone, but we encourage you to take others along for support and as a way to help them learn the ropes so they'll be ready when the opportunity arises. Incidentally, when you address a group such as the state Board of Education or the Senate or House Education Committee, take enough printed copies of your statement for each member, plus some for interested media persons. Speaking at such meetings can accomplish more than expressing views to board members or legislators. It can also increase your media recognition and lead to networking with other groups. If the organizers of your group live some distance from the state capital, as we do, you may want to empower one or more members to speak on your behalf at public meetings. We've tried preparing formal statements to be read, but this works only if the individual reading the statement is well enough informed to be comfortable reading the statement. Encouraging other group members to prepare and read their own statements at meetings empowers even more people to speak on behalf of public education.

4. *Be ready to expand your focus to include concerns of other groups and to network to achieve mutual goals.* We have found this to be critical to our burgeoning success. At first our concerns were mainly curricular, but our networking with other groups broadened our focus to include such topics as school funding, charter schools, vouchers, adult education, and proposed "parental rights" legislation (being proposed in national and state legislatures) that might allow parents to oust a variety of curricular practices and/or to demand vouchers for educating their children their own way.

One of the groups we began networking with is the Michigan Public Education Task Force, which includes representatives from teacher, administrator, and school board groups and unions, plus such groups as the League of Women Voters, the American Association of University Women, and the American Civil Liberties Union—all potentially powerful allies. In addition, we exchange mailings with other groups in the state and throughout the country that support public education, such as the Freedom to Learn network in Pennsylvania. By doing a presentation on MPE and its concerns and goals, we have even inspired the formation of sister groups in other states. We continue to draw on our MPE experience as we co-chair the planning for the National Congress for Public Education.

5. *Consider how you can best use your time and energy to be most effective.* In one sense we feel like we've already begun to do it all—that is, expand our membership, testify at board meetings and legislative hearings, write letters to the editor and viewpoint articles, speak on radio talk shows, and participate in local (and sometimes televised) panels on educational issues. But there are limits. For example, we talked about going to

Washington for the Stand for Children march but just couldn't fit it into our schedules. Now we're learning to draw upon each board member's particular talents and not expect everyone to do everything, and we're discovering our unique strengths as an organization and how best to use them.

6. *Consider the possibility that information may be your most powerful tool—and weapon.* We have concluded that one of the most important things we can do is use our professional skills to provide information, background, and perspectives on issues; to suggest resources for further information; and to recommend specific action. Ellen edits our bimonthly newsletter for members throughout the state, often focusing on an issue that's being discussed or decided at the state level, and sometimes including fact sheets that are short, to the point, and focused on specific topics. We encourage those on our mailing list to copy and distribute the newsletter and fact sheet materials. Though we're not a wealthy organization, we send complimentary mailings to selected reporters and media persons, members of the House and Senate Education Committees, members of the state Board of Education, and selected community and state leaders. We're not just being generous, for we realize that such dissemination of our materials is important if we want to influence public policy and the voters.

In addition to doing the newsletter, Ellen has prepared a hard-hitting summary of some of our concerns, "Michigan for Public Education—Why and Why Now?", which gives an overview of our stance on issues and provides talking points when we meet with groups. We both contributed to a flier on concerns about public education in Michigan that People for the American Way distributed to its statewide network of organizations, and Connie's fact sheets on public schools and charter schools have been distributed to over a hundred organizations through the Michigan Public Education Task Force. In addition, having gained credibility with this task force by preparing research-based materials on issues they care about, Connie is now beginning to disseminate her fact sheets on phonics, spelling, and grammar; others have been distributed by NCTE as SLATE Starter Sheets. Over a dozen are now available on Heinemann's World Wide Web page (http://www.heinemann.com) and published in *Creating Support for Effective Literacy Education,* co-authored by Connie and published in 1996 by Heinemann.

Another MPE member, Jean Williams, has established a World Wide Web page for us: <http://www.ashay.com/mpe>. This web page includes basic MPE documents, our newsletters, various fact sheets, and other related articles; all may be copied and used as needed. Another source of action-related information can be obtained for a fee: for $5 a month, People for the American Way will contact you (by phone, fax, e-mail, or pager) when action is most important on key legislative issues and, at your request, will send a letter or fax to your representative or senator on your behalf. To take advantage of this American Way Action Hotline, call 1-888-PFAW-ACT.

In short, by working with and supporting others in addressing broad concerns about public education, we are now in a position where we can begin to offer our perspective on curricular issues, supply information that others in turn can disseminate, and take action via the information highway. This is heady stuff. We realize that the disseminated information can influence voters if not always policymakers, and in the long run influencing voters may be public education's best hope in many localities and states.

7. *Agree among the leadership to allow individuals to initiate or take action without consulting the entire governing body.* This is a little scary, and indeed, we've been warned by one person experienced in the political scene that we should empower only *one* person to speak for the group. However, we've found that needed actions won't be taken if we have to consult every other person in our seven-member Board of Directors before taking action. For instance, with just a few days' notice we two discovered that the state Department and Board of Education was holding ten town meetings throughout the state to get input on public education. We figured that opponents of public schools and proponents of charter schools (which have essentially no public oversight in Michigan) might turn out in full force, so we needed to alert our members immediately. Ellen drafted an action alert, drew upon the "Michigan for Public Education—Why and Why Now?" statement to devise recommendations, and together we assembled two other sheets to send to members—all *before* we had consulted most of the other board members. We've come to understand one another and to trust each other's judgment—even if, once in a while, acting without everyone else's approval means we have to live with some action or statement with which someone is a little uncomfortable. This is simply the only way we can get much done.

8. *Share the public presentation tasks and the behind-the-scenes work as well.* All of our board members and several of our other members have actively represented the organization in a variety of formal and informal settings. For example, Pen Campbell, a strong parent activist and teacher but not yet an MPE board member, recently stepped in to help lead a session on advocating for public education at the Michigan Reading Association state conference. Over time we've come to enjoy the chance to speak to citizen and professional groups about public education in Michigan, where we encounter many people from all walks of life who share our concerns and our vision for strengthening public schools.

We share the behind-the-scenes work as well. For example, Ginny Little, a teacher and leader in on-line education, faithfully clips articles from state newspapers, providing research data that we can draw on as we produce materials; she also has taken the lead in obtaining financial support for MPE from foundations and corporations. All of us read stacks of reports from the Michigan Department of Education and publications from other state and national organizations. (Appendix B includes a list of helpful resources.)

As we read and research and write and speak, we find we're forced to refine our own thinking about the stands we want to take. And we discover the value of struggling to articulate our message to people who aren't in education, knowing that if we use expressions like "student-centered learning" and "critical pedagogy," our general audience will quickly tune us out.

9. *Consider what degree of formal organization you need in order to meet your goals.* Some of the first organizational details any group needs to take care of are quite basic: designing a letterhead, preparing a flier and membership form, opening a bank account, getting a post office box, and perhaps establishing a way to receive and send faxes. Even more important has been making personal connections and getting added to a variety of mail/e-mail/fax lists so that we can stay on top of current hot issues. All of these tasks emerged and evolved naturally as our group kept considering "What's next?"

At first you may not worry about a formal organizational structure. We went along for quite some time, in fact, without designating anyone as officers and without formally calling ourselves a Board of Directors. But when we got to the point of wanting to solicit members and membership dues, we realized that we needed to register as a nonprofit organization in Michigan—that is, we figured we'd better become legal. At about the same time, we concluded that we should apply to the IRS for 501(c)(3) tax-exempt status so that contributions to our organization would be tax deductible; this would allow us to begin to solicit grant support as well. It took almost a year between the time we came to this conclusion and the time we actually received our 501(c)(3) status: five months before we actually developed all the documents needed and decided how to fill out the forms (after all, we were busy being activists, too) and another six months from the time we submitted our application. The latter time span, we have since learned, is typical—perhaps even quick. A member put us in touch with an ACLU lawyer who responded to our questions about the incorporation and IRS forms and supplied some material we needed to include with the forms. In preparing the paperwork and documents for the IRS, one important thing we needed to do was develop a set of bylaws. Jean Williams, the librarian on our board, found books that could be used as a guide. As with so many other things, we found it was more efficient for one person to draft the paperwork and the group simply to make changes. (If you'd like to use our bylaws as a possible guide, fax your request to 616-327-5372, or write us at Michigan for Public Education, Box 1191, Portage, MI 49081-1191.)

In the process of applying for 501(c)(3) status, we found out that the primary purpose of such a group must be to educate through information. It's okay to admit you are advocating for public education, but you cannot promote any particular political candidate or spend more than 20 percent of your time and money trying to influence legislation directly. What you can do is disseminate information that will encourage people to act—for example, voters' guides that indicate the candidates' position on issues, the kind of guide distributed by the League of Women Voters, for instance. In developing your own organization, you might conclude that you need the flexibility to support political candidates, or even to run for office yourselves. In that case you may be eligible for 501(c)(4) tax-exempt status, but contributions to your group will not be tax deductible. Some organizations have 501(c)(3) status for part of their organization and 501(c)(4) for a branch that can then be overtly political. Your group will need to consider whether to apply for tax-exempt status at all and, if so, under what rubric, given what you need and want to do.

10. *Above all, make the decision to actually do something and follow through with your passion and commitment. Our slogan has become "Together we can make a difference!" And so can you.* We can't claim to be the voice in Michigan advocating equality and excellence in public education—not by a long shot. But we have become *a* voice. During a statewide teleconference, MPE board member Marianne Houston wasn't afraid to ask the state Board of Education president the tough questions, among them, "What evidence do you have that charter schools will improve public education?" To his irrelevant reply, she followed up with "You haven't answered my question." We needn't be antagonistic, but we must hold our elected officials responsible for policies and actions that have significant consequences in the lives of children and for a democratic society. We can do more than grumble about things we think we can't change. Instead, we encourage you to start thinking about whom you'll invite to that first living room meeting.

Appendix A: History and Goals

Michigan for Public Education began in the fall of 1994, when a group of educators, librarians, and other citizens began meeting to discuss their concerns about the attacks on public schools. At first, most of the concerns were curricular. Some members of the group knew that multicultural education was being threatened; some knew that effective teaching of phonics, spelling, and grammar in the context of reading and writing was being attacked as a departure from teaching "the basics"; some were especially aware of attempts to censor books and curricula dealing with a wide variety of topics, including critical thinking. All knew that in some school districts, a minority of parents and citizens had managed or at least tried to take control of the school board and/or the curriculum. All knew, too, that public education was being denounced by politicians and the media, despite substantial evidence for the successes of the public schools.

These concerns shaped the vision and primary mission of Michigan for Public Education: to research and disseminate accurate information regarding public education and effective teaching practices, and thereby to advocate for educational equality and excellence. More specifically, MPE's goals are to:

- support and strengthen public education;
- preserve First Amendment separation of church and state in the public schools, without censoring religion or denying its role in society;
- provide a challenging, quality education for *all* students.

We believe that a challenging, quality education will promote not only subject-matter knowledge but communication skills, critical and creative thinking, problem-posing and -solving, responsible decision-making, and civic responsibility. We further believe that education for the twenty-first century must demonstrate and promote democratic principles and respect for cultural pluralism.

Activities

Pursuit of these goals has involved MPE members in such activities as these:

- researching and disseminating information on current issues, such as charter schools and vouchers, state-level content standards, education in moral values
- publishing a bimonthly newsletter
- being interviewed by journalists and radio talk show hosts
- writing letters to the editor and viewpoint articles
- participating in panel discussions on education
- testifying before the state Board of Education and legislative committees on education
- speaking to professional, educational, and civic groups
- participating in the Michigan Public Education Task Force
- networking with other state and national groups having common goals
- fostering similar groups in other states

Donations to Michigan for Public Education are tax-deductible under IRS code 501(c)(3). MPE is registered as a nonprofit corporation with the Michigan Department of Commerce.

Michigan for Public Education Board of Directors
Ellen Brinkley, Penelope Campbell, Marianne Houston, Virginia Little, Connie Weaver, Jean Williams
P.O. Box 1191, Portage, MI 49081-1191, Fax 616-327-5372

Appendix B: Resources on the Radical Right, Education, and Religious Freedom in the Public Schools

Resource Manuals on Education

No Right Turn: Assuring the Forward Progress of Public Education, by Janet Jones (1993). Send $25 to: Washington Education Association, Instruction/Human Relations, Dept. jb, 3434, Eighth Avenue South, Federal Way, Washington, DC 98003.

The People's Cause: Mobilizing for Public Education. Rev. ed. fall 1995. Inquire of: National Education Association, Center for the Preservation of Public Education, 11201 Sixteenth Street NW, Washington, DC 20036, 202-822-7446; fax 202-822-7117.

Protecting the Freedom to Learn: A Citizen's Guide, by Donna Hulsizer. Washington, DC: People for the American Way, 1989. (Guidelines for combating censorship efforts.)

Books and Monographs on Public Education

Retarding America: The Imprisonment of Potential, by Paul Houston. Portland, OR: Halcyon House, an imprint of National Book, Division of Editorial Research Associates, 1993.

Exploding the Myths: Another Round in the Education Debate. Arlington, VA: American Association of School Administrators, 1993.

The Manufactured Crisis: Myths, Fraud, and the Attack on America's Public Schools, by David C. Berliner and Bruce J. Biddle. Reading, MA: Addison-Wesley, 1995.

Perceptions About American Education: Are They Based on Facts? by Glen Robinson and David Brandon. Arlington, VA: Educational Research Service, 1992.

Books, Surveys, Fact Sheets on the Issues

School Wars: Resolving Our Conflicts over Religion and Values, by Barbara B. Gaddy, T. William Hall, and Robert J. Marzano. San Francisco: Jossey-Bass, 1996.

Who Chooses? Who Loses? Culture, Institutions, and the Unequal Effects of School Choice, by Bruce Fuller and Richard F. Elmore. New York: Teachers College Press, 1996.

False Choices: Why School Vouchers Threaten Our Children's Future. A 32-page collection of articles. For a single copy, send $3 plus $2 postage to: Rethinking Schools, 1001 E. Keefe Avenue, Milwaukee, WI 53212, 414-964-9646; fax 414-964-7220.

American Families Speak: A Public Opinion Survey on the Christian Coalition's "Contract with the American Family." This study, conducted by Peter D. Hart Research Associates, refutes the Christian Coalition's claim of widespread public support. For a copy of this publication and a list of others available, contact: People for the American Way, 2000 M Street NW, Suite 400, Washington, DC 20036, 202-467-4999.

Fact Sheet on Vouchers. An 8-page summary, 1995–96; AFT item no. 111. For a free copy, contact: American Federation of Teachers, 555 New Jersey Avenue NW, Washington, DC 20001.

The Case Against School Vouchers, by Edd Doerr, Albert J. Menendez, and John M. Swomley, 1995. Concisely written and well documented. Send $10 (there is a reduced price for bulk orders) to: Americans for Religious Liberty, P.O. Box 6656, Silver Spring, MD 20916, 301-598-2447. Other titles available from Americans for Religious Liberty include:
Visions of Reality: What Fundamentalist Schools Teach (evidence that popular textbooks teach prejudice against other religions and cultures)
Why We Still Need Public Schools: Church/State Relations and Visions of Democracy
Religion and Public Education: Common Sense and the Law

Resource Manuals on Dealing with the Far Right in General

Challenging the Christian Right: The Activists' Handbook, by Frederick Clarkson and Skipp Porteous, 1993. Send $25 plus shipping and handling ($3.50 for the first item, $1.75 for each additional) to: Institute for First Amendment Studies, P.O. Box 589, Great Barrington, MA 01230, 413-274-3786. Various other titles are available, as is a newsletter, the *Freedom Writer.*

How to Win: A Practical Guide for Defeating the Radical Right in Your Community. New ed. Includes a CD of the information along with the manual. Send $25 to: National Jewish Democratic Council, 711 Second Street, Washington, DC 20002.

Other Sources of Information on Religious Freedom

Church and State. Monthly newsletter. Send $18 to: Americans United for the Separation of Church and State, 1816 Jefferson Place NW, Washington, DC 20036, 202-466-3234.

About the Authors

In the early 1960s KENNETH S. GOODMAN began studying the reading of authentic texts by urban and rural young people. His earliest miscue research, published in 1965, is probably the most widely replicated study in reading research history. But it was his article, "Reading: a Psycholinguistic Guessing Game" (1967), that began a revolution moving away from a view of reading as rapid accurate sequential word recognition to an understanding of reading as a process of constructing meaning—making sense—of print. That research is part of the basis for the whole language movement and disagreements over Ken's conclusions about the nature of reading fuel the current "reading wars."

Ken's research has received major awards in the field from NCTE, IRA, NCRE, and NCRLL. He is a past president of IRA, NCRLL, and the Center for Expansion of Language and Thinking, and an elected member of the Reading Hall of Fame. His book *On Reading* (1996) is the most recent and complete presentation of his understanding of the reading process. Equally influential, his 1986 book *What's Whole in Whole Language?* has been published throughout the English-speaking world and is available in French, Spanish, Japanese, Portuguese, and Chinese translations.

BESS ALTWERGER is a faculty member at Towson State University in Baltimore, Maryland. Throughout her career, she has collaborated with teachers to create inquiry-based, democratic classrooms. As a speaker and writer she has focused on developing whole language as critical pedagogy and teaching for social justice and equity. Bess is an active member of Whole Language Umbrella and currently serves on the Commission on Reading for the National Council of Teachers of English. She is co-founder with her husband, Steven Strauss, of Maryland United to Protect Public Education.

RICHARD I. ALLINGTON is Professor of Education and Chair of the Department of Reading at SUNY-Albany. He is also a research scientist at the National Research Center on English Learning and Achievement where he co-directs a project on state educational policymaking. Dick is a member of the board of directors of the International Reading Association and past president of the National Reading Conference.

ELLEN H. BRINKLEY, Western Michigan University, works with pre-service and practicing teachers of English language arts through courses on how to teach reading, writing, and literature. She also directs the Third Coast Writing Project. She is a former high school teacher who grew up in and first taught in Kanawha County, West Virginia, site of the 1974 protest over multicultural literature that James Moffett called the "storm in the mountains." In recent years some of her research and publications have focused on the political influences of Christian conservatives on curriculum and school policy. Her experience as grassroots activist and co-founder of Michigan for Public Education inform the chapters included in this text. She is also co-chair of a new coalition effort, the National Congress for Public Education, and her book *Caught Off Guard: Teachers Rethinking Censorship and Controversy* will be published in 1999.

CAROLE EDELSKY is a Professor of Curriculum and Instruction at Arizona State University. She is one of the founders of PEAK (Public Education for Arizona's Kids), a community organization that advocates on behalf of public education.

LINDA ELLIS is an Assistant Professor in the Elementary Education Department at Stephen F. Austin State University in Nacogdoches, Texas. She is also a trainer for the New Jersey Writing Project and has taught summer writing institutes since 1988. Linda is an active member of several regional and state reading education organizations and past president of two area councils of the International Reading Association.

YVONNE S. FREEMAN directs the Bilingual Education Program and DAVID FREEMAN directs the Language Development and TESOL programs at Fresno Pacific College in Fresno, California. Both are interested in literacy education for bilingual learners. They have worked with bilingual teachers in Argentina and Uruguay and spent a year as Fulbright scholars at the Universidad de Los Andes in Venezuela. The Freemans have published articles jointly and separately on the topics of literacy, linguistics, bilingual education, and second language learning in professional journals and books and have a regular column in the CABE newsletter. Their books include *Whole Language for Second Language Learners* and *Between Worlds: Access to Second Language Acquisition,* the latter receiving the

Mildenberger Award from the Modern Language Association for out-
standing research in the field of foreign and second language teaching.
Their third collaboration, *Teaching Reading and Writing in Spanish in the
Bilingual Classroom,* is published in English and Spanish editions.

SHARON MURPHY is Associate Professor and the Director of the Graduate
Programme in Education at York University, Toronto. Her interests are in
reading theories, assessment, and socio-political aspects of literacy. Her
most recent work, co-authored with Patrick Shannon, Peter Johnston, and
Jane Hansen, is *Fragile Evidence: A Critique of Reading Assessment.* She is
a co-editor of *Language Arts.*

FRANCES R. A. PATERSON is an Assistant Professor of Educational
Leadership at Valdosta State University, specializing in school law, the politics of curriculum, censorship, and professional ethics for educators. A former library media specialist and junior high school teacher, Dr. Paterson
received her law degree and doctorate in education from the University of
Oklahoma. She is the author of several articles and conference papers related to religious and political issues in curricular reform. She is also the
author of *Legally Related Religious Challenges to Public School Materials,
Curricula, and Instructional Activities: The "Impressions" Controversies,
1986–1994.*

CONSTANCE WEAVER, Professor of English at Western Michigan University,
is the author or editor of several books, most recently *Lessons to Share on
Teaching Grammar in Context* (edited, 1998), *Creating Support for
Effective Literacy Education* (1997), and *Reconceptualizing a Balanced
Approach to Reading* (edited, 1997). From 1987 to 1990, she served as
Director of the Commission on Reading of the National Council of
Teachers of English. In 1996 she received the Charles C. Fries award from
the Michigan Council of Teachers of English for distinguished leadership in
the profession. Connie is also a co-founder of Michigan for Public
Education, a nonprofit grassroots organization advocating equality and
excellence in education.

HALEY WOODSIDE-JIRON is currently a Ph.D. student in the Reading
Department at SUNY-Albany and serves as research assistant for the
National Research Center on English Learning and Achievement.